SLANDER!

an autotheory of six malayan films

REMY SHAH

This publication is the artist's first written book and will benefit anyone interested in intersectional writing, experimental art writing and artist book projects; cinema, media and performance studies; transnational perspectives and the Malay World.

Contents

Preface

We are more likely to remember Marlon Brando and Greta Garbo in our film consciousness rather than the likes of P. Ramlee, Sukarno M. Noor and Maria Menado, even though they come from the heyday of Singapore's film industry from the 1950s to the 60s as part of the Nusantara world.[1] I think that this dearth or gap can be revisited in the form of an artistic project disguised as a meta-novel. This project initially wanted to explore actors, non-actors, affect, human beings in conflict, re-interpretations, meaning, the slander of meaning, slander in texts, theory-fiction and 'Malaya' among other things. It wanted to prize noology over ideology—the contingency and fluidity of thought—and wanted to intermingle gossip and fiction, music and cinema.[2] It wanted to explore the colonial condition of pre-independence when the formation of a new island-state and its denizens was considered dangerous.[3]

It wanted to explore sets and artefacts of the 1950s and its aesthetics. It wanted to exercise in filling up voids with ellipses and premises about memory. It aimed to set itself up as a hybrid genre for a hybrid task. It wanted to explore Malay and sound/song fictions of a particular era. It wanted to generate speculative history.

I compare the photograph to the complexity of fiction and the novel and its trace: the publication is literally an emanation of its referents. From real bodies, which were there, "proceed radiations which ultimately touch me, who am here; the duration of the transmission is insignificant; the photograph of the missing being, as Sontag says, will touch me like the delayed rays of a star."[4] In this analogy I find the speculative fiction.

So the premise (and promise) of Slander started with this feeling I had:

If what I feel is constant fear and trepidation to do anything that might get me in trouble with some authority that I start to censor myself, then what I feel must be real and must be felt by others too.

Walter Benjamin wrote that in a Platonic state, poets are not needed as they are considered destructive and superfluous in a perfect community.[5] *Autonomy comes at a price, for some it's exile.*

Emotion can be a powerful thing against facts. They are real things; they can go around and meander in a book. Then you sense how powerfully emotions move compared to written law.

The slander of imagination—why did we not explore the Malay world that we formerly inhabited?[6] *Let's talk about Hollywood, and how it's tied to the culture industry of the colonialised world whose lingua franca is English. Till the present, we fixate on the ivory movie stars of yonder. In hindsight, maybe if we had explored certain scenes from Korban Fitnah (Victim of Slander, 1959) and other films, we would have appreciated how amazing they were! We had our own Brando that should have been entrenched in our popular memory!*

This insight came out of a fundamental encounter with the extensive text and research of film researcher Toh Hun Ping and after that, while working on a previous installation called A White, White Day based on Korban Fitnah.[8]

In a landscape of constant construction, upgrading and renewal, we seem to be falsely accused of being complicit with erasure of the past and accepting the status quo through our own silence. We become birds in cages, like the song Burung Dalam Sangkar in Korban Fitnah, or lost souls in the night, cut away from a natural history, its Majapahit past, while we are trying to reconnect with our Singapore spirituals.[9]

Like the protagonist in Korban Fitnah who chose to remain silent and even attempted suicide, there seems to be a kind of aphasia, an inability to speak in the changing face of modernity. Perhaps the slander lies in falsity—a falsity that lies in erasing, a kind of political amnesia.

So I come to this particular scene in Korban Fitnah when Hussein (Sukarno M. Noor's character) who plays an Orpheus-like character, backs against a blank wall and faces the prospect of confrontation or suicide. It is precisely at this point of entry into consciousness, I argue, where the transitional, suspended status of being-in-time produces a dynamic of prospective transformation. Like Paul Klee's Angela Novus, or the Angel of History staring back into the past, unable to stop the irrevocable change of progress.

Deleuze states that the use of philosophy is to sadden. A philosophy that saddens no one, that annoys no one, is not a philosophy. It is useful for harming stupidity, for turning stupidity into something shameful. So perhaps one of my objectives is to slander stupidity but also avoid falling into it by trying to uncover the physiognomy of a country in transition. So this inability to speak, this mute-ness is where art can speak, what we cannot articulate. I think that for so long, for many of us, we were afraid of the text. Hitchcock said "fear is a product of fiction yet not a product of falsification." We are scared to write for fear of slander. We seem to relinquish the text to historians, politicians, lawmakers and administrators, and relinquish that agency that forms their power over us.

But I would also like to attempt to make a book about subjectivity, desire and the nature of reality. And one that problematises certain thoughts and concepts and not to proposition—a dissolution of previous images.

So my methodology revolves around reading, writing, watching films, and then reflecting and dissecting and presenting. As disparate as it sounds, I aim to close the circle I have drawn as a form seen to be congruent with its content. I want to gradually build my general idea into an organised thought by writing about it diaristically to achieve this singularity of form and content.

For this project, I had been contemplating a manuscript/working novel or a loosely bound printed object like a book/zine (or an actual publication if possible). This will function as a kind of meta-novel: a diary, a manuscript, meditations and a story. The premise is to follow: the book is written in a diary format of the author constructing a story and ruminating on his research material. The main story focusses on the writer Remy Shah and a group of night-owls in a prata shop reminiscing (through Rashomon-like perspectives) about the heyday of Singapore's film industry and its bygone movie stars in a single evening. The story within their conversations tells of a struggling fictional actor from Indonesia who had been based in Singapore in the 1950s. My research material will deal specifically with our cinematic history (pre-independence films) and discourse of the era through books, songs and films and Malay folklore and other pulp fictions of the 1950-60s. Pulp fiction in both its aesthetics of production and its penchant for salacious fare to appeal to popular imagination. I was also interested in the study of deviance in novels that explore certain socio-economic groups. My other interest was in Singapore film-location history and their disappearance through rapid and relentless development.

I was looking at various hybrid publications that mixes fiction with theory, personal reflections and philosophy, research and experimentation and bricolage of various texts into new texts.

But alas! Alas! I either lost the ambition or the time and hence the need to simplify this project to its basic enterprise—that of its technical apparatus of presentation and the phenomenological reading of the films I was watching. The methodology remains the same but...

The devil, probably.[10]

I have a penchant for texts and titles like all Deleuzian schizos and it chanced upon me that the conceptual artist Stephen Prina's song, the incredibly West Coast-tinged and catchy The Devil, Probably sounded strangely familiar until I read an article mentioning Robert Bresson's late film of the same title. I had no opportunity to watch it yet; nonetheless, Prina mentioned the lyrics of his homage was actually generated by isolating 35 frames of the Bresson film where the character Charles tries to drown himself in the bathtub.

"What's wrong? Open the door! I was scared. What happened? /
What's wrong? Open the door! I was scared. What happened? /

You can't lie underwater like on a bed and then just wait. / You can't lie underwater like on a bed and then just wait. / It's impossible. Wait for what? / It's impossible. Wait for what? / Idiot! Do you know the mess you can get me into? / Idiot! Do you know the mess you can get me into?"

And that gave me the conceptual impetus to attempt this writing. I do realise now I cannot adopt the same method after watching two films from my list. I am not Prina, and inspiration trumps conception. However, I do appreciate this strategy as giving way to more creative freedom in writing.

The characters here are loosely fictional, except for artists and works of art; and places; and certain entities (only because I see the value of their fidelity to history); and any resemblance to actual persons may be intended but should not be construed as reality.

Lastly, I appeal to the reader to remain sensitive to any bias that may colour the reading of my text. I don't know, if one, in dealing with subjectivity, could ever write without fear and favour at the same time. I write from the perspective of an artist who lives in Singapore, in a time after the films were made. It is also a region of diverse ethnicities and communities, immigrant and indigenous, that has gone through its own process of rapid modernisation and decolonisation. I am aware that, as a writer, I may have been shaped and conditioned by certain narratives. I am also certainly not an expert or specialist in cinematic history nor the Malay World. Some of these perceptions may have also changed and developed with Remy's character throughout the writing.

JS, 14 February 2021

1. We can look at this term in three broad definitions in this context:

   i) Nusantara is the Old Javanese term of Maritime Southeast Asia. It means 'outer islands'. In Indonesia, it is generally taken to mean the Indonesian Archipelago.

   ii) Outside of Indonesia in Brunei, Malaysia and Singapore, the term would refer to the Malay Archipelago or the Malay realm. In Hans-Dieter Ever's *Nusantara: History of a Concept* (2016), Nusantara in a modern language usage, without national borders "refers to the sphere of influence of the Austronesian-related cultural and linguistic islands that comprise Indonesia, Malaysia, Singapore, the southernmost part of Thailand, the Philippines, Brunei, East Timor and perhaps even Taiwan, but it does not involve the areas of Papua New Guinea."

   iii) The former thesis could then apply to cinemas through the concept of Nusantara which speaks to the geographical, social, and cultural patterns of a region before the advent of film and nationalism in Southeast Asia. 'Nusantara cinema' could then be used as a strategy to evade national political boundaries. This is inspired by Mohd Erman Maharam's paper *Between national cinemas: reframing films from Malaysia, Indonesia, and Singapore.*

2. Noology is the study of thought, knowledge, and intellect. Noology, as it is defined in *A Thousand Plateaus* (1980) by Gilles Deleuze, is not only the study of images of thought, but also a 'historicity' for images. The modern subject who is subjected to a system of signifiers is therefore produced and has its genesis in previous relations of subjection. This book also serves as a personal study of intuition and comprehension, and hence "the contingency and fluidity of thought."

3. On 9 August 1965, Singapore separated from Malaysia to become an independent and sovereign state. Deep political and economic tensions between the ruling parties of both countries had brought about the separation, culminating in racial riots between the Malays and Chinese in July and September 1964.

4. Roland Barthes, *Camera Lucida: Reflections on Photography* (1980). Barthes precedes this with "The photograph is literally an emanation of the referent." The 'radiations' here include from film to digitisation. The advent of photography has also changed the image of thinking through technology, in which I take liberty for this analogy.

5. The *Author as Producer* by Walter Benjamin (1970).

6. I propose that certain imaginations, in our rapid modernisation, had been silenced to make way for other forms of imaginings. In this instance, the Malay realm diminished with Singapore's independence. In 'Malay', I use it not in the racial sense but in the geographical, social, and cultural sense of a region before the advent of film and nationalism in Southeast Asia.

7. *(Victim of Slander)* was directed by Indonesian filmmaker Usmar Ismail and was a joint Indonesia-Singapore production by Cathay Keris films in 1959.

8. *A White, White Day* was commissioned for the SAM exhibition, *Cinerama*, and is representative of my body of work, in which I complicate notions of representation and form by deconstructing the filmic image, breaking it down into its component phenomena of light, shadow and sound. Here, an installation of lightboxes appropriates the appearance and function of a cinema screen, transforming the space of the gallery into an atmospheric rendition of the

movie theatre. What is presented to the viewer, however, is an abstract play of flickering, scintillating illumination: the LED nodes in the lightboxes are controlled by a programme that is based on video data taken from the film *Korban Fitnah*. The title is borrowed from the name of a short story written by Andrei Tarkovsky, which served as a basis in the key episode of his film *Mirror* (1975).

9. Majapahit was a Javanese Hindu-Buddhist empire in Southeast Asia that was based on the island of Java (in modern-day Indonesia). It existed from 1293 to circa 1527 and reached its peak from 1350 to 1389, marked by conquests that extended throughout Southeast Asia. It is considered to be one of the greatest and most powerful empires in the history of Indonesia and Southeast Asia. I employ this term aphoristically to refer to the pre-modern in Southeast Asia, one before European colonialism and Cartesian conceptions of mind and body.

10. In the eponymous scene from Robert Bresson's film *The Devil, Probably* (1977), whose protagonist was acted by Matisse's great-grandson, a bus full of strangers engage with one another in a dialogue just before its distracted driver gets into an accident. In the unplanned conversation, they quip about humanity's futility against larger obscure forces that it cannot fathom, to which one of them replied "The devil, probably."

Conceptions of 'Malaya', 'malayan'

There are, in addition to the political needs of a group of relatively weak countries newly released from control by different Colonial powers, two uniting forces, not related closely but both operating throughout the whole region: first, the half-submerged ancient Indian culture that appears in dance, song, ceremonial and shadow-play, mingled with more divisive influences of religion, language and political structure; second, the close business, clan and family links of the overseas-Chinese trading community, which survives as a regionally cohesive force, whether governments like it or not, and partly in rivalry to, partly preying on, the Western economic pattern that has bound different parts of the region to different European markets.[1]

I like to preface that the subtitle of the book addresses the brief history that was Malaya and the precarious period before Singapore's independence, in relation to its filmmaking industry. 'Malaya' could refer to a number of historical and current political entities related to what is currently Peninsular Malaysia in Southeast Asia. British Malaya itself consisted of a loose set of states on the Malay Peninsula including the island of Singapore from 1826-1957, with a brief spell of Japanese occupation during the second world war. Singapore has always been in and out of Malaya.[2] This may have been largely determined by the delicate racial balance of Malaya and the strategic significance of Singapore, where economic and geographical arguments may have carried less weight.

Nevertheless, we are referring to a time where the English-educated were conditioned by the British Government with a nascent political economy that served colonial economic imperatives based on a 'cultural division of labour' that may have spilled over to another system of production such as film production.

Economically too, Singapore and the Federation of Malaya (1948–1963), of which Singapore was subsumed into Malaysia in 1963 until its own independence, were bound by a common currency, a common banking system, and very large number of businesses with branches in both territories, usually with the headquarters in Singapore.

As a problem of identity, I use 'malayan' with a lowercase 'm' to suggest a much fluid and looser form of imagining in a minor key, looking at films by the Cathay Keris production from the periods of 1958-63,[3] and to steer away from a discourse on national identity and culture instead, which is best, left to the grand-narratives of a nation-state. Cathay Keris Studio's history intersects the Malay film industry in Malaya, establishing in 1951 by its two Chinese businessmen and disbanding 22 years later.[4] Its roots lay in a network of cinemas that grew out of Malaya, distributing Hindustani films. So think of 'malayan' the adjective as an affect or flavour that permeates this book. Also as flavour, it would connote a different kind of imagination: landscape, people, and time.

I would like to also refer to Benedict Anderson's anthropological definition of the nation as that of an imagined political community— and imagined as both inherently limited and sovereign. The three main propositions put forward by the Anderson in the possibility of imagining arose historically when three cultural conceptions of great antiquity had lost their axiomatic grips on men's minds:

The first was that a particular script-language provided access to an ontological truth of which it was an inseparable part of that truth, for example, Latin.

Secondly, for similar ontological reasons, that society were organised around a higher power that had a religious centre such as a monarchy, whose access of power is spread centripetally.

Thirdly, a conception of time that did not distinguish the cosmological and divine from history, that connected men and their fatalities to the world of things and the origin of the world.

He ventures to state that nationalism was imaginable because of the relationships between a system of production and productive relations (capitalism), a technology of communications (print), and the fatality of human linguistic diversity.

This interplay of fatality, technology and capitalism provided the bedrock of assembling and assimilating differences of vernaculars mechanically into print languages capable of disseminating ideas through the market.

Does a 'Singapore-to-be' in this case, meet this definition? The fact that I think, write and print in English made possible by a post-colonial government serving the needs of a projected future in the linear time of progress says one thing. Or in someone's thesis, there grew a "tension between the general secular time of history and the spiritual time of gods and spirits" and "any attempts to 'de-modernise' society, such as by resorting to ancient, archaic practices and beliefs were seen as a threat to nation building."[5] So I am referring to a time of 'becoming-state', a 'not-yet-Singapore-the-nation-state'.

If according to Hegel, history is about the history of freedom and class struggle and the flattening of a hierarchy of society, then alternative versions of it will always creep up from the periphery through its more curious subjects.

1. T.E.Silcock, *Singapore in Malaya*, Far Eastern Survey, Vol. 29, No.3 (1960)

2. Ibid.

3. I borrow this loosely from Deleuze and Guattari's three characteristics of a 'minor literature': the deterritorialization of language, the connection of the individual to a political immediacy, and the collective assemblage of enunciation. An example of the third characteristic: Kafka's solitude opens him up to everything going on in history today.

4. Cathay's chairman Loke Wan Tho and Keris Film Productions' managing director Ho Ah Loke.

5. Norman Yusoff's thesis "Contemporary Malaysian Cinema" refers to what is often invoked in Malaysian horror films, but I think can also be applied and discussed in the film *Orang Minyak* (1958) in Chapter 2.

Life (anima—on the side of the mental image) is always already cinema (animation—image-object). The technological synthesis is not a replica, not a double of life, any more than writing is a replication of speech, but there is a complex of writing in which the two terms always move together, being in transductive relation.

Bernard Stiegler, *The Discrete Image.*

Chapter 1:

Che Mamat Parang Tumpol (1960)

The village idiot in the new city

7 April 2021

Nights are the hardest. Loneliness, harder still. Connection, hardest. How does it go from hardest, harder, to hardest again? We seem to have an inherent logic for grammar to be applied to living but language is not a condition of life but a construction for articulating concepts.

I'm on a bus homeward after an aimless stroll in Little India, I begin my introduction this way as it happens and I will see where this leads to.

11 April 2021

I should really be banging words out immediately after watching the film. It's a good habit, it shows discipline and it's conceptually faithful to the diaristic mode. But this is four days later… what am I trying to do? Writing from memory? Thank God, the stuff is out on YouTube too.

So the Asian Film Archive Office is at the National Library and not at the National Archives on Canning Rise. I realised this too late and had to email them to confirm that I should head to Victoria Street, where it is instead. The office is located on the sixth floor right in front of the escalator coming up from the fifth, just as Liping, the staff-in-charge and a young woman with red-streaked hair, had described in the email. It's a cozy little office with computers, desks, cabinets and film reels in canisters. Nice! I could cover the space in seven steps. Apparently, there's another one on the fourth floor and another branch somewhere in town. Why can't they consolidate their spaces? But a cozy office is less stressful. I know I could have watched the films online. But nothing feels like joyful work and disciplined research if I physically make it to the archives. Place is everything. It has a context and sense and it makes me focus more than being at home distracted by a thousand-and-one things.

00:00 The first thing I notice is the collage-style editing! I wanted to make collage for this project, as in collage with drawings. It seems whatever I do is collage anyway. The title fonts are a wacky cartoony sort of Bauhaus design. Maybe too cartoony for the fonts I want to use for *Slander!*

02:05 I am introduced to the idyllic *kampung*/beachside. We never had houses this close to the sea, maybe in Sentosa Cove if you had seven million dollars now. This is where our protagonist Mamat feels literally at home. I am introduced to fishing here (as usual fish and water in my work). I am thinking it's the East Coast before reclamation and old Bedok. Mamat is alone fishing, his bait pulls his whole weight down into the water but only to reveal a tiny fish, so you know metaphors abound here—Mamat but is both the fool and a small fry in the big sea. I need to head home to sleep.

12 April 2021

I'm at the *prata* stall near my apartment, the very stall I said I would write from, except I'm the only night owl reminiscing about films from Singapore's heyday. I'm not exactly reminiscing—these films were made way before I was born. But I'm tapping speculatively into this time—my father would have been seventeen here! My Tinder notification comes on my phone, I turn it over—I will not be distracted.

4:45 Mamat hastily leaves after being bitten and beaten by ants and a falling coconut. His neighbour picks up his straw hat which he leaves behind and tosses it vertically into the air. In the vertical progression like a nod to Stanley Kubrick's *2001 Space Odyssey* 'bone' scene (wait, Kubrick hasn't made this film yet! Could he have watched L. Krishnan's classic!), it dissolves into a crop-shot of a modern high-rise building. Architecture. Offices. Suits. It's a press room.

5:20 onwards, I'm noticing the black and white grid windows and it's looking uncannily like my display system! This is perfect, exactly when the *modern* is introduced!

6:11 The black handprints. This is quite a nice idea and plot device. The Black Handprint Gang is a Chinese Secret Society in the film and they stamp their mark on territories they want to claim and people they want to beat up through a black-inked palm print. I like that I can now use my artsy semiotic terms like the print is a sign, a trace and an index. Not to mention another metaphor of being black-marked or -listed. I'm also thinking of Alfian Saat's first collection of poetry called *One Fierce Hour* that had a palm print depicted on the cover. Was he also inspired by this film? A palm print does suggest the self and a right to mark.

7:35 I'm reminded of the Cheong Soo Pieng painting here called *A Dream of Tropical Life*, popularised in Ho Tzu Nyen's depiction of and deconstruction of this painting in his *4x4 Episodes of Singapore Art*. Here, the idyllic *kampung* life giving way to creeping modernisation is transposed into Krishnan's cinematography where Mamat's role as singer and storyteller of the village reads the omen-like news from the papers delivered to him, one that announces a reward given to anyone that could provide more information on the Black Handprint Gang.

10:01 The introduction of several things into the *kampung*/forest/beach scene occur. First, it's the arrival of Mamat's cousin Puteh, who is seen as a role model and the epitome of a successful modern man by Mamat's mother. Mamat is also the antithesis and foil to Puteh's white-collar aspirations. Next it is the introduction of a complex industrial machine into the forest, which is Puteh's white (early Alfa Romeo-ish) automobile. It duly gets punctured by nails on the ground left by Mamat when he was repairing the stairs by the porch.

Lastly, it's the introduction of the colour white in this scene. It's funny I say this for a black-and-white film, but it is important to see it as the contrast against the backdrop of a godforsaken place (implied here by Puteh). *Puteh* means white in Malay; he wears white from head to toe like a PAP politician[1] and comes in his white car. The colonial and epistemological implication of this is obvious, and it offsets the greens and browns here even though you can't see them here. White is the aspiration here from the modern man (Puteh) to the white buildings in the city seen previously whereas Black here is seen in the negative, associated with lowly gangs, criminal activity and dirty marks. The car is seen here as a real disparity in a *kampung*; a modern mechanical, not so well-oiled machine as opposed to the languorous, humid forest and *the lazy native.*[2] Mamat is depicted as a good-for-nothing *kampung* boy here, but I would argue to say that Puteh, being learned, is not any better. He is still a struggling writer. How does he afford the clothes, rent and car anyway?

12.43 A scene of Mamat chasing Puteh's errant tyre along the *kampung* grounds, if not for the silly comic tone, it can be shot beautifully like Francis Alÿs chasing a reel of film in Afghanistan; it is the same trope. This trope like our old film reels could be released to unleash new meanings and connections.

13:13 The *kampung* house interior is shot brilliantly by the DOP! The tracking-out shot of Mother to Puteh is thoughtfully done and unfolds space like never seen before. I'm thinking they are unlike Ozu's stills and how he shot the Japanese interiors but I need to come back to this with concrete examples. It's more *Citizen Kane* tracking with the deep focus. Again at 19:57 with the tracking-in shot of Mamat in the doorway.

20:20 onwards, Mamat flips through Puteh's failed manuscripts in a chest he had left behind. Like Max Brody, he is tasked to burn/dispose of all Kafka's failed stories. Puteh had interesting titles.

The Muslims have started Ramadan. Not too long ago it was Lent and then the weekend of Good Friday and Easter. I'm neither religious nor have I been practising, but I respect the rituals of abstinence and fasting, I think it makes you a more spiritual person in touch with your body, if not a more disciplined person. I told myself to avoid drink and cigarettes until Wednesday, partly because my asthma has been acting up. Right, I'm going back upstairs to feed my cat.

13 April 2021

Did not get much sleep in. I stayed largely awake thinking of the *Wayangmalam* project that I had launched, an online platform of moving images and text. The formatting of the text and editing held me up, so those hours spent will be useful here. They say morning is the best time to write. I knew a writer who was a close friend of my ex-wife and he said that he would wake up really early before his kids went to school and get as many as a thousand words in (or was it 500). I'm not trying to match that habit but it helps to stick to a method.

22:00 *Scooter, radio and Hong Kong.*

I referred to my friend Hock Peng's copious film research of early film location history and he had laboriously traced the *kampungs* in the film along the East Coast. So I was right!

The archetype of a lost wandering soul—the artist—a man walking along the beach with his guitar, deep in thought. Fatimah in her *kebaya* runs to him (the fool even has a beautiful girlfriend!) and chides him for not calling her. Mamat is more interested in how everyone, especially his mother, thinks he is useless. Fatimah expresses faith and devotion to him and strategically informs him of a storytelling competition, another plot device, that Mamat can enter. I'm starting to notice the sound does not behave atmospherically here; they sound like they were overdubbed in the studio. The guitar, the birds and the beach feel much too separated in the quiet to be part of the same environment. The musical and landscape (the beach) combine into one like in most early Malay films that continue in Asian films mostly via Bollywood. The musical, comedy and plot are inseparable.

It's important to note the inherent musicality of the Malay world. In this world Malays, Indians, Eurasians and Chinese unite in a common language of music. I grew up in a very musical family; my first band was with my sister and cousins and we would sing and then perform together at gatherings. This was before I discovered the guitar and before my full introverted personality set in. But music forms the backdrop of my childhood where the matriarchs led us around the TV for soap operas, *Sandiwaras* and Hindustani films. There is no Other in music. Everything becomes one.

Mamat:	***Mamat:***
Sampaikanlah cita-citaku	*Please convey all my hopes*
Buat kita bersama-sama	*For us together*
Mencari pekerjaan	*To find work*
Menjadi wartawan	*To become journalists*
Kita kan bahagia	*We will be happy*
Untuk selama-lama	*Forever*
Sampaikanlah cita-citaku	*Please convey our hopes*
Buat kita, bersama-sama	*For us, together*
Fatimah:	***Fatimah:***
Ku doa supaya berjaya	*I pray for success*
Buat kita bersama-sama	*For us together*
Scooter, radio dan Hong Kong	*Scooter, radio and Hong Kong*
Tidaklah aku perlukan	*I don't need them*
Ku cuba doakan	*I will try to pray*
Buat kita berdua	*For the two of us*
Ku doa supaya berjaya	*I pray for success*
Both:	***Both:***
Buat kita bersama-sama	*For us together*

25:42 Lovely shot of Fatimah by East Coast beach, circa 1960.

Fatimah's intentions are clear at the end of the song after much beating about the coconut trees. She wants him to be a journalist. Period. To get a good job. She wants the same thing as most mothers and future wives of the day. Does she not like hanging out by the beach anymore? Will they sing the same songs in the city? But most importantly, she wants him to have ambition. Does ambition go hand-in-hand with progress? This thing called 'ambition' is an eye towards the future, a projection that has not happened yet. When faced with the prospect that you may fail, ambition becomes anxiety. Or maybe not having ambition in an ambitious world creates one.

Mamat spirals into a dilemma, contributed by the comments made by the two most important women in his life about his uselessness and lack of ambition respectively. He walks, sighs and sulks over the sad soundtrack. Everything he does is wrong, so he steals one of Puteh's stories and signs it off as his own to be mailed over for the storywriting competition.

Because of The In-laws

I'm back at Al Fahah coffeeshop and the time is perfect after mutton biryani to work on more text while I wait for my Carousell meet-up. I'm almost dying for a cigarette but I shall persevere.

31:06 The postman delivers a mail to Mamat on bicycle, which announces that he is the winner of the storywriting contest, much to his elation. Unknown to him but revealed to the audience previously was that his win was a fluke (as much as we now know necessary) caused by a distracted Chief Editor. So Mamat achieved the impossible, and by no means was it a devious device but a serendipitous series of events in the right time and place that provided the maximum gain for the most minimum of effort. It reminds me of the Wittgenstein anecdote where a composer drops dead, but not before accidentally leaving an extra note on the last score she was working on during the fall, and thereby altering the course of music history when the new conductor picks up the dusty score after a long absence. But you know, it happens like shit happens. You know philosophically comedy has a place in Marx: "History repeats itself first as tragedy then as farce."

37:15 *Kampung man in the city.*

I see the Victoria Theatre's clock, some extinct buildings and the street where Mamat, dressed smartly, is enjoying a city tour on a trishaw. I assume this to be somewhere at North

Bridge Road. He looks up and it says Union Building (ok, so this is closer to Chinatown, Tras Street), confirming this is another bygone building called Denmark House at McCallum street.

38:16 Almost a minute later, it cuts away to a low vantage perspective of a highrise building with contrasting boxy windows. The grid. Mamat does not know how to take the elevator, nor can he tell plain glass from air. It feels like an illusion and wonderland where people walk through doors and disappear into black boxes. A note: back in those days, local women wearing *cheongsams* and *kebayas* everywhere were very attractive. Why does the office feel like a minimalist set to me? Why are there strange signboards at the various doors with strange titles instead of professional labels? Is this one of L. Krishnan's absurd touches?

At one of the cubicles Mamat asks:
Are you Mr. Anjang Akal Panjang (Pak 'Witty Mind' Anjang)?

A chubby woman replies:
Yes, but I don't like to be asked that except on Fridays.

Next, she gives him a little guitar-lele and asks him to play a song. A musical duet breaks out. So it is one of the rabbit holes that Mamat, our Alice, has stumbled upon in his serendipitous journey into the modern world. Again, music here serves as intermission and uses a traditional theater format where the lyrics are a narrative dimension into the scene they are talking about:

Mamat:
Riuh-rendah,
orang kerja, sibuk dan bising
Pelabuhan kapal di Telok Ayer Basin
Satu masa waktu malam aku di sana
Aku berpegangan tangan dan berasmara

Bilaku senyum, si dia pun ketawa
Bilaku tengok, giginya tinggal dua
Aku sudah jawabkan tertanyaan kamu
Kau sekarang mesti jawab soalan aku

Soalanku wahai Pak Anjang Akal Panjang
Berapakah tingginya dari sini ke bulan?

Lady:
Kalau mahu tahu si bulan indah permai
Jauhnya bulan, tangan tak boleh sampai

Mamat:
Oh, Panjang Akal, panjang pandai berkata-kata
Tak sampai tangan ke bulan sudahlah nyata
Kau tentu tak boleh jawab soalan ini
Di Singapura berapakah banyak teksi?

Lady:
Soalan kamu boleh aku menjawab
Banyaknya teksi hinggakan tersendat

Mamat:
Pak Anjang Akal Panjang, oh bijak laksana
Memang sungguh bijak pandai sudahlah lama
Dengarlah kali ini soalan yang terang
Siapakah namanya yang berdiri di depan?

Mamat:
The hustle and bustle;
people at work, and noise
The harbour at Telok Ayer Basin
One night I was there
I held hands and romanced

When I smiled, she laughed too
When I looked, only two teeth were left
I have answered your questions
Now you must answer mine

My question, dear Pak 'Witty Mind' Anjang
How high from here is the moon?

Lady:
If you wish to know about this moon so lovely
So far away, the moon, my hand can't reach it

Mamat:
Pak 'Witty Mind' Anjang, clever with words
That the hand won't reach the moon is evident
You surely can't answer this question
In Singapore, how many taxis are there?

Lady:
Your question can I answer
So many are the taxis until they're jammed

Mamat:
Pak 'Witty Mind' Anjang, oh so wise indeed
Truly intelligent and has been for a long time
Listen this time to a question so clear
What is the name of he who stands before you?

Lady:	***Lady:***
Rupanya cantik, rambut ikal berjambul	*His looks, pleasing, his wavy hair in a quiff*
Di depanku nama Mamat 'Parang Tumpul'	*In front of me stands Mamat 'Blunt Machete'*
Mamat:	***Mamat:***
Pak Anjang Akal Panjang, ku tak tanya lagi	*Pak 'Witty Mind' Anjang, I won't ask anymore*
Sampai di sini, Mamat hendak mintak diri	*At this juncture, Mamat will take his leave*
Lebih baik kalau kita berunding saja	*Better if we were to just discuss*
Lain masa kita akan berjumpa pula	*The next time we will meet each other*
Lady:	***Lady:***
Kalau begitu sudah tujuan kita	*If that is indeed our intention*
Both:	***Both:***
Biarlah kita kekal selama-lama	*Let us remain for as long*

42:10 A jazzy uptempo break and then at 42:48, a transition to a cha cha! A time when all men knew the cha cha and wore their hair in quiffs.

15 April 2021

1.10am, Al Fahah is packed with late night denizens. Hump day. Worse time to write in a crowd. Might as well, as I forgot my notebook and earphones. It's like I made up for the cigarettes I avoided the days before. I want to squeeze some passages out before I sleep. Morning class tomorrow.

I want to mention screens here. As I was watching the film from the PC screen at the AFA office, I thought the size of the monitor was perfect for the display system. In a way it's not cinema anymore, so that technical mode of projection does not make sense, and neither is it a TV monitor, which would suggest the comfort of a domestic home entertainment. So it is not the 1960s where you would go out to watch a movie like this in a cinema or the 1980s when they used to have classic re-runs on primetime TV like the P. Ramlee stuff and the

Bujang Lapok stuff, when my grandmother was still alive. It's now relegated to a digitised database in an archive and perused through a computer screen for research purposes.

45:00 Press Room. Cue McLuhan. Cue the Gutenberg press. Cue the onset of how the printed word changed the human from an aural and formless environment to a literate, rational and visual one. Cue Walter Benjamin and art made in the age of mechanical reproduction. An assembly line of machines and papers getting inked. Mamat inadvertently gets his hand dirty with ink and spreads the stain as he shakes the hand of the Chief Editor. The handshake that sets off a chaotic chain of events. It's the blackmark of the village oaf in the city, the unruly element as much as modernity is the irreversible blackmark on our environment and the human need for systematic progress and utilising every ounce of resource we have. Who remembers the tragedy of Macbeth (will these hands ne'er be clean?) where the blood-stained palm symbolises the guilt of evil deeds? Whereas in this vaudeville comedy, the black handmark is really the stain against the machine. We have names for this—crime, viruses, riots, clowns, rebels, outcasts, poets, enemies, graffitians, *orang minyaks,*[3] individuals etc.

16 April 2021

I'm trying to remember the film that I watched last night called *Mouchette on Mubi* by Robert Bresson. His severe style, his austere style and maybe what you would call a religious experience, what Werner Herzog wants to get when he watches films. To put into perspective, it's miles apart from the Cathay Keris films, and it's made seven years after *Che Mamat Parang Tumpol.* And I'm not trying to value this kind of film as a higher art form over Cathay's lower forms of entertainment. I see the value or art in both. I'm more interested in the conditions of the milieu that would produce films as such.

Europe's long history of film, modernity and individualism and loss of religious beliefs with Southeast Asia's burgeoning communal identity in flux and its own modern form—a hybrid of traditions. Anyway in *Mouchette*, what strikes me is the lack of emotion and drama in the film and protagonist that stirred the most emotions in me.

They were Bresson's vehicles. A conjecture—Bresson has a keen interest in both images and their historical references to paintings; he draws from his interest in portraiture in Western painting a kind of 'look' for his characters. So the disinterested barmaid really looks like Manet's barmaid in *A Bar at the Folies-Bergère* and at the end of the film *Mouchette*, our martyr in a dress, rolls herself down a hill into a lake to drown like Ophelia, only that this is never shown.

46:48 At first I thought it is the Singapore River, but it's too wide an expanse. Then it reminds me of the water-body that I used to drive over via the Yishun Dam, but HP's research confirms that it was the Johor-Woodlands causeway before the political split. Before the jams and delays. Identity here was more fluid between new Malaysia and Singapore. Did you need passports to go through? It was Puteh driving then from Malaysia to Singapore. Did he come from Johor or Kuala Lumpur? Was he Malaysian or a Singaporean expat? And those clouds over the causeway are the fluffiest I've ever seen, like they were painted on. How did L. Krishnan get so serendipitous here?

48:52 This is when it really turns into satire, which I analyse as tapping into the social and political anxieties of the day. I want to call this the Doctor Strangelove effect when the Chief Editor declares war on the Black Handprint Gang and calls the civil and defence brigades with both of his telephone receivers over his ears.[4] This is when the Police on their patrol bikes first make their appearance as a convoy. Later you will see how ridiculous it is when the army is roped in what looks like a parade. There is some display and symbology of law and order and a nationalist showcase of armed forces. This of course is a farce when you know the only culprit here that started the fire was our clown and scapegoat Mamat. I want to head to bed early as I have a long day ahead tomorrow and I'm looking forward to my dinner date with Sofia in the evening.

17 April 2021

It's funny how the country I live in is so defined by its aspirations. Projections about what we can be. Look out at the skyline and you see a futuristic metropolis in its wave-like architecture. And the current trend for art seems to be veered towards possible futures and alternatives. So it seems anachronistic for me to delve into a project like this. I put a picture of the old Cathay building on the wallpaper on my iPhone because I did not want my date to see—as the first thing—my children on it. But dinner with Sofia last night went better than expected, we had a good time talking over Lebanese food with drinks. Today when I woke up the grainy black-and-white image looks strangely befitting of the vertical format, filling up the whole screen and performing its architecture on my iPhone. You wonder if it is the image or the building or the medium that makes it compelling here. I would argue how the medium imprisons its subject in its reality and influences your perception that creates an image of memory.

Screens. We are all so separated by these mirrors called screens. Everyone is on their screens; take a look around you. I'm in a new Vietnamese joint down the street and it has that chic and cheap decor that's also prevalent in Bangkok. I love it. The food is not bad either. It's been raining nonstop the whole day and I'm taking refuge here. Traditional Vietnamese coffee!

50:20 Mamat picks a scooter from a row meant for journalists. You could ride without a helmet in those days. In fact, I associate the scooter with Southeast Asia, it's still prominent on the roads of Malaysia, Thailand, Vietnam and Indonesia, and people still ride in them without helmets, sometimes in pillion of threes. But the scooter is more prominent in the outskirts of the main cities.

At this point Puteh has reached the Police Barricade and passes through.

I'm figuring out how my text functions here. It's how writing does not correspond to film time but has its own rhythm, much much slower as it chomps and stretches down the reams of time that is inversely proportional to the time stamps here.

7≥≥ ≥≥≥≥≥≥≥≥≥≥≥≥…………………………≥≥≥≥≥/9…………………7./////
////////////.6y≥/.

The text here created by randomly putting my journal on the keyboard of my laptop.

Condensed milk. This is the distinct flavour of the coffee I'm drinking. Georges Perec wrote a whole novel in a cafe in Paris where he tried to write everything he observed in the 'infraordinary'. This was 1974.

I cannot begin to tell you how invaluable HP's early film location research is, he has done all the legwork for me. And I can't begin to tell you how serendipitous this has been to my place in time. In Mamat's rare and scenic scooter tour, he sings as he scoots along the places that no longer exist:

Mamat:
Ho hooray! Ku berjalan-jalan
Hatiku senang, riang,
menjadi wartawan hooray!
Ho hooray! Ku berpusing-pusing
Pancari berita penting untuk
menghapuskan samsing

Skuterku yang handal sekali
Lambretta namanya ini, buatkan dari Italy
Lari kencang, belanjanya kurang
Dengan Lambretta ni
kutangkap Kumpulan Tangan Hitam

Ho hooray! Ku berjalan-jalan
Hatiku senang, riang,
menjadi wartawan hooray!
Ho hooray! Ku berpusing-pusing
Mencari berita penting untuk
menghapuskan samsing

Skuterku yang handal sekali
Lambretta namanya ini, buatkan dari Italy
Lari kencang, belanjanya kurang
Dengan Lambretta ni
kutangkap kumpulan Hitam

Mamat:
Ho hooray! I'm out and about
My heart is light and gay,
being a journalist hooray!
Ho hooray! I'm going all over
To get that big story
to take down the gangsters

My scooter's truly reliable
Lambretta is its name, Italian-made
Rides like the wind at low cost
With this Lambretta,
I'll catch the Black Hand Gang

Ho hooray! I'm out and about
My heart is light and gay,
being a journalist hooray!
Ho hooray! I'm going all over
To get that big story
to take down the gangsters

My scooter's truly reliable
Lambretta is its name, Italian-made
Rides like the wind at low cost
With this Lambretta,
I'll catch the Black Hand Gang

Chinatown (Nanyang Siang Pau Building)

South Bridge Road before large-scale urban renewal

Bras Basah Road (Old Cathay Building, this was on my iPhone wallpaper and will be a recurring image in one of the next films I am watching)

Shenton Way and the Merdeka Bridge (an aspirational symbol of the Singa here for independence)

Mountbatten Road (The Dakota Crescent Singapore Improvement Trust flats, one of the first flats to be built and soon to be demolished)

Old Airport Road (SIT Flats which are already demolished)

And then he rounds up somewhere from Frankel Avenue to where I am now, Joo Chiat Road! Home of the Black Handprint Gang and their lair at 171.

At some point in time, Wahid Satay, the actor who plays Mamat rode his scooter along the road where I now live. A decade ago, I wrote a poem about my impressions of Joo Chiat (reading this now, a slight uneasiness):

Joo Chiat is the underbelly of Singapore
Its road ate the intestines to form the town
Its stalls are eyes that open to these intestines
That is part viscera part dirt
Everyone smokes in Joo Chiat
Caucasian mothers with kids
Ah peks
Hajs with goaties and
Prostitutes and
Bohemians
Feeding the roads with cigarette butts tossing them to their long mouths on their sides that ate the intestines, as if they weren't enough everyone wizened and hardened in Joo Chiat no matter the age
Artists took some of his viscera and dirt and smeared it on their skins
They weren't enough Chinese women with makeup and perfume
So the Vietnamese girls brought their soaps
No, Joo Chiat is the long gamine legs of a dirty whore
That part when the moon gets eaten by worms!
Great communities flourish and great food left over

56:03 Malay man by a kind of speakeasy bar at 171, thinking of an Edward Hopper frame here. He orders a ginger beer instead. The Black Handprint Gang henchman literally bumps into him and discovers he's the man they have been waiting for.

I am totally exhausted, I fell into a short nap after I came home. I am in love with the poetry of my life—a little studio apartment in a single building where I live. Mine is perhaps the smallest at the side of the airwell of the building, a module facing other modules of apartments, where each window offers a television glimpse of my neighbors' lives, like Krzysztof Kieślowski's *Dekalog*. In my apartment are more modules of furniture, appliances, artwork and shelves of books that mirror the outside.

My cat sleeps at the side of my pillow under a postcard of a Lucian Freud painting of a man resting with his dog.

Before this I went to 171 Joo Chiat road and it's not replaced by Hotel 81 Sakura (this is 181 as HP described though it's in the same vicinity). Instead, it's now a new self-care therapy boutique joint for the pampering of oneself.

18 April 2021

I tried to watch Terry Ong's *Untitled* (Sebuah Film U-Wei Hj. Saari, Sofia Jane Hisham Sebagai *Perempuan, Isteri & ...?)* last night before I slept, an adaptation of Malaysian director U-Wei Hj. Saari's seminal film of the same title. It's 12 hours long, and not quite like Douglas Gordon's *24 Hour Psycho*, I only managed slightly more than 1/6 of the video loaded on *Wayangmalam*, breaking it down in two nights. The video is quite riveting I may say, like watching stills very slowly unfold. Without sound or dialogue, this is pure image-hallucination going into a dream zone, yet lucid enough for me to still be distracted and check my phone and come back to it. I made some screen captures of shots I thought were resonating. There are strong images of violence and sexuality which I think must be missing from contemporary Malaysian cinema; I'm speculating because of its recent fallback into conservatism and fundamentalism.[5] Is this good for cinema? At least this film was balls out and still is gutsy for its time.

1:00:19 I forgot to mention there is also Hokkien in the dialogue spoken by the Chinese baddies, common for its time where everyone could speak street Malay and pepperings of Hokkien.

The army is mobilised to go after a gang of 2+1. Troops marching, tanks rumbling, machinery and signal equipment; our army is a mix of local and colonial counterparts. A quick look at history will provide you this:

> *Prior to the formation of the army, the responsibility of defending Singapore fell solely on the British forces stationed on the island as well as two battalions of regular soldiers and volunteers from the Singapore Volunteer Corps (SVC). The two regular battalions were the First Singapore Infantry Regiment (1 SIR) and the Second Singapore Infantry Regiment (2 SIR), formed in 1957 and 1963 respectively.*
>
> *The basis for the establishment of the Singapore Army was to ensure that Singapore was equipped to conduct its own defence preparations and to reduce its reliance on the British. To build up the nation's defence force, one of the government's most urgent tasks was to secure command over the battalions. When Singapore was part of Malaysia, 1 SIR and 2 SIR were placed under the command of the Fourth Federal Infantry Brigade of the Malaysian Army in Singapore.*[6]

Is this a display of our burgeoning military forces and independence? Just as how early paintings in the Western canon served the Church. I suspect here this is part propaganda to display something their viewers may not have seen at that time. One can only look at how the police and army are portrayed here to a sophisticated extent that is contrasted with the buffoonery of the criminals and the village simpleton here. One discovers too in a bit of scholarly trivia how the Lumiere brothers were themselves engaged with a little propaganda of their own when their films portrayed a narrative and spatial privilege of the ruling class over the workers. Similarly, the epic film *The Birth of a Nation* (1915) by the pioneer D.W. Griffith portrayed blacks as uncivilised, rampaging buffoons.

19 April 2021

I'm at the bar near the college where I work. Feeling exhausted again. I had a nice time and dinner with XY last night, missed her company, she had a new bob haircut that looks really good on her. I collected four hard disks worth of data from Sim Lim Square, had the old faulty ones transferred to a new single external hard disk.

1:03:00 *Soap and Beer.*

I have no idea why you would have soap powder and a beer brewery together. My guess is that the business of selling soap products is just a cover for the illegitimate or *haram* business of producing alcoholic drinks. The Manchu gang leader has a speakeasy bar on the ground floor and a brewery in the basement, both of which their legality is questionable. What is interesting is that Mamat accidentally produced a new substance of soap and beer (without drinking much of it) in the brewery and drowned the triad leader in three barrels of the concoction. I mean, materially that's absurd yet artistic—drowning in an alcoholic foam bath. Like an installation artwork based on the substance between the cleansed and the impure. And what is more symbolic about the new Government cleaning the streets up than to cleanse the sins of the community then by killing the ringleader with a swimming pool of alcohol and lye agent, in an overt effort to keep the place *bersih* (clean). Of note is the font used for 'Soap' for the products. Note the letter 'S'. I am thinking that old modern, kinda pre-computer generated typography, of hand and mechanically created signages will make a good typeface for 'Slander'. I have to close my laptop now, get the bill and head down to Geylang Serai for my second jab of the Covid vaccination.

20 April 2021

Today I take Bus 33 back and it feels like the same route Mamat took on his scooter from Bras Basah Road. I see the Dakota Crescent SIT flats as a pale shadow of their former selves, all hoarded up, one block is wrapped in blue tarpaulin, ready to be demolished. Then, past Old Airport road and now here, I am in the Vietnamese joint, been coming here recently, I'm on the comfy couch for four now. I can't seem to work from home, I'm always exhausted and lonely there. Over here I can work with food, drinks and the buzz. I think I'm able to knock out words everyday, maybe even a thousand if contemporary life wasn't so distracting and if my mind wasn't so restless.

1:07:36 Now Mamat is identified and wanted as the leader of the Black Handprint Gang with a $10,000 reward tag on a poster. I would like to recreate this visual. I also love the comic sequence of Mamat's entry and escape from the Black Handprint Gang backyard shed in Joo Chiat. I think it will remain iconic in my memory as one of the highlights or the climaxes of the film. It is real physical comedy that is choreographed as a complex sequence of actions in a maze of rabbit holes and takes place in the backlanes between the spaces of gangsterism and movie posters (the industry), both of which no longer exist.

Village idiot in the city

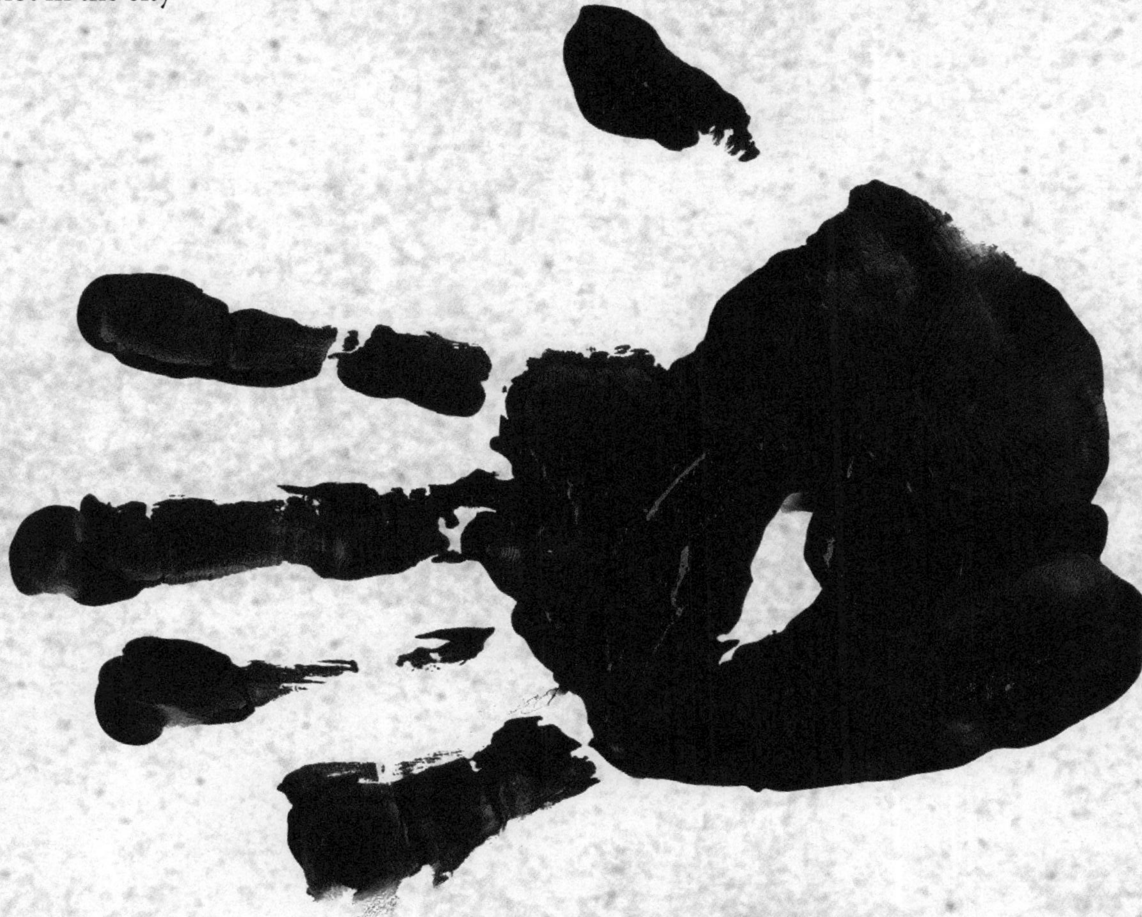

Mamat opens the window
He pokes his head out of the very poster he is wanted for
Sees Puteh and retreats
Slamming both doors against Puteh's nose
Picks on a loose end of a wooden panel from the shed
And inadvertently see-saws it down from the other on
Puteh's head
Escapes out of the narrow slot caused by the loose panel
Runs out the back alley
Sees the police
Retreats back into the hole of the shed
Again pushing the panel in and see-sawing back down on
Puteh's head
Puteh picks down the same panel
And see-saws back up at the other end to whack Mamat on
the buttocks
Pushing him with such force Mamat breaks a large hole in
the other side of the shed
And escapes from it
Running around the alleys
And ending up in a theatre

Wahid finally assumes the role of the absurd actor in this film. I remember one of the most powerful performances and videos I had ever seen was Steve McQueen's *Deadpan* (1997). McQueen had assumed the role of Buster Keaton in his seminal comedy, the 1928 *Steamboat Bill, Jr.*, where a house facade literally collapses on him through the window opening. McQueen transformed comedy into a taut and suspenseful Beckettian play and inserted his Black identity into the history of film through his body.[7]

21 April 2021

Technically I'm not even a writer, who am I trying to kid? This is pretentious. Who is going to read this conceptual dribble? I don't have anything left in me to write tonight. What did I sign up for? Last night I fell asleep trying to watch Agnes Varda's film *Cleo from 7 to 9* (1962). It's an incredibly, incredibly modern film compared to the Cathay Keris ones, but these are really directors at the forefront of filmmaking meant for the intelligentsia and not burdened by narrative, budget, propaganda and mass entertainment which was important for the day. I can't even remember the half of it but I know conceptually the film happens in two hours of the protagonist's life. It brings to mind Beckett's quote: "The creation of the world did not take place once and for all time but takes place every day." What's with me and French thought anyway. Why am I so attracted to that way of being?

I am at Al Fahah, and I see a fat Indian man with two heavily perfumed and scantily clad Filipino women, this is a quarter to 11 at night. I am sure they were paid and I am sure he's having a threesome later.

1:09:53 I am trying to recall the movie posters outside the theatre here that Mamat stumbles across. For sure I recognise Charlie Chaplin. What's he showing in 1960? Chaplin's almost done by then, it cannot be *A King in New York*; it doesn't match the visuals. I would always like to think it was *Modern Times*, so I can dissect it and make a correlation here. Also maybe I recognise that Wahid Satay could have been the Chaplin of our time, there was also Mat Sentol. These comic geniuses.

The version on YouTube is too poor, I can't make them out, now this is the real difference in watching on such a platform—you lose a lot of life and context. I would have to go back to AFA to retrieve the footage again. OK the *mamak* is chasing me out as I'm hoarding a whole table with my laptop. Got to run.

It is real physical comedy that is choreographed as a complex sequence of actions in a maze of rabbit holes and takes place in the backlanes between the spaces of gangsterism and movie posters (the industry), both of which no longer exist

25 April 2021

A three-day lapse, where did the time go? More cigarettes, alcohol and sleep in-between but I couldn't find the time nor the mood to write. I fell into a funk and needed to escape elsewhere and not through writing. Yesterday was spent with my two sons Jaxxon and Jagger, this morning I returned them to their mother and that's that.

I want to escape conventional tropes about modernity. What can I uncover here? I feel a dearth of works here that deal with the self and individualism through modernity, through the outsider. The reason why I'm doing this project is I see a real value in fiction, research and autobiography and where they meet art. And I have always liked the idea of a project unfolding in time.

1:10:45 The absurd actor. The only redeemable elements of Wahid Satay's fame and career are his images immortalised on film. Otherwise, his characters are as fleeting as our *kampungs* and film industry. Only images survive them. But what do these images want then? There was a mass extinction 252 million years ago called the 'great dying', where 96% of all marine life perished while two-thirds of terrestrial species perished. There are no images of such.

Recent study has pointed to the cause of the 'great dying' as the spike in Earth's temperatures. I have a similar analogy to the demise of a particular world from the 1950s to the 60s, called the 'long disappearance'. What caused it? Modernity? Capitalism? Globalisation? Nationalism? Or just time? But our modern machines, recorders and devices—themselves as artefacts today—were there as accomplices to all the changes that happened.

Anyway, this scene is quite meta in the way Wahid is playing Mamat who plays these characters on stage but is actually Wahid himself in his natural form as a comic performing his sketches. In this sense, this is Mamat's true calling—to be an actor (and this meta-fiction is further explored in a parallel world where he is a successful actor in *Rasa Sayang Eh* (1959) and his way of capturing and embracing the absurd in an ever-changing world that he is struggling to keep up with. He says he is trying to save his neck by going around the world, namely Japan, India and China. He explores and pokes fun at the stereotypes—his former but short-lived Japanese ruler during the occupation and his fellow migrant neighbours from China and India, but never addresses the stereotype of his British colonial administrator. Was it because they were partly funding this project with Cathay? Or was it because of sentiments of the day? His Japanese stereotype is solemn and mournful, his Indian talkative and naive, his Chinese wise and scrupulous. His multiracial audience is in stitches until he gets identified by his pursuers.

26 April 2021

In the scorching April heat, our impressive skyline does nothing for me. In fact they all look more hostile, baring their teeth. All teeth. In the Marina Bay area, look at the Esplanade, the Marina Bay Sands and the Central Business District buildings, all waves and teeth. Yes, a lot of money goes into glass and metal and more intricate architecture, a playground for the rich. Money makes money and these buildings are made of money.

I'm nearing the end of this film. I have five more to go. Perhaps this is possible, but I have not reached that intensity yet.

1:22:28 A scooter in the office, after a whole sequence of physical comedy involving the throwing and falling of water, noodles and raw fish on faces, heads and body parts. The fruits of our labour and natural resources are as out of place and time as they are on the two buffoons who defected to the city.

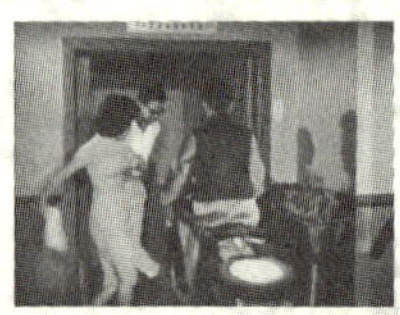

Mamat returns with the scooter riding into the premise of the office itself, but rides himself unintentionally into a prison van. He really is the chaotic misfit in this new modern world. In the police station, and I guess this recurs in L. Krishnan's Cathay world, superintendents are highly disinterested, grumpy and pill-guzzling middle-aged Malay men. The superintendent (the long arm of the law) dismisses the chief editor (our emblem of modern democracy/activism and freedom of speech). Both of them dismiss Puteh, who is nothing but a failed writer, and Mamat, the joke that unexpectedly gets caught up in this system because of his actions.

Mamat returns by boat to the *kampung*, does he live on an island? Pulau Ubin? Fatimah waits loyally and encouragingly. Later on, both the policeman and postman bring along good tidings of monetary reward and job offer respectively: for having drowned the gang leader in his own beer; and a position of actor in the theatre troupe he had stumbled across.

1:33:06 Love on a scooter. He returns to the city with Fatimah on the bike and at the end of the film, breaks the fourth wall by waving to the audience.

Some notes:

Failure—I'm thinking how failures can thrive in a system, like the comic, the actor, the writer, the artist. To fail over here is to not have accomplished material goals and reached certain status in life. I am like Mamat too, a total misfit who has failed and does not fit into the system. Maybe I am looking at the outsider here who has failed to stay 'inside'.

Digitisation—It is very hard to call this cinema. I have only watched these films in the context of computer screens only made possible by digitisation. The loss of dimensionality, depth and resolution from the actual reels is flattened on a computer screen. At the beginning of each film I watch, there is a notice informing me of the digitising and restoration process of old films with before-and-after pictures. I could never ever imagine walking into the theatre in the 1960s to catch a film and experience this cinematically. So this really becomes an anecdotal exercise in fiction and film-watching and also annotated in the way that this is written in fragments.

Slapstick—Liping already pointed this out to me after I finished watching the film, that slapstick was the form of the day, and the Malay comics thrived in this genre because I think it communicated with a wider audience, plus it was hugely entertaining. I respect this form of physical comedy as an art perfected in early silent filmmaking before the advent of sound through the likes of Charlie Chaplin and Buster Keaton. But for the Malay sensibility here or should I even say Southeast Asian one (you will even see this in Thai comedies), our humour appealed to a particular vernacular audience. However, slapstick wasn't the only form that was popular, there was the usual crime drama in the style of film noir; romance; and horror too, sometimes a hybrid of everything.

I'm wrapping my night, typing this in bed and I'm recalling a few hours ago I was taking a walk with XY from the Esplanade towards Lau Pa Sat under an overcast sky and I felt alienated from these skyscrapers in all blocks and shapes in the CBD area. They were spectacular to look at but I could not connect to them. So it was great to chance upon artworks in the heart of the downtown area. Not all of them, some are just bland corporate commissions. But outstanding is Han Sai Por's granite slabs where you can walk through called *Progressive Flow*. She's like our Richard Serra but she's a planet of her own, a spritely old woman with steady arms and stronger fingers and balls of steel to make and carve out works on tons of marble or granite with her bare hands. Another feature was the Ascott Building, a beautiful colonial/Art Deco facade that wraps a street corner, majestic and old world reminiscent of London and New York. A quick read on Wikipedia acknowledges it as once the tallest building in Singapore, back in the 1950s, surpassing the Cathay Building and then overtaken by the Shaw Centre in 1958, if it wasn't the towers of the two major film companies in Singapore. Designed by pioneering architect Ng Keng Siang, it was originally called Asia Insurance Building.

When Asia Insurance Building was the tallest building in Southeast Asia, along with the other highrise Pickering Street flats, there was a record number of people who would jump to their deaths. Existentialism has always been foregrounded against the background of modernisation. Existentialism gave rise to meaninglessness in a world of cold and chaotic progress. Albert Camus proposed in *The Myth of Sisyphus*, three options to confront this reality. One is physical suicide which will end your life, the other is philosophical suicide which is conceding this reality to a higher power to give your life meaning. The last is to embrace the absurd and realise that we are free. In this sense, Mamat, our ignorant fool, has chosen the third option.

At the 7-Eleven, before I headed back, I bought four packets of these tasty chilled chicken breasts that I could keep in my fridge. At the counter, the elderly staff would always say the same things to me. *Wa you really like this ar. You can eat this cold one ar? Wa I cannot, I eat only warm food.* I must have gone there more than 10 times to buy these snacks and either she cannot remember me or that it is really her way of communicating with me.

1 May, 2021

Labour Day. At various times of this endeavour I am wondering why this work will be called *Slander!* I'm also thinking whether this writing could serve the reader just as well without her watching the films. I am thinking about Roland Barthe's *Death of The Author* and that the role of writing is to destroy all points of origin. Need I supply supplementary images here? What role does fiction and text play here then?

I was also reading both Timothy P. Barnard's *Blindness, Modernity and Tradition in Malay Films of the 1950s and 1960s* and *Decolonization and The Nation in Malay Films (1955-65)*, both of which are very useful and substantial but I did not want them to cloud my reading of the films here or even adopt, as I mention, the usual academic tropes. I want to depend on a more phenomenological enterprise of experience, reflecting on these films and their production through my subject. Hiroshi, my curator who had also been instrumental to this project and pointing me to references that may be useful, arranged for a meeting at The Museum's office to talk about the impending show. I was definitely a little intimidated and stressed when a boardroom of people entered from various departments to ask me about this project and I am now wondering how personal I should be here now with the institution in the picture. These are important questions and predicaments.

But as you can tell from the gap in writing, I'm struggling to keep up the daily reflections; I may have over-promised here. I am either emotionally exhausted or malnourished, I can't tell and to have some degree of vulnerability and honesty in a project is frightening.

To free up a mental space and distance for this needs a kind of clarity and vision… or should I just move completely by intuition and with the utter mundanity of my life?

Notes

Chapter 1: Che Mamat Parang Tumpol (1960)
The village idiot in the new city

1. A member of the People's Action Party, Singapore's dominant and ruling party that has been in power since its independence in 1965.

2. A derogatory term used to describe indigenous races in Southeast Asia. Syed Hussein Alatas analyses this as a colonial construct: see *The Myth of the Lazy Native: A Study of the Image of the Malays, Filipinos and Javanese from the 16th to the 20th Century and its Function in the Ide*ology of Colonial Capitalism (2010).

3. This could refer to freaks, especially in the context of the next chapter. Also, how minyak here refers to crude oil which stains.

4. *Dr. Strangelove or: How I Learned to Stop Worrying and Love the Bomb,* known simply as *Dr. Strangelove*, is a 1964 black comedy film directed, co-written, and produced by Stanley Kubrick, starring Peter Sellers in various roles, including the title character.

5. Filmmakers like U-Wei Hj. Saari and Yasmin Ahmad challenge the status quo of Malaysia, a conservative and mostly Muslim country, with their films, by tackling taboo subjects.

6. With acknowledgements to the National Library Board of Singapore.

7. In an interview, McQueen thinks the term 'body' is a pretentious artsy term.

Chapter 2:

Orang Minyak (1958)

Malaya's premier bogeyman strikes back, again

1 May 2021

1:50 I notice immediately that the timestamp on YouTube does not correspond to the AFA version and is at least two minutes faster because of the restoration introduction for the AFA copy. This version online is a lot poorer too, higher in contrast so much so the introduction is literally a void of shadows, which gives an interesting effect: the Orang Minyak is introduced by his silhouette seen creeping, dissolving into or emerging from the shadows, behind the brick walls here. The 'oily melting' title and credit fonts are so interesting to look at, gives it a graphic novel quality.

Yusof B. has been doing a great job with the music for both films so far, again this is directed by L. Krishnan about our mythological bogeyman. We are now approaching the genre of horror in 1958 Singapore.

3:15 He creeps into a bedroom of a woman who is lying on the bed, her back turned towards us, sarong-wrapped, her shoulder blades exposed. The scene blacks out, the oily text of the opening credits of the assistants appears over the screen: A.Rahman, Tan Beng Sim, George Paterson, Tan Peng Suan, Ramalingam K.Rajoo… . A door opens, a woman screams (presumably after having discovered a body), pandemonium, the Orang Minyak is here. Shut your doors, shut your windows, get off the streets and retreat back into your homes.

4:28 Ok, it's that police Superintendent from *Che Mamat*, so it's the same universe here, boy is he working overtime. Now he has to find a serial murderer. The video clip is hissing from the audio track. He takes his pills with water again. I wonder what his prescription was for 1958. This film is made two years earlier from the last, he looks leaner. Also this clip has no English subtitles, poor sound quality and as my Malay is half-par, I have to depend on a purely phenomenological reading on my re-watching.

5:25 Mak Wan rents the dodgy haunted house. Why? Is she a Malaysian expat? Or renting was the norm then and our notion of property was vastly different too?

6:04 Some kind of rice harvest ritual and dance. Interesting. You definitely do not see this now. Again, this is the *kampung* side and all the village heads and other dignitaries gather around to witness. The detectives from the previous scene—the only presence of the city—visit. The ritual gets interrupted by another piercing scream. Have you ever wondered why it's always a woman screaming and not a man? I want to see a contemporary horror flick where a scene is interrupted by a grown man's scream. Because to this day, a woman's scream is heard: visceral and victimised and a man's scream is silent, seldom heard but is symbolic and visual, like the paintings of Edvard Munch and Francis Bacon. Let me rephrase this—a woman's scream is often heard and seldom seen and a man's scream is often seen and seldom heard.

2 May 2021

As I was walking back home yesterday along the back alleys, I recounted my relationship with screen recordings. I remember before the advent of digital downloads and streaming, you had pirated DVDs. They were always sold near the markets by a male figure with a lookout, and they were packaged cheaply in poor res printing paper and plastic. The video quality itself was just as bad, the footage was obviously taken by someone who went to the cinema with a camera and tripod and recorded from the screen; sometimes you would see shadowy figures during the beginning or end of the film passing by the camera's viewfinder. I remember as a BA painting student, I would paint from film stills. These were done without any software but manually with a film SLR and a tripod set to the right speed to record from my TV. The results were always unexpected and painterly. It was this filter that was attractive. As a young adult in the 90s, I used to rent VHS films from the old grumpy Jewish uncle with the bushiest eyebrows at Tanglin Shopping Centre. After all this disappeared, it was the age of torrents and downloading these little seeds on the internet that are shared within the community but you never know what you were going to get. This is my version of technology which is very archaic and is rooted in the technical re-production of obsolete formats.

How the body always resists and needs to be maintained.

Lately I have been occupied with the thought of how the body has its own autonomous needs. It always resists your lofty aspirations and plans as it wears against time towards entropy: that it will break down eventually. It needs to be maintained in modern life in spite of this. So the body needs to eat; it needs to shit; it needs to sleep; it needs to heal and repair itself; it needs to be maintained when its nails and hairs grow; it needs to fuck. You never tell it what to do. If you are in a hurry and you need to pee you have to wait for the last drop before you flush. Was it Charles Bukowski who said there is nothing better like taking a shit and Milan Kundera wrote in the *Unbearable Lightness of Being* that "shit is denied and everyone acts as though it did not exist." So it's a constant struggle with logic, rationale, and what the body naturally wants. In fact morality is based on resisting what the body wants, whole philosophies are built around the body-mind dichotomy or singularity. There is no escaping the body. I bring this up because I've been so fucking lazy and tired, and so full of shit. I wanted to put in a few lines about the film *The Wind will Carry Us* by the Iranian film director Abbas Kiarostami that I had watched but I can't remember now. But it was an incredibly poetic yet mundane film about how the modern was encroaching on the traditional, and something about waiting for a 100-year old woman to die. I think the protagonist was a photographer or a filmmaker disguised as an engineer. But the most potent scene was a woman milking a cow in the dark and the protagonist reciting a Sufi poem of the eponymous film. How is such mastery possible?

21 May 2021

Ok, so this is a long lapse. I had been so busy with work and balancing my projects and dealing with my own emotional needs that I fell into a funk. Or maybe I'm burnt out, I can't tell. It's like exercising: once you stop, it's hard to get on the treadmill again. Moreover, we are almost in lockdown again, we can only go down to buy food. It will be funny to look at this writing years into the future when we can put the pandemic behind us. But apparently the several clusters of community infections are spreading like wildfire. On top of that, we still wonder about where our lives are going, and what's going to happen with our livelihoods. Which comes back to this writing. Why am I writing this, what's my interest in wanting to delve into films of the late 50s. It's best again not to rationalise and intellectualise my motivations here. Maybe I'm doing it because I don't want to be forgotten as an artist. I told Hiroshi I'm partly doing it for the money as I need to move house and buy a property of my own. What will the institutions think of this? I told my intern I never really plan for stuff and that I'm a circumstantial artist. What a load of crap that is. It's because I cannot follow through with anything.

7:34 The YouTube version is awfully poor and dark. I made a note in my book about the set design of the backdrop which I cannot see here. Basically, it's a painted landscape that serves as a distant background. I like it, it reminds me of theatre and early filmmaking before the advent of CGI. If I ever made a production like a film, I would want to incorporate props like this and everything that deals with theatre and the craft of its own making, no illusion, our audiences are not fools. It's the Brechtian effect which I love.

8:22 The 'Gents' tailor signboard has a nice font, probably hand-painted (semiotically referring as well to the gentlemen of this film and their well pressed trousers), and the grids over the windows, the only source of light besides the signboard in the alley, reminds me of a set design again. Very surreal and noirish. It's a black and white world before the advent of neon and colour. Electricity and photography in its mid 20th Century stage.

9:33 While the cop is getting strangled by the Orang Minyak, I'm thinking about two things: one, what is that silly contraption in the cop's hand just as he was about to be snuffed out? It looked like the end of a shisha pipe, did he want a last drag of tobacco? Or was it a weapon? His asthma inhaler? Two, this Orang Minyak, an icon of horror, must have captured the imagination of the public to psychoanalyse repressed men plagued by the ills of modernity the way the Pontianak did for the monstrous feminine and revengeful woman.

22 May 2021

I did about a 1.5 km swim in my lap pool downstairs. Swimming equals meditation for me. Someday I wish to make a work about a swimmer performing as a clock, swimming endless laps, becoming Sisyphus himself. There is something about this circuit breaker (light) we are having from the pandemic that gives me more time to myself. After dinner, I fell asleep at the second Kiarostami film, *Taste of Cherry*, from the box-set I borrowed, the kind of peaceful slumber after a long swim and sniffles after, where my body is telling me it's done with cigarettes and alcohol. And I woke up at the most phenomenal moment in the film: a man preparing to be buried alive under a lightning streaked night sky, just moments before, scene of his car undulating down the road from the hills (I gather now to be a typical Kiarostami shot), a Rückenfigur where the man contemplates the city line, goes to his hole, and between flashes of light and complete blackness, the director leaves us to fill in the details before cutting to a poor daylight video of a scene being made where director and actor, some Iranian soldiers, are all seen together. Beautiful.

11:18 *Special 53*

Special 53 is possibly the Police HQ, or command centre or operations room. It's the second time I hear the police radioing using this code term, after *Che Mamat*. This time they are calling for an ambulance, but we already know the detective is dead.

12:10 While Mak Wan and Lehah are talking in the house (I'm lost as there are no subtitles in this version), I am wondering about the different social classes of the Malays back then. Mak Wan seems well-off enough to rent a mansion with a Chinese servant (was this usual for that time?) and a personal assistant. What kind of work did Mak Wan deal with? But her dressing is more typical of common folk rather than a matriarch or a socialite. Another thing—is Mak Wan a spinster? I mean, where is the rest of the family? Or is she a convenient plot device?

13:45 Because there are banana trees outside, this isn't the city. It is where a traditional *kampung* house would be. But this is a well-built piece of architecture. A grand house in the boondocks. I want to know more about this house. I checked HP's research and he covered the other film called *Serangan Orang Minyak* (there were several in this franchise, just like Jason and Freddie Krueger). But the premise is the same revolving around a colonial-era Anglo-Malay style bungalow. I am trying to understand the symbolism of this. Was it an attack on the elite Malays who were behaving like colonials?

23 May 2021

Good day today: I exercised, cleaned up my house a bit, hung some artwork and got some good work done with my interns. I am going to meet Sofia later at the beach; I had told her our sand comes from Malaysia and she was amazed. So I'm looking forward to that but before that I was hoping to bang out a couple hundred more words.

From my notes, I indicated that I was going to do a reading of films made in Singapore during the late 50s to the early 60s just before independence, when its identity was in flux. Dear reader, am I doing that now? I am not sure. Is this an experiment? Yes it is. Is this art? I'm not sure either. Another note: the Malay women here are not wearing the hijab and tudung here. I only noticed this trend, which some call the Arabisation of Islam in Southeast Asia, became more prominent in the 2000s till the present. The Malays here are synonymous with Islam; with my looks, I can pass of as a Malay person. And I had always been surrounded by Malay friends and Muslim relatives. The thing is, I'm neither of the three main races but really the fourth here, the Other. I feel like one, and I'm always seen as one. That gives me passes to weave in and out of different communities. Even my artworks have no real identity. Lastly, we are looking at a film where everyone is not safe from the Orang Minyak, loosely translated as 'The Oily Man.' But who is the Orang Minyak hunting for? He likes to rape women.

I'm writing at a slight disadvantage here because of my language handicap but I will use this as an excuse to advance my reading further. I am noticing now the *baju kurung* of Lehah and especially of Mak Wan could be of superior thread, they look glossier, setting them apart from the *kampung* sorority. And the shadows cast on the surroundings are really harsh, what kind of lights did they use those days in film sets? But I guess it fits into the film noir/horror genre here.

18:15 Mak Wan's Chinese manservant Ah Wan makes an appearance here and lo and behold, it's that dude from *Che Mamat*, the triad leader. LOL. What's he doing here with the Manchu moustache? He's even shiftier here, eavesdropping on old Mak Wan. Of course maybe in L. Krishnan's universe again, it could be his humble beginnings as a servant before joining and rising up the ranks of the Blackhand Gang; this film is made two years earlier. If not, he clearly is a go-to actor for Kirshnan. Whatever it is, the Chinese are made into stereotypes here of being shifty or criminal, based on the last two films.

19:32 I really love this scene and it looks like something Quentin Tarantino would have studied if he looked at old Cathay Keris films. Anyway, Mak Wan retrieves a pistol from her bathroom cabinet and goes out into the forest with a gun in a *baju kurung*. How badass is that. What is she trying to do? Hunt? Look for Orang Minyak? Target practice? She nearly shoots Rohiah, her niece, under an Angsana tree. But one suspects the Mak Wan's heart is fainter than the resolve of the iron pistol. And all femme fatales like Rohiah wear body-hugging *kebayas* while the dowdier women are draped in *baju kurung*. Did we really have guns then back in 1958? It would have been hard to imagine. What was the law like involving the use of firearms for a civilian. How much did a pistol cost? How many people died from gunshot wounds in 1958?

KEJATOHAN BANK UNION

21:43 Newspaper headlines of Union Bank collapsing, and the person that absconded with the money. It gets politically interesting here—tying the gruesome murder cases by the Orang Minyak with the financial collapse of a main bank. I am trying to corroborate this information with our history but I cannot find anything that matches bank collapses (of that period) on the internet. The greatest case of a bank collapse here is of Nick Leeson when he squandered 1.3 billion from the Barings Bank in Singapore in 1995. Maybe, it was a figment of L. Krishnan's imagination. We have a strong culture of Chinese dialect-based banks in their history. What I found was that in the 50s, the Aw family, owner of Tiger Balm and Haw Par Villa, was the first to set up a bank after the war that catered to ordinary folks, middle-class families and to a broad-based multi-racial clientele. Other local banks sprung up, namely, Overseas Union Bank (OUB) which was established in 1947, Industrial & Commercial Bank (ICB) (1953), Bank of Singapore (1954), Far Eastern Bank (FEB) (1958) and Asia Commercial Bank (1959). Many of these local banks ended up being acquired by OUB in the seventies and eighties. And as you know now, OUB has merged with UOB to form the super three in the land of acronyms with these two: DBS and OCBC. So money has never slept here, we know this, but I would like to know what went behind the money that grew the city. Was it as clean as the tall gleaming buildings we have today in the CBD (Central Business District)? What is money's connection with power, sex, violence and the outcast, at least in this film? So money is linked to dirty dealings in the city here—the innocent framed, a serial rapist and murderer is on the rampage. How was this monster produced then? Who is the Frankenstein here? I suspect the Orang Minyak is impotent and only becomes powerful in hideous form, in front of a beautiful woman, and relishes in her defilement and demise. But as misogynist as this sounds, I will advance this theory further by saying he kills her as he is unable to consummate the endeavour because of his impotence, or the consummation or rape is unable to give him the ultimate gratification.

24 May 2021

I have to admit I am at that age where the body is starting to betray the custodian; some of my parts are not working as well as they used to. I think the body is a vengeful teacher—treat it well and it rewards you with unknown pleasures, ignore it and it wreaks havoc on you. Or am I just very tired and stressed, or anxious? But there were some very awkward moments with Sofia last night and I hope she wasn't offended when she left. I woke up today feeling like shit and got a bit better after meeting Hiroshi and talking about the work. His gentle and open handling of the project is exactly what I need.

23:22 Filmed shots of dark fluffy clouds and lightning. Nice and rare. Of course this is added for dramatic and narrative effect rather than an artsy effect *a la* Ozu's pillow shots. I realise there is also a comedic effect between Mak Wan and Lehah. Lehah is always seeing things and ghosts, and screaming, and Mak Wan never sees this and always rubbishes her. Hilarious. By now we establish the house is haunted. You will see later how L. Krishnan splendidly turns this into a whodunit thriller revolving around the premise of the bungalow.

25:30 Dancing ceremony. Festive party. Looks so good since we are all stuck at home sixty years later. Pubescent dancers in a courtship dance with violin and traditional drums, the girls with small perky breasts under the *kebaya*, I remember the exact feeling I got as a kid looking at the Indonesian sculpture in my house of a nude figure with a straw hat, like a seductive rice farmer, probably Balinese. It sounds like *ronggeng*, a traditional Malay *joget*. Again the performance here is shown in its entirety. I suspect two reasons—to glorify local culture here and again to acknowledge the musical in Malay films. I love the portrayal and camera angles of the dance; you have vantage points as an audience which is different from a live experience. My interest in video and film lies in these perspectives too and the idea of their cuts—truncating/dissecting time. I think this is highly original which I don't remember seeing from Western films.

29:59 Now just medium shots of only the feet dancing and their sequences. Kudos to Krishnan here for being inventive, I see his remarkable talent and how he deals with the semiotics of image-making.

39:15 *Siapa Tu? (Who's that?)*

Jumping now to Rohiah changing to her negligee, how risqué was that in that time and how is this even possible now? It's a sexual representation of a woman about to go to bed. After turning off the bed lamp, she hears someone creeping and opening the door, a sliver of light cutting in. *Siapa Tu?* Is this the Orang Minyak? No it's Bakar, her lover, now disguised as Mak Wan's gardener Cik Ahmad. What is going on here? She covers her modesty with a shawl (as if that was necessary) and embraces him excitedly. They spent the night talking in her bed, and wondering about how Bakar was slandered into being the scapegoat for taking the bank's money. He suspects the money is hidden in the house. And then the electricity goes out again in the storm from outside. In the blackout while trying to light the candle, the couple hears a noise from upstairs, prompting Rohiah to exclaim yet again: "*Siapa Tu!*"

I need to sleep even though I'm not sleepy, it's half-past two in the morning and I am chatting half philosophically, half nonsensically in my chat group, while half-drunk on Sauvignon Blanc.

I would really hate to be full of myself here. I would. Every artist is perhaps narcissistic and attention-seeking and approval-seeking. It's best to avoid these pitfalls and even though I'd like to think that what I'm doing is great, only time reveals mediocrity from great work. I have no say in this and thank the greater forces for that. Maybe that's why I decide to bury this in pulp, or a kind of kitsch. Those kinds of things are blameless. I miss hanging out in the bar with Carl, the barman. This shitshow makes us so damn isolated and lonely. It makes families closer and lonely people lonelier.

25 May 2021

The devil arrived early today just as I got out of sleep. As usual, Horlicks my cat dashed for cover behind the oven when the intercom buzzed. It was James Baldwin's *The Devil Finds Work*, about his memoirs watching films growing up as a black person. It was going to be one of the many books we will photocopy for the installation.

What does the writer do here as a proxy? What do past films reveal about us today? Can this be an alternative form of history? I thought about these questions in the toilet while looking at a MUBI post on Instagram.

Chris, or rather X—he goes by the symbol—messaged me on the phone that he was in the neighbourhood accompanying his mother for an acupuncture treatment. He decided to leave her at that and asked if I wanted to hang out and have coffee. I said it wasn't compliant with the new Covid measures so why not just hang out in my apartment before my meeting. We got some iced coffee and tea from Al Fahah and went up to my place to chat over the drinks and cigarettes. X's life is perhaps more chaotic than mine, yet I would seek advice from him. Why would I ask someone who is well adjusted and hasn't a clue. I'm drawn to people who have lived and people who have the least conventional lives and families, because I can relate to them. X says I think too much and cannot live in the moment, I said I'm trying but it's easier said than done! Then the conversation digressed to music, fashion and art. Sometimes, they are not so separate from each other, that's how we think and that's why I think we can relate to each other. I had to cut the meeting short because of my college meeting on Zoom so he left to wander around the neighbourhood until his mother was done. While I was having the meeting, he buzzed me again about some BTO HDB flats I should really consider buying instead of a resale.

Somewhere around 37:30 as Rohiah is talking to a personnel from the bank (I lost this part of the plot because of the language barrier), the saxophone sounded familiar in that key register. Later it dawned on me that it was similar to the main notes played on Ornette Coleman's *Lonely Woman*. Interestingly, Coleman's piece came out in 1959 via Atlantic Records, in the seminal album *The Shape of Jazz to Come*. This is one year after *Orang Minyak* came out. Before Coleman came to New York in the early sixties, he was an outcast even in his own community in New Orleans, getting beaten up by fellow black persons for being different. He said, "I was looking for a music that I could play without feeling guilty for doing something. To this day I haven't yet found it."

43:31 Bakar and Rohiah have a lovers' interlude under the pavilion and in the garden forest, declaring their love for each other in song. I don't know who's sexier now—Rohiah in her body-hugging *kebaya* or Bakar in this unbuttoned safari shirt with chest hair peeking, a *songkok* and the traditional *baju* belt around his waist. Perhaps Bakar wins here, as he showed more skin and looked like he worked hard under the sun before. Somehow the actor who plays Bakar, who also is a recurring actor in Krishnan's world, resembles P. Ramlee—or his leaner brother. Like maybe he's the second choice in the casting director's list.

49:35 Orang Minyak on the roof of the colonial bungalow. Looks like sundown. Silhouetted. What was it like to be a stunt double those days? He creeps through the window, Lehah as usual sees him, but her scream is delayed five seconds later. When he recedes back into the dark, his eyes glow a menacing—I would imagine—red or yellow. It reminds me of the black monkey demon in the dark forest with the glowing eyes in Apichatpong Weerasethakul's excellent *Uncle Boonmee Who Can Recall His Past Lives* (2010).

Everyone gets out of their rooms to find out what happened. The railing grills above the staircase cast ominous shadows like another set of black bars on the wall, emphasising the caged-like atmosphere. I forgot to mention Inspector Dasuki added to the list of characters, he has come to investigate the strange happenings in the house, and has taken board in one of the rooms of the house offered by Mak Wan.

51:58 This scene wasn't necessary but it was necessarily artistic in the sense that Krishnan sought to capture the beauty of flow and space between two floors of the bungalow as both Inspector Dasuki, relaxed with a *Lucky Strike* cigarette dangling from his lips, and an apprehensive Rohiah walked down the stairs—cuts elegantly and diagonally across the frame of the picture, contrasted and lit in high keys of blacks and whites.

26 May 2021

Vesak Day.

Last night I read ten pages of Baldwin's *The Devil Finds Work* and at once felt overshadowed by his devastating eloquence. I imagined a voice between Morgan Freeman and Gil Scott Heron. I don't know if that's my version of a strong black voice cause I've heard Baldwin speak in an interview on YouTube, which I remembered as more English-accented and crisp but my reading voice becomes somehow this cross between the revered actor and the gifted but troubled singer. This morning I decided to take it easy and slow. I just need to chill. I had also decided to lay off the cigarettes and drinks until tomorrow's appointment.

52:28 Rohiah retrieves the pistol, this time from a different cabinet, hearing something approaching from the door. The music builds the suspense, only to discover that it's Rashid

Dubar from the bank. She quickly leaves the gun on the desk behind her. Okay Rashid is dodgy and involved in some shady business, probably behind the embezzlement. While Rohiah goes to look for something, he looks for what appears to be a blueprint of the house behind a shelf, tearing a portion of it, only to be caught by Rohiah who insists on him returning it to her. A struggle ensues when Rohiah grabs her weapon and in the scuffle just by the stairs, Rashid gets shot from somewhere. It wasn't Rohiah. Inspector Dasuki is alerted and runs out of his room. Rohiah quickly hides the map in her bosom. Rashid Dubar is dead. The inspector covers his face with a handkerchief. Mak Wan and Leha also come out from their rooms. Bakar and the Chinese servant join them. We have the whodunit ensemble of characters now. Inspector Dasuki takes another handkerchief to pick up the pistol, inspecting it thoroughly. Now I understand from the spoken Malay that Rashid is the nephew of the boss of Union Bank. And he was shot in his own house which was rented to Mak Wan. Inspector Dasuki also reveals to Mak Wan that Rohiah was engaged to the absconded employee, whom she denied knowing earlier. They were interrupted by a shadowy figure on the stairs, Inspector Dasuki goes out to investigate, Mak Wan slyly hides the pistol in her baju. The family doctor arrives for the body. The Chinese servant shiftily slips out. He returns with another character, having caught him loitering outside—it's Rashid's driver Daud. He discovers his boss is dead. The doctor tries to take something from the hand of the body but is spotted by the inspector. It is one portion of the blueprint. The inspector keeps it. They remove the body. Nice play of placing all characters in one setting by Krishnan.

1:02:09 I like this scene where Rohiah retrieves her portion of the blueprint from her blouse and hides it in a French loaf of bread, while no one is looking. It's now a piece of paper with some vital information on it embedded in baked dough. The significance of French Baguettes, Chinese servants, and

English houses with Malay tenants is interesting. The piece of paper, which suggests another space hidden within the space of an organic edible substance is also intriguing and clandestine, suggesting various stories and myths about information and communication hidden in foodstuff. Mak Wan tells Ah Wan to keep the bread in the kitchen. The inspector stops to inspect the article, raising tensions for both Rohiah and the audience, but to her relief, doesn't find it.

I fell into a nap which is good, albeit a short one; for years, I've been having much trouble sleeping. I woke up, checked my Facebook and found a quote by Buddha that said something like the problem of all human unhappiness lies in not facing reality squarely. Serendipitously, an article came on too, advertising Sneaker Pimp's long awaited album in 20 years and a preview of their new single *Squaring The Circle*. How long had I been staring down things into circles and spirals? I sent some affectionate emojis to Sofia and then proceeded to check out Horlicks. I don't have his grace and peace, this furry creature at the right of my pillow. The fella is so peaceful I cannot locate a heartbeat when I tried to lie on him as a pillow, hoping to be one with him, listening to his innards. Instead, lots of wheezing and heaving sounds.

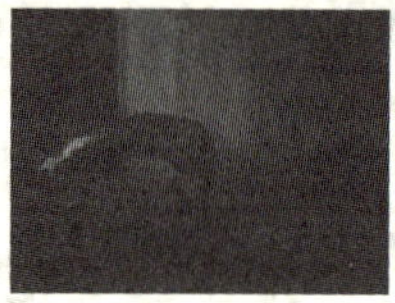

1:04:01 This is one of my favourite scenes of the whole film and it is to be repeated later in the movie again. A hand creeps in like a spider and tries to unlock a window from the outside in the blackness of the night. Its fingers fiddling with the latch to what sounds like an eerie theremin. Its dark stained limb at first resembles the Orang Minyak's, just as it manages to lift the latch open with its finger to enter the room, you realise then this is not how the bogeyman would have entered. It seemed more human and desperate. The camera zooms out, revealing a man, still within the shadows, dressed in white shirt and black pants. Something is amiss that's being added to the puzzle. This short scene is choreographed very well and adds a real edge and psychological flavour to the film. If anything, it's about exteriors breaking into interiors via a surrogate of the body, introducing an unexpected element into the architecture of both the plot and the building. It heightens the psychospatial element that creates fear in the audience. At least in the few L. Krishnan films I had watched, many scenes involved people breaking into interiors through windows.

1:06:32 It's too dark to see here on the YouTube version, but I made a note about the timestamp where the Orang Minyak is changing into the monster. He looks up at the window and throws a rope into it, makes it taut and uses his super powers to glide-walk up into the opening, where Rohiah is resting. The minute when he enters is quite phenomenal, because behold the man—in all his gleaming glory—is the first time you see him in the light. He looks rather crude, and rather sympathetic like Quasimodo. In the abode, he spots his beautiful prey sleeping, holds and observes her face for a few seconds:

Over here let's take a pause and review,
At the licensed still frame (from Cathay)
in a much higher resolution.
In stillness you see so much more;
The still entombs where the moving image fleets.

First I notice the grain of the still,
Then I notice that Rohiah's shadow is of the
same value as the Orang Minyak.
A man of the shadow,
Black as his companion the night, who stays outside.
Hiroshi calls him the "monstrous outsider."
The outsider, uninvited, breaking inside.
He casts a glance at Rohiah,
Who is dead to the world.

This is longer than a glance.
A lingering gaze of the outcast, cast upon her face

But unreturned.
From here you see his upturned nose
Like a pig,

Maybe he is a wild boar.
Everything crude and profane:
Oil, pigs,
But it is still a micro-moment
Of sympathy for the devil.

Then he attempts to undo the buttons of her blouse when she wakes up. Never has Rohiah seen such a hideous thing, and knowing who he is, too frightened to do anything, goes into a catatonic state. The Orang Minyak proceeds to undo her blouse, before Bakar chances upon him and as he attempts to catch the elusive monster, he slips out and disappears.

Never has Rohiah seen such a hideous thing, and knowing who he is, too frightened to do anything, goes into a catatonic state

27 May 2021

Last night it was supposed to be the eclipse of the Flower Blood Moon of spring. A total eclipse. For Capricorns, we are supposed to harness the energy of the moon by decompressing and resting. But I know this too well. This eclipse is a reminder to take care of myself and to find solace within because we run around so hard all day all week. Or so I was told. How do these horoscopes end up being so true? I did take it easy. I was going to anyway, so I spent most of my night sleeping and listening to meditative music on my bluetooth speaker.

1:09:00 It is quite a funny remark Mak Wan made upon telling the lovers how she knew Mr. Ahmad the gardener was Bakar in disguise. She said she's had many gardeners before, but never has she seen one with starched pants, one who wears shoes in the house and who didn't know his plants.

So much for the modern man.

28 May 2021

I turned off the air conditioner. It is so much more conducive to write in silence and heat. Nothing will survive the 50s except the reproducibility of their copies. In art, in America, individualist Abstract Expressionism was giving way to consumerist Pop Art. Both art forms, as critiques, have become kitsch today. I would argue to say even more so for the former since the latter has more awareness of its milieu. I could never stand to see another action painting done by yet another student and another artist in a Jackson Pollock revelation, even without the benefit of a Marxist reading that the autonomous self inevitably gets subsumed by capitalist machinery. Can any artist safely say they have not been affected or defined, in the way they make art, by gender, race and socio-economic class?

If they have not and had this complete freedom, then they must be somewhere on top of the food chain. But even without this, another action painting is just awful to the eyes and says nothing. In coming back to the idea of kitsch and this project, which lies at the heart of the italicised expression *Slander!*, pulp (aesthetics) has its place in the populace within the desiring-products of society and it is likely *kitsch* if it satisfies at least one criteria set by these esteemed/established versions: *a la* Clement Greenberg, it is the opposite of the avant-garde, the product of industrialisation and urbanisation of the working class hungry for culture, but without the resources and education. Via Milan Kundera, he talks about how it is the aesthetics of the over-sentimental and the melodramatic in political ideology. In its extreme totalitarian form, it rejects all individualism, doubt and irony, such is that the artist is unable to create unusual works. When you know you've seen a certain kind of work (product) a dozen, hundred times, you know you are in the realm of kitsch.

But kitsch is the flavour I'm looking for against my better melancholic self. It has to come from something manufactured yet has a critical distance to it. The reproduction of form takes precedence over any expression, and any expression is a form able to be reproduced again in logic or strategy, through shape, size, scale, seriality and repetition. The very instruments of infinite reproducibility in capitalism is made technically possible by print and photography.

1:12:19 The same figure in white shirt black trousers climbs out of the room through the window and goes to another one from the outside, unlatches it the same way he did earlier on to clamber back into its interior. However this time, Lehah sees the hand and screams yet again. One starts to think that the actress who plays Lehah was hired for her particular scream. She seems to see everything but gets rubbished again this time by the Inspector, to which Mak Wan jumps to her defence.

1:16:00 Inspector Dasuki frisks the suspicious doctor and retrieves a portion of the map. Later on, as he is about to lock the door of the room, he catches the doctor trying to hide another fragment of the map, after which another struggle ensues. And I forgot to tell you that our dear family doctor here, besides being in cahoots with the Dubar family to frame Bakar and embezzle the money, is also played by the same actor who was the editor-in-chief in *Che Mamat*. So while we know that he has a face to play a senior distinguished professional-type, we also know that he has a way with those 1950s black dial telephones. If you remember how in the previous film he activated the country's entire defence force with two receivers, here, while struggling for the pistol on the desk, he promptly knocks out the inspector cold with one like a club, and then gags him after. From now till he binds the inspector's wrists with his own handcuffs, it's almost a full minute of silence on film. This is splendid directing and acting where tension is built up with camera movement and editing and the terse all-too-human desperation of the actor's face. Another point is that the doctor really has a nice haircut that would still look good today—with his *songkok* knocked off, his stylish floppy fringe (in a Hugh Grant kind of way) is revealed with a slope fade cut at the back. He is a pretty good-looking middle-aged man.

After this, the plot heightens and accelerates into two search parties for the unknown in candlelight (after a blackout in which real intentions are also hidden). Actually, I'm not even sure now whether it's the money hidden in the house they are looking for or the Orang Minyak. Just before this, the last and mysterious character had been introduced. Bruised and concussed, presumably it's the mysterious figure in shirt and pants that comes through the main door, despite repeated warnings to the tenants not to open any doors. He cannot remember anything, but unbeknownst to the cast, this fella is up to something as well. They leave him with Ah Wan.

1:23:00 The men and women separate. The men continue on the second floor, the women go upstairs. Is this somewhat sexist or old-fashioned, or simply illogical and foolish? What was the scriptwriter's reason for this?

29 April 2021

Woke up late, close to eleven. Remembering four things the ex told me that stuck with me. First is that I live in my head. Second, I'm a slow-moving particle. Third, I'm never satisfied with anything. And fourth—that I can't have everything.

1:24:53 This is such a claustrophobic scene of three women climbing up a very narrow staircase in the dark. I am tempted to dissect the whole mansion through screens of scenes involving its architecture like staircases, rooms, cells, trap doors, windows, compartments, levels. It's not so much Gaston Bachelard's *The Poetics of Space* but rather the psychosis of space. This is best exemplified by Alfred Hitchcock's horror film *Psycho*, which focused entirely on spatial relations shot in various interiors, using non-elaborate sets. This, and the shooting of his film in black-and-white, kept his budget low. Norman Bates' vertical house is contrasted with his horizontal motel. In the cinematic masterpiece of a scene involving the stabbing of Janet Leigh in the shower, the scene is voyeuristically dissected into a construction of cuts, involving seventy camera setups, no less, for forty-five seconds of footage. Considering Krishnan's own horror piece preceded *Psycho* by two years, one could also imagine that his camera setup to be somewhat rigorous but not anymore objective here in his editing to unfold the space of the Bungalow like a maze and labyrinth through his lens and cuts. The floors, levels, staircases and perspectives act as psychospatial elements of the film. I want to probe this a bit further by reading what the new tenants of the mansion inherit as a metaphor.

Earlier I spoke about the house being a colonial-era Anglo-Malay style bungalow. A more appropriate architectural terminology would be a colonial-vernacular house, and more specifically a Compound House. One that is adapted for Europeans in the climate and one which has a unique interior layout. 'Compound' here is etymologically borrowed from the Malay '*Kampung*'. So the inheritance here from the colonisers is problematic when the original owners of this complex architectural system have left the building, leaving the house to its new tenants to run the show. It doesn't exorcise the ghosts of its past and one needs to find and join patches of its blueprint to inherit its real treasure which otherwise leaves a motley crew ensemble to solve its riddle. And it's hard to keep order in the house if your tenants distrust one another, allowing your ghosts and monsters to fester and grow stronger.

Malaya's premier bogeyman strikes back, again

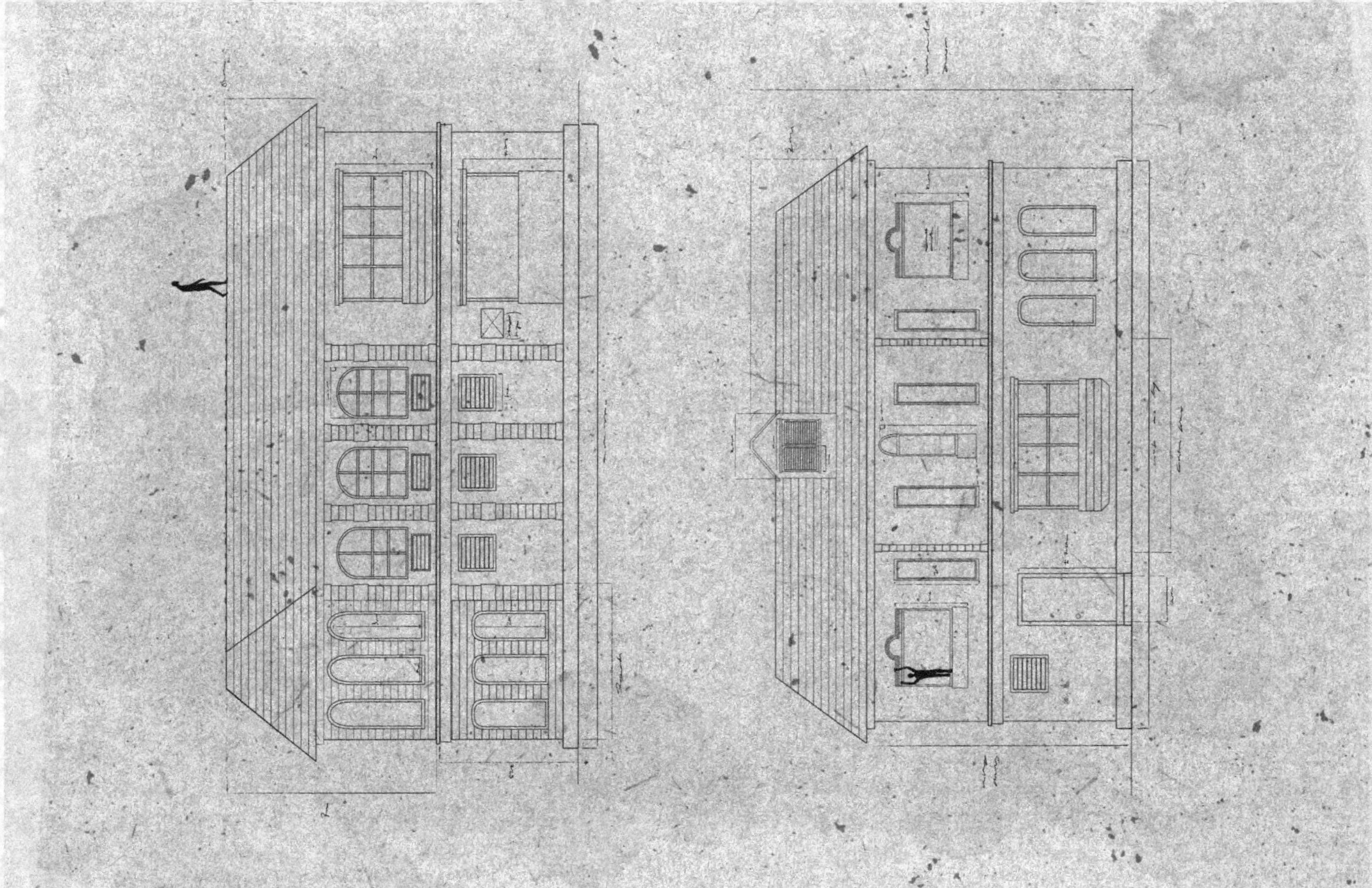

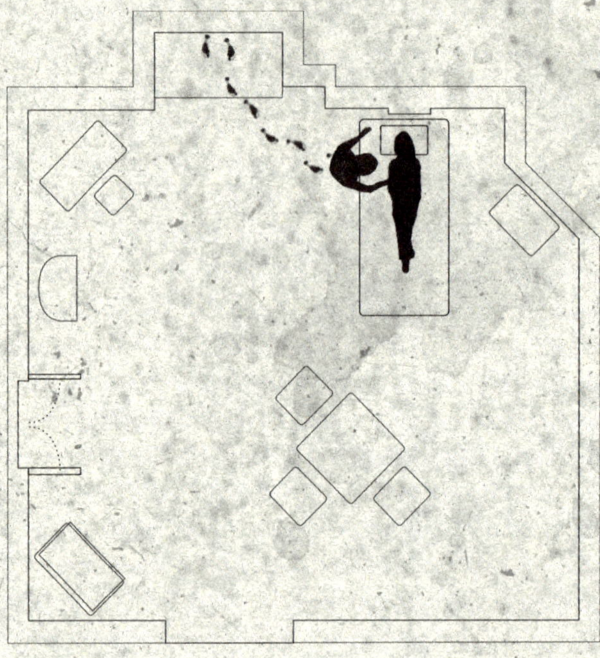

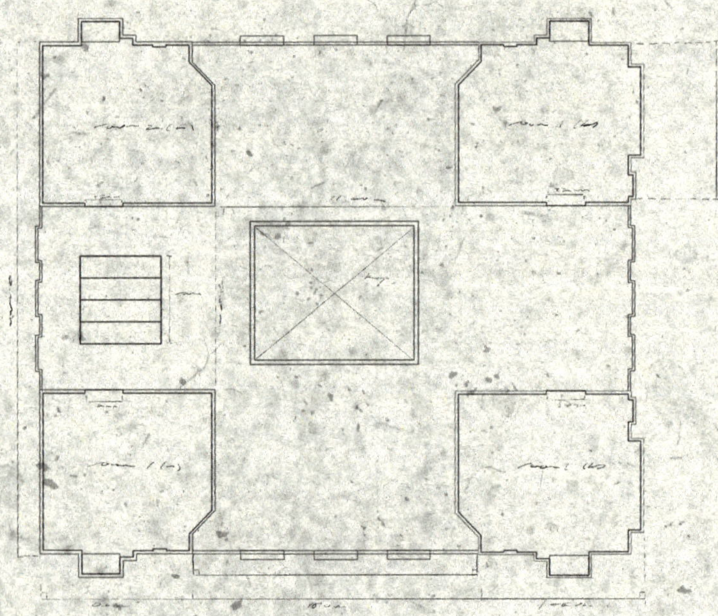

31 May 2021

Literally the 11th hour of the last day of May. Master procrastinator. My mind is a coil of snakes. I think in fragments. I write in them. Malaysian humour—some whatsapp post of a FB comedian poking fun at Malaysians about the vaccination and other impersonations. And I told the messenger it's quite close to local Malay and Indian humour without the Malaysian politics. And it dawned on me that the brand of humour was tied to a political identity. A hundred years ago, we were perhaps part of the same entity Malaya with different borders marked out by the British. And then I thought about images and what images want from us, from hidden archives and forgotten films and the restless dreams that we generate. I think they shut the floodgates of emotions by shutting them in their portals, together with our memories. Wait, images are not memories. Images lie to us and have their own agency. They don't make us remember, they estrange us from memory. They tell us what to think. An example of this: XY sent me an image of my son Jaxxon and I on the water breaker by Sembawang beach. It was a lovely image. I was trying to tie his shoelace when the wind caught his hair and at that moment he had frozen spikes on his head, smiling a gleeful smile. Another image showed both Jaxxon and Jagger coming to me against the littoral curtain of the sea, painted flat in the picture. It looked religious like I'm some prophet with my long hair and pin striped trousers. But I did not remember these moments like that; it was what the camera captured, albeit with XY's hands. I say hands because we shoot with our hands these days on our mobile phones, whereas before the camera was synonymously attached to the eye.

This mundanity of the diarist format seems like a lazy excuse to want to write an actual book of fiction.

Now I'm transitioning and am starting to understand things that are falling into my life. I (or it?) take(s) a long time.

'The Malay World' is problematic, I realised. But what

does this mean, other than it's a construct like anything else, a construct of an identity/category in the forming of a nation through the census. But language is interchangeable and here I mean 'Malay' is a pack like 'Chinese' or 'Indian', to deliver it immediately to the reader. To 'unpack' them also requires time. But who needs an exegesis here when that's not the point.

I'm trying to find the difference between Benedict Anderson's print capitalism (tied to media and the national) and colonial capitalism (perhaps tied to subject and power). I think they can be synonymous and problematise one another.

There are three types of pictures. One that entombs, one that immortalises, and one that propagates.

Words fail me. Sometimes I try to find the word but it escapes me, and the words I have in my lexicon do not quite describe what I'm thinking or feeling. And I find the membranes of my nasal passages tightening and I breathe a little harder.

1:27:33 We are nearing the end of the film and the mystery of the Orang Minyak.

The dark is the abode of the Orang Minyak, and there is no fight against him even in candlelight, because it makes his shadows accomplices to murder. With this, the monster strangles Daud to death from behind. You may only defeat him through strength in numbers, not when you stupidly abandon the group like the men. To keep from fainting, apply tiger oil to your temples like what Lehah does.

Because this is not a scene by scene plot breakdown, I will end here to say they found the money in a basket, discovered that the Orang Minyak is actually one of them involved as an accomplice to the loot and also discovered the identity of the mysterious stranger. With a rather abrupt ending to maybe keep to the timing of exactly one hour and forty minutes, Krishnan has a tendency to break the fourth wall at the end, this time by painting the words 'the end' on the money basket held by one of the actors. I suspect this is less of a Brechtian effect than to pander to the audience and their fears by saying "Hey, it's only a film."

It may have worked for local audiences then, but I came off feeling unsatisfied with the lack of a psychological edge to the roots of how the Orang Minyak came to be. I guess this could be explained from the franchise of the other Minyak films like the sequel *Serangan Orang Minyak* and the period fable version *Sumpah Orang Minyak* by Shaw Brothers starring P. Ramlee. All were released in some fervour between 1957-58.

HP's research states: "In the final months of 1957, certain parts of the city of Singapore were in a state of pandemonium. An 'oily man', whose last incarnated appearance caused widespread hysteria in 1954, was on the prowl again, this time terrorising women in the residential estates of Clementi, Alexandra, Ayer Rajah and Changi."

There was a real and recurring "serial molester who covered himself in a mixture of coconut oil and soot to elude capture."

In dispelling the myth further by delving into its origin, in *Sumpah Orang Minyak*, a marginalised member of a village suffering from a skin disease makes a pact with the devil to transform himself into a handsome young man, very much like the actor who played Inspector Dasuki. However to keep his side of the bargain, he has to rape a number of women as an oil-covered monster. These motivations then seem to converge in this film I'm watching where sorcery, myth, rejection, greed and lust combine to create a modern monster.

In looking at these archetypes of the haunted house and the bogeyman, I remember as a child, it was stoked in my imagination how my grandmother used to warn me that if I do not behave myself, the Orang Minyak will come in the night and take me. I noticed very vaguely how this term was also used discriminatorily against darker-skinned people in jokes too.

Again blackness was associated with something unsavoury and insidiousness, creating a perceptual myth around oil, black, crude, smell, outside-ness and ugliness.

Chapter 3:

Rasa Sayang Eh (1959)

The actor or laugh in the airways

23 June 2021

What do we do with time? Too much of it and we don't know what to do with ourselves, looking for the next fix, the next distraction. Too little of it then we complain and get stressed out. Just what do we occupy ourselves with?

I took a break, but also a week off to spend time with Jaxxon and Jagger during the school hols. Our model warship is still not complete, not with the three-minute attention spans of these kids. We have added two penny boards that I've tucked away at the top of my cupboard. Two days ago, I was looking at Tony Hawk videos—damn that feels tempting to take up skateboarding, on top of the things I never finish doing or learning.

But finally, I'm back at the keyboards. 80 laps at the pool the night before helps to get me back in focus, and prevent the mind from turning to corners of useless thoughts. I can finish this.

Rasa Sayang Eh (1959)

It feels like we're never moving past the end of the 50s and we end up in comedy again.

2:09 Credits. Soundtrack. We all know this familiar ditty as kids and the Malay title translates as 'Feel The Love.' Listening to the mambo-infused version here brings back memories of the dance musical TV programme in the 80s called *Kelab Dondang Sayang*. I would always chance upon the programme being on TV while at my cousins'. Again, together with the *Sandiwara* soap operas, my grandmother loved to watch these programmes. This is particularly familiar with Malay, Peranakan and Eurasian families. Dondang Sayang consists of two singers in a hall having a repartee about love and good deeds, singing and dancing to Malay *rebana* drums, gongs, guitars, tambourines, and flutes. The history of this musical and poetic form traces back to Malacca in the 14th and 15th centuries. It was a popular form of entertainment among the Malay royal families and nobles, before spreading to the public. Dondang Sayang found its way to Singapore in the 19th century when Malacca came under British rule as part of the Straits Settlements.

3:17 L. Krishnan back at the helm again. Wahid Satay is back on stage, his persona is that of a jester. In a parallel cinematic universe this is Che Mamat again as a successful comedic actor belting out "Rasa Sayang Eh." It would translate Into English poetically as:

Rasa sayang, hey!	*I've got that loving feeling, hey!*
Rasa sayang sayang, hey!	*I've got that loving feeling, hey!*
Hey, lihat nona jauh,	*See that girl in the distance,*
Rasa sayang sayang, hey!	*I've got that loving feeling, hey!*
Buah cempedak di luar pagar,	*The cempedak tree beyond the fence,*
Ambil galah tolong jolokkan;	*Pick the fruit with a stake;*
Saya budak baru belajar,	*A youthful learner I, so hence,*
Kalau salah tolong tunjukkan.	*Be please to point out each mistake*
Pulau pandan jauh ke tengah,	*The Pandan Isle is far from land,*
Gunung daik bercabang tiga;	*Three peaks on the Daik Mountain;*
Hancur badan di kandung tanah,	*Though the self has rot in the sand,*
Budi yang baik dikenang juga.	*The good deeds are never forgotten.*
Dua tiga kucing berlari,	*Two or three cats are running around,*
Mana sama si kucing belang;	*The cat with striped is the one superior;*
Dua tiga boleh ku cari,	*Two or three (gals) can easily be found,*
Mana sama adik seorang.	*But not the same as having you, my dear.*

Pisang emas dibawa berlayar,	*With golden plantains sail away,*
Masak sebiji di atas peti;	*Whilst on a chest lies one that's ripe;*
Hutang emas boleh dibayar,	*The debts of gold we can repay,*
Hutang budi dibawa mati.	*But debts of kindness last through life*

5:00 But unlike Che Mamat, his character suffers from extreme anxiety around beautiful women. So you can't have it all. You are either a bum with an encouraging girlfriend or an esteemed comedian who cannot face a pretty reporter in a white dress without getting an extreme case of the hiccups that culminates in a lack of oxygen and his falling to the floor. His manager is introduced as the 'Laurel to his Hardy,' or is it 'Hardy to his Laurel'? He asks the stage personnel for a glass of water while tending to Baning (Wahid), and upon getting it, drinks it himself and proceeds to cast some sort of spell on Baning to 'cure' him of the dizzies.

Again I am making do without the English subtitles in this poor copy.

24 June 2021

6:12 In the dressing room, the manager expresses his concern for Baning's mental health. But Baning is not only afraid of women, he is afraid of doctors too. He tells the manager off, and the manager breaks into tears. So the manager is easily offended while Baning is easily scared. I look around the room and find checkered sarongs for draped curtains and a photograph of Baning above his mirror. It's got a changing cubicle within the room and a nice dining table for two. Baning's arms are spindly and thin in his sleeveless ensemble and he just applied what looks like pimple cream on his cheeks, probably having a breakout from too much makeup.

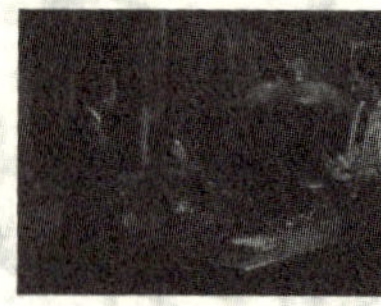

7:50 Why am I not surprised that the Chinese triad leader and man servant is back here as a Datuk Rashid Dubas. He is playing a Malay character now—he's lost the annoying Chinese accent. I looked him up and found out that he's a Malay actor called Dollah Sarawak. He sure had me convinced that he was a Chinese person all along! Which makes me think he's quite a good actor after all, and quite versatile too at that. Here, four men in the dark-lit office room set in the late 50s, one Datuk seated wearing his traditional *songkok* and garb, one in a suit, another in a sporty jacket, another in a shirt and fedora, all discussing and hatching a plan behind closed doors. Love the noirish feel.

26 June 2021

11:59 Samsudin, a character, gets shot in the dark rubber plantation after getting chased by the two of the four shady characters mentioned earlier (Datuk's henchmen who look more like jazz musicians). The forest/jungle is always associated with crime and guns in this cinematic universe. And violence, fedora hats and modern jazzy clothes were rife then. There is a bit of espionage going on about a mysterious map (which is largely going to be an object of contention here) that the shadies want but which, gets intercepted by Samsuddin who smuggles it to the mask-maker for the theatre, who in turn uses Baning as a mule to smuggle the map to someone in the theatre. But unknown to the mask-maker, Baning is planning to make a trip to KL (Kuala Lumpur) first before heading down to Singapore which tells me that this is taking place in Penang. Before Samsudin falls dead by the telephone, he makes a call to Abdul Salam (the actor who played the chief editor and the doctor in the earlier two films) and instructs him to receive the map at the airport from the unsuspecting Baning.

14:29 A note: back in the day in this Malay world, the men who wore *songkoks* were kind of debonair actually; headwear as fashion status symbols as opposed to ethnic/religious identity.

14:54 Some of the best scenes here involve Baning getting on a commercial airplane for the first time. I wonder how L Krishnan shot this then: was it on a real air liner or was it staged in a movie set design? There is a shot of the plane taking off and another overhead shot of the plane flying over the coast of Penang. Was this borrowed footage? If it wasn't, how did Krishnan get the bird's eye shot? No drones then. The introduction of a plane here continues the ambition of the director in introducing modern elements of transportation into the increasingly cosmopolitan lifestyles of its denizens. Where before the car was an incongruent element in the *kampung*, and was the vehicular bridge between commuters in Malaysia and Singapore (later on in cinematic history the train will also be introduced in the other films), the notion of speed is amped up to serve the need for interstate distances and time of espionage and travelling professionals, and the relations between these nations and neighbours. Paul Virillio wrote a whole book called *The Aesthetics of Disappearance* about how the need for speed in the modern world has contributed to the disappearance of the time/space dimension of past and traditional elements, through the motor of cinema and technology, such that our viewing of environments become different as looking through the window of an automobile or a plane. Such as that our modes of perception have also changed or adapted, where previous modes are abrogated for the present, to serve a different reality. Virilio has been quite radical in claiming that speed has in fact been the primary force shaping civilisation, militarising society as an engine of destruction.

Comedy (and filming) here is exercised in the metabolic bodies of these passengers in the time capsule of the plane, providing much fascination for the viewer:

As the plane is flying at great speeds,
its passengers are stationary in their leather bound seats
and still balancing to the vertiginous speeds of the aircraft
and defining their intimate spaces within the confines of a long tubular capsule—
Baning mistakenly takes his beautiful co-passenger's seat belt (amidst hiccups) for his own and buckles them together.
The female co-passenger bumps her head against the ceiling as she tries to change her seat.
Baning loses his balance and spills hot coffee from the stewardess' tray onto the same woman's lap.
Beautiful Eurasian air-stewardess (let me list the Eurasian stereotypes—stewardess, radio personality, musician, MC etc.).
Long unavoidable conversations on the plane, as Datuk Rashid requests Baning to come over to the seat beside him to speak with him.
Baning tries to find his way back to his seat without losing his balance,
accidentally holds onto the head of the same female passenger.

The plane flies down and along the left coast of Malaysia toward KL.

27 June 2021

I'm in my favourite Vietnamese joint, and already they are trying to cut costs, aggravated by the five weeks of social distancing measures in the ongoing pandemic. You can't order single skewers now, you have to get at least five in a bunch and they don't even provide serviettes this time.

A Japanese tourist in a Hawaiian shirt is seated diagonally across me, very pleased with himself. His face is flushed, probably from one too many mojitos on his table. He signals to the waiter to order another one. Minutes later he is smiling and whispering to himself. He sure is content. I am mildly fascinated by this, perhaps a little envious. He glances my way and I smile back, catching the Vietnamese waiter watching me eat, while sitting in the opposite diagonal direction. Waiter's job is done and perhaps he is fascinated by me as well. Said waiter always gets my order wrong: I ask for chicken heart, I get squid. I order five skewers, he gives me four. But all is always forgiven in this cafe where lonely men, couples and long lost friends find some kind of temporary refuge in this joint.

Earlier on, lying in bed, I was thinking about how we are occupied with so many useless distractions that make us so careless with our lives. I was thinking about how Jordan Peterson the psychologist said that mental illness and depression is a problem of complexity and not so much one of illness. We make our lives so damn complicated, and when we are hit with catastrophes, we blow out at our weakest points. I was also thinking about Heidegger and what he said about anxiety—that it points to no object but the void—being conscious of existence itself, revealing the hidden-ness of Being. I feel we are distracted from the problem of Time, or the problem of ourselves being temporal beings.

18:25 The plane, which looks like an early model Boeing, lands in Kuala Lumpur Airport. It was a time when airports were modest. I think they resemble train stations. A photographer spots Baning and asks to take his picture. Baning puts on an air of being an important star. Abdul Salam appears to offer him a light when Baning cannot find his lighter for his Lucky Strike cigarette. The airport must have reeked of cigarettes then, something we cannot fathom today. Salam says "Salam" thinking Baning will respond that he is the deliverer of the map. Instead Baning, thinking Salam meant 'salam'

('greetings' in Malay), greets him back. Salam goes to prod Baning again, *Salam*, and tells him he is asking for something. Baning now thinks he's a well-dressed beggar and offers him some coins. The comedy is wearing off on me. It's not funny watching this on a laptop in 2021.

I met Ariel, after a long time, and we had dinner and drinks together over at my apartment. I brought her to the rooftop for smokes, and it was only today that I realised I had never bothered to take in the view of the east coast at sunset. I am going to read a little more before I hit the sack.

28 June 2021

Agatha Christie has a formula for getting work done. First she writes her story in her head. Then she checks herself into a cheap filthy hotel or a fucked-up one for whatever time she needs to write. The room she has will discourage her to sleep when she wants or to get up as late as she wants, it will discourage her from lounging or having guests, basically enjoying herself, so that she is unable to procrastinate further and have nothing to do but just get the pages out daily until she gets her book.

I wish it were that simple today, I think the first step is to flush your mobile phone down the toilet and despair for a night or two. And because this endeavour is more diaristic then all-out fiction I can't vomit a story in two weeks. The agony comes from a Sisyphean task to churn out from the writing machine every day. It's impossible to have a writer's block but then it's also a task to sound interesting when perhaps maybe your life is really boring as fuck and who gives a shit.

So I'm in Without.U (the Vietnamese joint), my cafe of choice which functions as a space to make me write. I pick a table right at the corner next to the bar so I can watch the main road from a distance. The tropical sun outside contrasts with the black decor of the cafe. Hanging over the bar, there's a neon sign in handwriting that reads 'Cocktail - Tea Or Me?'

Everything is so badly decorated it's good. Kitsch in the right place. We are all getting used to the pandemic and I can't imagine going out into the world without a facemask.

Back in the years 1957 to 1958, there was a pandemic too. Dubbed 'The Asian Flu' (also known as the Singapore virus), it was thought to have originated in Guizhou, China and then travelled to Hong Kong before spreading Singapore in April '57. The virus infected 30 marine workers living in a *kampung* on the offshore settlement of Pulau Brani, then a settlement for both the British army and the local sea gypsies. In the *Singapore Stories* website, a segment reads:

> *The island of Pulau Brani (Pulau Ayer Berani) was home to four main villages—Telok Saga, Selat Sengkir, Masak Timah, and Spedo. The islanders were primarily composed of Singapore's Orang Selat and included those who had migrated from Singapore River. Over the course of the 19th century they were closely connected to the British army base on Pulau Brani, which provided the Brani men with jobs such as marine engineers, lighthouse attendants, and ferry service crew. Another company that provided ample jobs for the residents of Brani was the Straits Trading Company which had set up a tin-smelting factory on the island.*

A poem comes to mind, Edwin Thumboo's *Island*. While not an exact reference, I am making filmic images of kids of different races by the sea.

> *Once*
> *There was a quiet island,*
> *With a name.*
> *You must believe me*
> *When I say that sunlight,*
> *Impure but beautiful,*
> *Broke upon the bay, silvered*
> *The unrepentant, burning noon.*

There were persons in this place.
Too young to know the sea,
Aminah cried;
Harun, who followed crab and tide
Ambitiously, learnt
To keep the spray out of his eyes.
Their father in his bid
To make a proper life,
Lived the way his father did.
Mangrove and palm
Unfold in brittle shades of green.
Houses on stilts, boats drawn up
The sand, the makeshift pier, village shop,
Smoke from kitchen fires,
All frame a picture.

Romantic. Nostalgic.

But images change.

The Asian Flu peaked in mid-May and petered out over a month later. An estimated 680 lives were lost to the pandemic. I read Camus' *The Plague* during this pandemic and vaguely remembered the plot as lasting less than a year. It has been one-and-a-half years and our current virus shows no signs of burning out.

20:19 I recognise Merdeka Square (Malaysia's own Padang next to the renown Masjid Jamek) in KL from its spires, minarets and architectural design. Built at the turn of the century featuring Indo-Saracenic and Neo-Mughal designs, "it was here the Union Flag was lowered and the Malaysian flag hoisted for the first time at midnight on 31 August 1957." We used to bus here from Singapore to play gigs when I was in my twenties. Those were the days I really felt like a touring rock musician with our six-hour bus journeys. Bands would play there to cater to the larger market in Malaysia and a much more vibrant, less sterile scene where we were always welcome like brothers. It's quite surreal now to think we did those things as kids!

22:12 Baning and his manager stay in Grand Hotel. And the Datuk too. And Abdul Salam. So you know lots of action is going to happen here. Baning sleeps in striped pajamas. How cliché is that? Who does that? In the 50s? Ok my boys do that. I probably slept in them when I was five. Actually no. I'm trying to remember my photos as a kid. It's such an archaic idea, or such a boy-boy thing.

23:00 A very strange, surreal and inventive scene by Krishnan. After being given sleeping pills by his manager, Baning starts sleepwalking to a non-diegetic soundtrack in what sounds a lot like avant-garde music (dissonant strings). The soundtrack is actually interactive with Baning's somnambulant state, and features what looks like a Kuleshov effect between the tap in his bathroom and his body in bed (interesting, earlier on his manager was struggling to get water out of the modern pipes). Baning ends up in the room of his female co-passenger from the plane (a Doctor Faridah staying in the same hotel), asleep in the other twin bed. Well, it's not every day that you wake up next to a beautiful stranger in your boy-boy pajamas. Such are the perks of a famous Malay comedian in the 50s.

29 June 2021

A really early morning today. Film shoot and interview with the installation. Even though Hiroshi and I are not morning people, he seemed to struggle less with his radio voice and organisational memory. I couldn't stick to the script and had to follow really planned instructions like where to walk and even how to turn.

Decided to take it easy after coming back and doing a little maintenance and housekeeping. I'm back at the *Sider Bar*, my usual after-hours hangout and happy to see Carl and Buen again. I got my usual Aspall in a glass, my laptop and I'm a happy man.

26:40 Shower scene. At the hotel, in what seems like a common unisex shower room. Baning in one cubicle and Doctor Faridah in another in the same shot. Their two towels hanging side-by-side in the middle on the rack. Their hands touch as they reach out for their towels and the viewer realises that Baning is in the women's shower room.

28:54 While Baning is at the doctor's, Abdul Salam is rummaging through his room and finds the box with the mask where the map is hidden. The actor Yem seems to reprise his role again as a shady map-hunter character. L. Krishnan never explains nor describes the contents of this particular map and its value and importance. It never goes further than being a plot device. I also understand now from the Malay Wikipedia that Baning is in KL to seek treatment, on the advice of his manager, for his nervous disorder around women. He is advised that he will be cured eventually when he finds his mate.

29:22 He chances upon Faridah again in the clinic, and tells his doctor that technically they met in a plane, and slept and showered together in the same hotel. At this point I am paying attention to certain depictions also in the film: they have a Chinese nurse. In the last film, they had a Chinese manservant played by a Malay actor. While I assume this scene to be in KL, one gets a sense its predominantly Malay cast perhaps catered to an audience seeing a film that represents modern professional and cosmopolitan Malays and their Chinese servants and staff. No insinuation here but pure observation. I had been sending my dad to the hospital for his routine checkups, and most of the nurses are usually Malay or perhaps Filipina. This has to account for living in a Chinese-majority country, but back in the late 50s Singapore also had a Chinese majority. So it is quite interesting that the films (and the cultural capital produced) back then catered to a Malay or rather Malay-speaking audience whose films depicted a Malay-majority representation and identity.

5 July 2021

I am overcome by a mood I can't put my finger on. It is like the tiredness has given way to something and then given over to many distractions. Bingeing on Instagram and Netflix. I wake up several times a night, I catch Horlicks staring at me both intently and nonchalantly. Is he curious about me and watching over me? Or maybe it's the only time I look more vulnerable than he is. I know when I wake up, I have always observed how my hands curl inwards like balls. I am forgetting Jean, I cannot remember my mother and we had stopped mourning for my grandmother. Everyone becomes occupied with their lives. History becomes memory that exceeds us. Melancholia becomes a project to locate myself in this temporality.

I was at the *zi car* stall just now trying to figure out this poem by Charles Simic and all I get is a kind of David Lynchian dream logic—bizarre and surreal images:

> *My thumb is embarking on a great adventure.*
> *"Don't go, please," say the fingers. They try to hold*
> *him down. Here comes a black limousine with a*
> *veiled woman in the back seat, but no one at the*
> *wheel. When it stops, she takes a pair of gold*
> *scissors out of her purse and snips the thumb off.*
> *We are off to Chicago with her using the bloody*
> *stump of my thumb to paint her lips.*

31:44 Musical interlude. Women in *kebayas* singing about *baju*. My scribbled notes read: "skimpy dress"; I guess they are singing about dressing and *kebayas* and decorum. Every musical interlude feels like you are attending the same performances in real time with the characters.

35:56 Plane scene. It's a noticeably smaller plane in the sky. I assume they are heading for Singapore. Ok it's a ridiculous edit, because it's like a little passenger plane and not a commercial airliner that it's supposed to be. No budget? No footages? Nobody noticed? Baning declines a cigarette offered by the Datuk. I still can't imagine smoking in stuffy planes then, and the other hazards and risks. Meanwhile Muhamud, Datuk's henchman is rummaging through the luggage at the back and finds the map in Baning's mask. You get a tiny glimpse of the contents but this film copy is too poor and faded to make out anything. Datuk tries to pry himself out of his seat from a sleeping Baning on his shoulder before taking the map from Muhamud.

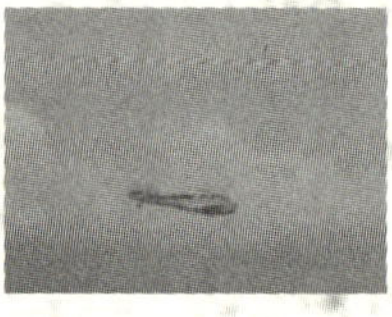

36:58 Rare bird's-eye view of Singapore but I can't tell where it is: picturesque rows of low-rise buildings and shophouses, but definitely not *kampungs*. I must admit I want to do the minimum here and close my laptop. I am tempted to turn on the TV again.

6 May 2021

There were persons in this place,
Too young to know the sea.

Last night I had to wash my sheets again because of the sand I brought back from the beach. That's twice in a row in three weeks. The first was with my kids, the second was with XY. Some older teens were frolicking in the water at sunset. I recorded them briefly on my iPhone. They seem to be so carefree, only interested in the sensuous caress of the dying light; of water; of sand; and of the opposite sex. I noticed they were of different races too.

37:28 Datuk in his abode wearing a Hugh Hefner bathrobe heehee. Actually looking at Baning putting on cologne afterwards and I thought he reminded me of my granduncle. His features, his body type, how he would use Brylcreem in his hair..[1]

The cologne that Baning splashed on himself was called *Soir de Paris (*Evening in Paris). *Ernest Beaux created the perfume for French perfumer Bourjois in 1928. Established in Paris in 1863 to manufacture make up and face powders, Bourjois has been making perfume since 1900. Evening in Paris was originally sold in a cobalt blue bottle designed by Jean Helleu. The scent was discontinued in the late 1960s, and revived and reformulated by Chanel in the early 1990s.*

I like to think the scent of a time and place could be distilled and bottled and brought to the present. You could order one from eBay now.

Baning is visiting Faridah's clinic wearing a bowtie and suit, cologne and his *songkok*.

40:00 I didn't notice this before watching this at the AFA but it all makes sense now. I thought it was a peculiar scene where Faridah sanitises her hands at the end of her workday. There was a bar of soap instead of a dispenser. And there was no tap but a basin in which she washes her hands. Now I understand why Baning's manager struggled with the faucet earlier on. And Baning had a strange sleepwalking experience with the recurring image of the unused and unturned faucet. Baning and his manager were waiting for something to happen with the faucet but no water ran out. It was a symbol or thing of anxiety that would unleash the flow of all modern trappings. Modern sanitation and sewerage systems did not come in until the 60s and after Independence and a period of rationing. So modern taps and automated flushes would only exist in luxury hotels.

It was a symbol or thing of anxiety that would unleash the flow of all modern trappings

42:50 Baning, obviously smitten with Faridah, shows up at her home on the pretext of seeking treatment. I don't know if I had mentioned this earlier, but Baning, on advice of his manager, was in KL, enroute to Singapore, to see the doctor for his condition around women. And the only cure, as consulted by his Doctor, is if he falls in love with one.

Baning takes six spoons of sugar in his coffee. So we all know he not only feels the love but he feels the sweetness of it all.

43:57 The actress who plays Faridah is called 'Kasma Booty'. I mean this was 1959 but I think a name like 'Kasma Booty' would spell 'sex symbol' in today's world. Faridah lives in a nice house. It's good to see such a modern woman in 1959 enjoying the perks of her profession.

7 July 2021

49:50 Inspector Dasuki returns! In case you didn't know from watching *Orang Minyak* before this, Dasuki was the mysterious man in the last part of the horror film who turned out to be the inspector (in a plot twist) that the Orang Minyak was impersonating. So this is really cool that Krishnan is tying *Rasa Sayang* to *Orang Minyak* in the same cinematic universe! Where perhaps Dollah Sarawak has a doppelgänger in the manservant Ah Wan and the Datuk here or maybe it's that one of their characters could be undercover here; Yem who played Abdul Salam was the doctor in *Orang Minyak*. Or it could be that all main detectives in Krishnan's film universe are called Dasuki. Over here, he is tall, proud and suave. A smoking debonair devil in a suit, speaking in measured steps, introduced halfway into the plot, a mediator between good and evil, much like the previous impersonator Dasuki in *Orang Minyak* where the devil was literally the *devil*.

51:43 Inspector Dasuki goes to Datuk Rashid Dubas' house to investigate. His place, which I originally thought was a hotel room/suite (maybe it is since I don't know where the Datuk is from), is something of peculiar interest to me. It's an interior that warps time in that the passing of time happens here. It has something to do with the lattice patterns and the lamps and the ornaments on the wall and the patterns on the floor. I don't know how to explain this more adequately but it is something of an affect—a time-image. An example is this scene, where the previous scene transits into this one and dollies out to reveal the interior of the men in the room. I am pretty sure Krishnan and his DOP are aware of this subtle ingenuity. The patterns are a repetition that multiplies space into more hypnotic spaces. It would not have been possible without the ornaments and patterns or else Krishnan would not have needed this wide shot in an otherwise standard conversation. The only example I can think of is the hotel interiors in *The Shining* by Stanley Kubrick. Here, Krishnan is creating a *mise-en-scène* where he establishes a conversation that leads to the suspense/tension/discovery of the other map that the baddies were not aware of. The movement of the camera moves from a wide to tighter shot to focus on the individual emotions of the three men, enhanced by the soundtrack. I will come back to another scene later again to talk specifically about this interior with the ornaments and patterns.

8 July 2021

There are a few brown glue stains high up on the walls of my apartment. They are left behind courtesy of the previous French tenant whom I have never seen. Besides leaving her g-strings under the furniture, she left one of a pair of chopsticks, I presume the other one went with her hair bun, and she had a penchant for gluing really kitschy shit on the walls because her wall nails did not hold adequately. I don't know if it's a case of apophenia, but one of the brown stains looks like the Angel from Nirvana's *In Utero* album and the other looks like Goya's *Saturn Devouring His Son*, though at night it just looks like a blob. Am I prone to religious symbolism? As a kid, I was told to say my prayers at six every evening to an altar of figures: Christ, the Virgin Mary and a Saint or two. I remember asking myself why they were all caucasian-looking. I would have been none-the-wiser had I read into that more critically beyond mere bewilderment.

52:55 I thought I was getting bored with *Rasa Sayang* but maybe I was getting too distracted to finish this project and my attention is going elsewhere. But these scenes onwards are what is pulling me back into writing.

Again here you find all the baddies breaking into Baning's room through the hotel window. A world of cat burglars and thieves. Where before the psychospatial aspects of *Orang Minyak* lay in the navigation of the colonial bungalow, the plot here revolves around the transient and liminal qualities of hotel rooms and their habitability for travellers (both welcome and unwelcome) and espionage.

Hotels are the interiors of espionage.

These spaces are hardly neutral despite giving very little away, as much as the inscrutable countenances of the house 'breakers' and the 'breakees'. Spaces here from *Orang Minyak* onwards, to this film and the next film involve some form of 'transgression', rather than an 'invitation' to space. *Che Mamat Parang Tumpol* started politely enough, with Mamat being invited to the city and to the press room. There was harmony but a contrast too between spaces of the city and *kampung*. In *Orang Minyak, space* was transgressed by the bogeyman who broke into spaces of the city.

There is a point of contention here between Hiroshi and I here in that I think the Orang Minyak was terrorising women in the city, and symbolising all that was evil and unruly from the *kampung* but Hiroshi corrected me to say it's the other way round: he was terrorising women in the *kampung* and symbolising all that was unruly in the city. He is right to say this in theory, and this is corroborated by the wonderful reading of *petrohorror* by Yogesh Tulsi called *An Oily Mirror.*

So I ruminated on this for days as to why I thought this way. And what I can only come up is that this is my personal psychoanalysis from Hiroshi's, which I begged to differ: he is a creation of society then, so he is a modern myth. But he also symbolises all that is our irrational fear of the unknown. I also seem to have a romantic notion of the *kampung* and there was hardly a *kampung* depicted in *Orang Minyak*; he breaks into a colonial-vernacular house which is a remnant of both colonialism and a modern piece of architecture. Why then is the *kampung* considered evil and unruly, well not to me actually, but to the modern mind where the outside, nature, and tradition are something that we have to control, contain and overcome for our rapidly urbanising city. When I say evil, I mean it is much older, that points to an origin to where the myth originated which is depicted in P. Ramlee and Shaw Brothers' period version *Sumpah Orang Minyak* set in the past. And even though Yogesh Tulsi excellently points to this film as a displacement of modernity onto a supernatural past, I would point out that all myths is the present mythologising the past as a narrative in modernity.

The Orang Minyak cannot speak for himself due to the fact that he will always be a complete Other, an Other in totality—a construction or projection of our fears onto another. He is ungraspable and slippery like our shadows, but he cannot speak for himself and will always be misunderstood and slandered into other representations.

But back to the break-ins, the reader might misunderstand this as a kind of chronology as the films become more transgressive where in actual fact *Orang Minyak* was made first in 1958, followed by *Rasa Sayang Eh* (1959) and then *Che Mamat Parang Tumpol* (1960). Nationalist elements and the disparity between the *kampung* and city only became apparent in *Che Mamat*. Whereas before—crime, horror, espionage was rife and the cosmopolitan Malay identity was much more fluid and seamless.

So, Datuk and his fedora-donned henchman break into Baning's room first, gingerly walking in the shadows looking for the other half of the map. They hear a sound and see another shadowy figure by the window and they go to hide in the wardrobe/room. Datuk accidentally leaves his cigarette holder that contains the other map behind. It is Abdul Salam, who breaks into the window with the same expression as he did as the doctor in *Orang Minyak*, so thank god Krishnan kills off his character here when he gets discovered by the Datuk—that's one too many crimes in this cinematic universe, he gets his comeuppance here. But before this, he displays his fine dagger-throwing skills when he sees Mr. Fedora in the mirror and throws the blade at a ridiculous angle through his heart to hang him up smack on the cupboard door. He gets interrupted by a whistling Baning who enters to hang his tie unsuspectingly on the corpse. As he goes out to get sleeping pills from his manager, Salam comes out to continue his search but gets intercepted by Datuk with a gun. Datuk discovers the map is with Din, the mask-maker, who is staying in Room 21 at the Royal Hotel and gets Salam to call the hotel operator. And that's the last of Salam. Datuk leaves the room through the window alone.

1:02:01 When Baning discovers the two dead bodies in his room and inadvertently gets slandered for murder, he takes off to hide from the police. And this is the beginning of the body count that leads right to the next film *Sumpitan Rachun*. This dark city, where policemen wore khaki shorts then, underscores these narratives.

9 July 2021

It's 8:46pm and it's raining outside. My apartment is perfect for rain. It's a hole in the building that traps shade. It's my man-cave yes. It is made for the term 'holing up' and it's conducive to reading and sleeping. It's a longish room with everything I need. My kitchen is also my desk; my bed is my lounge.

I broke one of the temple frames of my spectacles as I had sat on it reading on my bed. The bifocals are useless and I much prefer being 'immersed' in a book without any contraptions, but now I have to call Ray Ban for a service appointment to hopefully replace them. I also came down with a cold after my swim last night. I just downed some Panadol with Coca-Cola and hope I can write this away. I think I have to do an Agatha Christie to create the conditions to write.

Why do I keep returning to *Orang Minyak*? Now I'm thinking about Rohiah just before the Orang Minyak broke in to have a glimpse of her. That moment when she was awake, she wasn't feeling fear but anxiety of what is to come. Of feeling unease in that house. I am also thinking of Shinya Tsukamoto's industrial cult film *Tetsuo: The Iron Man*. Now, this is a modern horror flick in 1989, *The Iron Man* could well be Japan's horror icon of the eighties as compared to the *Orang Minyak* of 50s Singapore. Where the Iron Man is the ghastly bastard of man and machine, a fetishistic figure of cyberhorror, Orang Minyak is the shadowy and slippery monster of petrohorror. The oil-industrial fuelled modernity of the 50s versus the techno-industrial excess of the 80s.

All that is deep needs a mask.

This is apparently from Nietzsche, but I got the quote from Abbas Kiarostami.

Kiarostami once watched a French film twice for six hours straight in a cinema, and not understanding a single thing about it because it was in French without any subtitles. So he watched the three-hour long movie the first time, went out and bought another ticket and watched it again. In the darkened space of the cinema he depended on the visuals and sound to make an impression on him without deciphering the dialogue. Years later he would watch the same film, this time with subtitles he could read and realised he understood the characters wrongly.

Kiarostami mentioned the first generation of Iranian filmmakers made films about real experiences, what they felt and saw. The second generation made films about what they saw in the first generation films and made what they felt. The third generation filmmakers made films about what they saw in the second generation's. The fourth generation made films about techniques.

Kiarostami warned about American cinema. That it was more powerful than American military that it pervades almost every cinema screen across the globe. He says ninety percent of film screenings in European festivals are allocated to American cinema.

1:01:41 This scene is reminiscent of a scene in *Werckmeister Harmonies*: Valuska assigns some drunkards in a Hungarian bar at closing time the roles of the sun, the earth and the moon respectively. As they dance, rotate and orbit around one another: the earth around the sun, the moon around the earth, they come to a point where they are in line—the human sun bows down and they become an eclipse. At this point Valuska narrates:

At that moment
The air suddenly turns cold.
Can you feel it?
The sky darkens
And then goes all dark.
The dogs howl,

Rabbits hunch down,
The deer run in panic,
Run, stampede in fright.
And in the awful,
Incomprehensible dusk
Even the birds...
The birds too are confused
And go to roost,
And then... complete silence.

And then the *Werckmeister Harmonies* are introduced in the soundtrack. I say reminiscent because this scene in WH is incomparable as one of best opening sequences in cinematic history.

This great pathos by Béla Tarr is contrasted with the intentional bathos of Krishnan's drunken men in a bar scene. I like this scene for a particularly different effect. Baning is fleeing from the scene of a crime and tries to run away from a policeman who gives chase. He slips into a bar, puts on a beret as a disguise and joins a group of men to sing a rendition of *Rasa Sayang Eh*, their version of the *Werckmeister Harmonies* in this film. In fact, I'm so intrigued by this scene three-quarters into the film that I wish to experiment in writing here that we could very well start *in medias res* here as the beginning of the film. I feel dreams always have this logic.

Rasa Sayang Eh (1959)

1:01:41 Wahid Satay plays a character here who seems to be fleeing from something. He slips into a bar, puts on a jazzy beret as a disguise and joins a group of men to sing a rendition of *Rasa Sayang Eh*. This version sounds slightly melancholic and bittersweet with a piano intro and then a more upbeat verse and chorus. It is funny they are singing something about 'feeling the love' when all their cells are numbed by alcohol. A policeman enters the bar and we know he is the one Wahid is running away from. All the men in the bar appear half-drunk, and the five of them stand and dance in a row and put their arms around each other's shoulders to sing in unison. Wahid looks like a natural comic performer. The policeman inspects them and then walks around the bar before leaving. After that Wahid's character tries to slip away but falls knocked out to the floor. The men, assuming him to be dead drunk, find a key in his pocket that says *Royal Hotel Rm 21.* The crowd gathers to lift him just as the scene blacks out too.

10 July 2021

I had a bad dream. In the dream Jean and I were still married and I get called up by Jagger's school to find his missing bicycle and water bottle. At the school I'm received by Gary, the same guy who helps run the elderly home my father is in. Jagger is in primary school but this feels like a phase out of kindergarten and his teacher is a young Caucasian woman. I rummage through the catacombs of Jagger's school and meet people along the way. The school looks like it went through an earthquake or a flood. I'm losing the details as I write this down the way all dreams slowly dissipate as you try to remember in trying to enter their kingdom again.

But the gist was this, along the way they try to tell me things about what a brat Jagger is but I refuse to hear it and try to defend him and raise my voice. At some point Jaxxon is with me and wants to get in on the action but I don't seem to acknowledge him, lost in my indignation. At some point Jean gets roped in and his teacher is talking to her. I find his bottle and Jean says something in support, then when the teacher pulls her aside and asks if I am always like this, Jean jumps sides and becomes a woman ally. Now I feel trapped trying to defend my bad behaviour in school. Now I feel I'm the one with the problem and I wake up.

Horlicks comes to me and meows. I literally brush him aside. He then climbs down to play with a crushed paper ball.

I push up the blinds, no light rushes in, it seems like it just stopped raining from yesterday.

After I brush my teeth, I open my coffee jar to smell the beans. It is my litmus test against Covid. I message Jean to tell her I can't take Jaxxon and Jagger today.

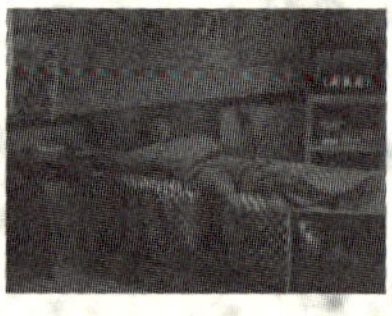

1:07:28 Baning wakes up to the sound of the telephone in his hotel room. But this is not his hotel room. He is still in his 'going-out' clothes. This sense of placeless-ness and bewilderment sets the mood for what is to come. He finds out from Faridah, on the other end of the phone reading the papers, that he has been apparently slandered for the murder of two people the night before. This is a point where Baning's life takes a turn from whatever it was before. Although comic, this is a crisis not to be taken lightly, at least not philosophically. He is a person now, politically and legally reduced to that of mere life. To make this less abstract, he is a fugitive now without his former rights and freedom; he has known no other way of living but now he has to *run* for his life. He can't even remember whatever happened last night, let alone defend himself against overwhelming evidence. He will have discovered three dead bodies by the end of the day, and that will be too much for one soul to bear if not for comedy. We are only sensitised to death, at least in film, according to the mood of the film.

1:13:00 It is daylight. Faridah breaks into Wahid's original hotel room to find some clues related to Baning's theatre masks. The site of transgressions. The transgression of space. She hears a sound and sees another shadowy figure by the window and she goes to hide in a room. An older man (looking like some Datuk) and his moustached accomplice break into Baning's room, gingerly entering in full daylight looking for something. The Datuk seems to be looking for something he left at the scene, perhaps the night before. He goes into the room but does not see Faridah behind the door.

1:17:22 Baning and Faridah discover a piece of a map in the cigarette case that Baning kept, which ties in to the puzzle of the purported object left behind in the hotel room by bigshot Datuk Rashid Dubas. The map in a cigarette case is mysterious and nothing is explained about the contents of the map nor the motives of its coveted nature.

1:19:37 Baning's manager visits Selamat Restaurant and tries to order some cheap and free food from the Mamak, patronising him with his order. We realise Mamak is Baning in disguise as an Indian Muslim man. Even though Wahid Satay's portrayal and comic timing is spot on, his performance can be seen as patronising to Indian Muslims in today's context. Forming the largest ethnic minority within the Malay Muslim community, they receive little attention and are often sidelined by Malay-dominated Muslim institutions. Being both Indian and Muslim is a bit of a predicament which I can empathise with, an 'other-ness' predicated on not fitting into the synonymity of race and religion. It is funny not so much because of Wahid's comic timing, but because his character Baning, when confronted with his 'bare-life' crisis, chooses to identify, and take shelter and refuge with the under-represented.

1:23:11 Datuk receives an important guest at his mansion, supposedly to receive the maps, in exchange for large amounts of money. They are in his pattern-laced living hall. Faridah is on the second floor eavesdropping. She is disguised as a maid of the house. Just what is on the map? This is never accounted for. I only have speculations. In 1959, Singapore held its first general elections in which all 51 seats in the Legislative Assembly were elected and gained internal self-government. The People's Action Party won a landslide victory with 43 seats. At that time the British in Singapore were increasingly forced to deal with the prospect of decolonisation and their intelligence wanted to still retain control of the city state.

Also the spectre of communist violence still hung over with insurgents reaching their final legs in the Malayan Emergency. The contents of the map could perhaps relate to any of these elements in history: independence, anti-communist, communist, pro-colonial. Or maybe I'm reading too much into this; espionage could be on an industrial level with rival businesses. Or maybe it's the same map of the house from *Orang Minyak* in Krishnan's cinematic universe where Ah Wan, the doctor and Inspector Dasuki all return again from the past.

1:24:31 I wish to mention Datuk's living hall again. It's an interior that warps time in that the passing of time happens here. The lattice patterns and the lamps and the ornaments on the wall and the patterns on the floor, all when shot by Krishnan create something akin to an affect—as I mentioned earlier—as a time-image. A good example happens here in this excellent scene: in a matter of 25 seconds, the camera zooms in on the wallpaper and focuses on the two lamps on the wall, slowly moves to the left, hours pass, it has made a full circle and comes back to the lamps. The camera zooms out, it's evening and Cik Mat, Baning's manager is on the couch, drunk with a hostess. He has been lured into a trap to reveal the whereabouts of his fugitive charge and star.

11 July 2021

Assuredly I labour here and I labour within myself; I have become to myself a land of trouble and inordinate sweat.[2]

Displacement is a serious matter. We use this term a lot in art school and it is always so superficial or just something you lift from theory. Besides place, you can also be 'dis-placed' by parent, by race, by gender and by time. It is getting exciting yet incredibly difficult to write about what I am feeling. It was Slavoj Zizek who mentioned that you can find 'foreignness' at the beginning of philosophy. That philosophy is not the discourse of those who feel the certainty of 'being at home'. 'Not-being-at-home' to cite Heidegger must be conceived existentially and ontologically as a primordial phenomenon as opposed to the familiarity and assuredness of the everyday world, our tranquillised default state that falls away to indefiniteness (or nothing) when one is anxious. In anxiety, one has a feeling of the 'strangely familiar' or 'the uncanny'. But a concept that Sigmund Freud would also develop to talk about what is repressed in 'the uncanny'. In the long term, this sense of placeless-ness becomes a form of melancholia that is 'irre-placeable'.

This points to a kind of deficient being of being-alone, but I had a comforting thought though. There is always something of you that is reflected and part of the world, and you cannot be any different from the world you come from. You are not a 'being' cut from the background but that you belong to it. And if you are able to think it, something in the world must reflect that.

I also have a theory as to why we write. We write to read even if it's for yourself. And that's where the diarist exists peculiarly to the novelist. You objectify your subject. You externalise the internal through language and text. Your voice becomes a figure that both passes and activates the reader.

When I went down for breakfast, I felt naked when I forgot my face mask. Like you would have forgotten to put on your bra or briefs. Our respiratory apparatuses have become private. I predict a dystopian future not far from now, as in the case with our kind, where newfound fetishes will be developed alongside the dining places for mouths and noses.

I'm reading the gay couple across my table at the *teochew moi* place:

> Even though one is Indian and the other Chinese, they resemble each other from their haircuts to the colours and cuts of their T-shirts and shorts. From the way they

walk, their body language, to the cadence in their speech—well-spoken and educated. Because I see them checking out other men. After a while, I decide they are not really together but dating. The intimacy is not there. There is a certain degree of formality and self-objectifying there. With real couples, you only see one object or entity. After a while I decide they are just friends as they are talking too loudly. That's just too much performance for the gaze.

1:23:33 And so Cik Mat, Baning's manager. is being plied with drinks by the hostess with her hand on his lap, and he's reciting a pantun:

Kau berikan aku minum lagi	*You give me another drink*
Mari sayang, mari kemari	*Come on baby, come here*
Nanti aku cakap tidak berhenti dendang sayang	*I will speak continuously, my love*
Bila nanti diri, aku tak sadar diri	*And I will get ahead of myself*

Datuk comes downstairs in his Hugh Hefner robe to ask him about Baning. In his drunken state Cik Mat reveals Baning is staying above Selamat Restaurant in Sungei Road. Seeing Dollah Sarawak from playing a triad leader to the shifty manservant Ah Wan to the Datuk Rashid Dubas, I realise he is still playing the gangster, only that he is much more sophisticated here. But wait, I also remember the name Rashid Dubas was used in *Orang Minyak* for the bank employee who got killed. Well, I spelled it 'Dubar' instead. But Krishan seems to be recycling names here as well.

1:28:00 Inspector Dasuki's cigarette-smoking shadow appears after Baning is kidnapped from his quarters by Muhamad and his accomplice. It's a bit absurd that I know it is him now when my earlier notes asked: "Who was the shadow?"

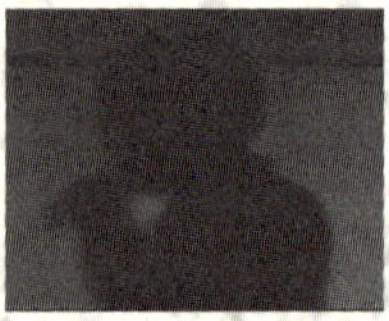

1:30:00 This scene is somewhat like a silent film and slapstick interlude and a showcase of using the interior architecture of the Datuk's house as a prop for the physical comedy: Muhamad and accomplice chase Baning in his striped pajamas around the house, under the tables, through doors, up and down the staircase, and in and out of rooms. Baning finally hides under the serving trolley in the kitchen where Faridah is working.

12 July 2021

I'm at Placebo, the college cafe as the library was closed. I wanted to borrow more films but did not account for the school break. And I don't know what's with this place, it's like winter in here. I have two hours before dinner with Sophia again.

I've been thinking about the scene in *Orang Minyak* again: the moment when Rohiah awakens and sees the Orang Minyak in the attic, inadvertently returning his gaze. I remember

Timothy Barnard's trope of blindness in Malay films, used to convey a disability to see the ugliness in a modernising city. In a way Rohiah was confronted with this instead without forewarning and in this instant, and, unable to turn blind before this encounter, goes into a catatonic state where she is unable to move or respond. It has been said that the causes behind catatonia is a systemic response to unrequited fear. The most common symptom is stupor, which means that the person can't move, speak, or respond to stimuli. Of course this is an extreme example of an encounter through horror. But I imagine fear can be manifested in the long term for individuals and collectives and their only response is to not attract its attention: to go numb in your daily life, not moving much and not speaking about it.

Kafka.

Kafka wrote a lot. Reams and streams of writing. But what I remember about his stories is that they had no context of time and place so any story feels like you are estranged in a foreign place. But this placeless-ness also made his stories timeless and therefore universal. I am only saying this because I'm thinking in chronological order, these films that I have watched become more contextualised in place and values as the years go by. Of course this is only premature conjecture but *Orang Minyak* and *Rasa Sayang* drew a common modern Malay identity without spelling it out and its scenes of places could be of anywhere. When *Che Mamat* is introduced, there is a dichotomy between *kampung* beach and city architecture, along with its named buildings, its police, its military and the values of living in the city versus living in the *kampung*, and Mamat's mother and girlfriend's aspirations on him to live in the city.

1:33:21 The servant-in-charge brings the trolley out to the hall for Datuk's dinner, unaware that Baning is under the trolley. Datuk is reading the papers. The camera dollies towards an article whose headlines read "Oily Man!" This is a nice sly reference to the *Orang Minyak* and also Krishnan's way of acknowledging the same cinematic universe where time runs parallel or contiguously. The trolley too is a fantastic human-mechanical prop in the film.

That explains the temperature drop. The sky is darkening and it's about to rain. There's hardly anyone left in the cafe save for a noisy table of two girls and two boys, whose eyes are only on one girl. I look at my table to pay the bill and realise it's the same number I always pick without knowing. I try to beat the skies to buy some ciggies across the road but it's too late. It's pouring hard now. I love the weather.

From a distance, I see a colleague holding the hand up of another colleague, helping her down the wet slope. I didn't know they were dating.

15 July 2021

I didn't know how much I had drunk till I woke up. My head felt like a ton of bricks. I wanted to be in the dark for a while listening to the rain. I hear drilling sounds in the background, it has to be the construction across the road from my block. Covid and financial woes had halted the construction since I moved two years ago. Things always feel like they are never gonna be built but when they are finally ready it feels surreal.

The lamp posts are from another time. Said the tour guide to an elderly group on Joo Chiat Road. I looked up, he was right. Why haven't I noticed them before? Maybe I did but have forgotten these sentinels. At once, I felt proud to live in a heritage estate.

1:36:28 It is at this point again that the ridiculous shadow of Inspector Dasuki appears and we know the film is coming to an end. Faridah and Baning discover the secret compartment behind a landscape painting that holds the map.

1:37:49 Faridah is an image of defiance standing on a chair when she gets caught taking the cigarette case out of the secret compartment. The heroine will not come down to Datuk and his cronies.

1:38:55 Inspector Dasuki finally appears in Datuk's house casually smoking his cigarette on a holder and casting a side-glance, much like David Caruso in *CSI: Miami*; his lurking shadow had been the prelude to his appearance—reality and truth finally caught up in 'the big reveal' scene. No one sees him come in but rather, he just appears like an image of cool authority. Three policemen also 'appear' on the upper floors as 'statues of the state' immortalised with their stern countenance. The long arms of the law have come and are here to stay. This play of perspectives and their symbolism is further extended to the next cut when Krishnan unusually employs an overhead perspective of the policemen (law) that is reminiscent of a surveillance camera by depicting the criminals being apprehended by the Inspector and his officers.

Referring to my notes: I probably said this before but Baning looks like my granduncle with his quiff, his chiselled features and his spindly build. This granduncle used to live with my family, rode a bicycle to work as a security guard, had a sailor tattoo of a couple kissing in an embrace on his upper right arm and would pull down his pants to flash his butt to my sister and me. Sometime back, a long time after he passed, my cousin remarked on how my arms reminded her of his.

Notes

Chapter 3: Rasa Sayang Eh (1959)
The actor or laugh in the airways

1. Brylcreem is a British brand of hair styling cream for men, popularin Singapore with street barbers in the 50s and the 60s.

2. *Confessions,* Saint Augustine, Book X, Chapter 16.

Chapter 4:

Sumpitan Rachun (1961)

Cowboys, Malays and Indians

I hear the birds in the morning outside while my body is lying in darkness. I feel the chills that come as the night ends its shift and I sense the atmosphere in the air that feels like the hour I am thinking—daybreak. We have internal, natural clocks that we have forsaken for mechanical/digital timers that dictate our whole lives. Three years ago, I stopped wearing watches and I took all notifications away from my mobile phone. I hear the birds again. Bird. *Guak, guak, guak, guak* in four counts. Five seconds. And then again. I reckon it's the common mynah. I hear they are smart as hell. They have to be, to live in the city. When I was in Tanah Merah, where old Bedok was, in a house in the hills, the bird I heard was the koel. A slow *ko-oo, ko-oo, ko-oo.* It's funny when I think of bird sounds, they bring me to places.

When my eyes adjust to the light, I find Horlicks pondering over me from the floor. It dawned on me that cats don't know what breed they are. Knowledge and epistemology are not their domains. Understanding and interpreting and slotting everything into categories so that we may find meaning and use aided by language is what we do. That breaks it down really simply for me to understand what being is—I imagine I'm a cat. If I don't know what breed I am, then it's a construction from what is. So I tell Horlicks:

"Horlicks, you are a stray!"
It doesn't seem to get into him.
"Horlicks, you are a stray, just like me!"
He makes a tiny meow.

In being in the world, we have little epiphanies everyday: premonitions and revelations. Nothing grand, it just becomes part of the mundanity of your life. Mine came in a smoke from my cigarette beside the Mecca mall of electronics. I was born to make these images, and it's almost a morality or a responsibility to make these images adequate. Of course this sounds pompous. And they haven't happened. So this is an exercise, or an excuse. Derrida said the archive is about the future of what is to come. I hear him. The sounds I hear in the revelation is a mix of radio, drone and voices in a key. Only I hear it. It's like that new Apichatpong film *Memoria* (2021) showing in Cannes where Tilda Swinton hears a rumble that only she can hear and decides to go to the heart of the sound in the Colombian jungle. I had been loath to give him the benefit of a genius but I think I may be envious of something I do not understand.

While in the midst of thinking and writing, one uncle points to my cigarettes on the table. I thought he was a cleaner or a safety distance officer and I said I wasn't smoking here. He pointed to my cigarettes again and asked if he could have one. I was more than happy to do so. I thought of a friend who said that smokers are not selfish people and suddenly that made sense.

Then my mind drifted to the recent schoolboy-killing in River Valley High. It was big news. What could have possessed a 16-year old to wield an axe in broad daylight and butcher another boy in the school toilet? It feels so senseless and beyond reason. Like so many things in the world. And I became very concerned for Jaxxon and Jagger.

It was in another bizarre dream that my sons turned into chocolate syrup. Well rather in that dream they were two of three boys, of which they were my brothers and my father was a younger version of himself like what I am now so I assumed him to be the father of all three of us. In the dream, I had just woken up, and their great-aunts from Jean's side reprimanded me for feeding them a mysterious snack that turned them into brown goo with only their heads floating in a tub of chocolate. Not in a grotesque way but in a 'Thomas the Tank Engine' meets 'Willy Wonka' kind of way. My dad was appalled at my breath as I had just woken up and he covered his face with the newspaper he was reading when I tried to question him. Then I woke up.

Sumpitan Rachun (1961)

During Malay cinema's golden age, this film would have been under the broad category of action cinema, which could comprise anything ranging from war movies to physical action and thriller elements made in the form of crime dramas such as *Sumpitan Rachun*, translated as 'Poisonous Blowpipe'. This genre is said to be mostly inspired by Chinese films and Hollywood noir films.

1:42 *Don't believe all you see*

S. Roomai Noor, the P. Ramlee stand-in or lookalike returns to yet another L. Krishnan film as Assistant Superintendent Latiff, our debonair hero detective who was the debonair gardener/banker in *Orang Minyak*. As a kind of prologue and disclaimer, again sans English subtitles (am trying to remember the version that I watched at the AFA), he is sitting at his desk in uniform and breaking the fourth wall to tell the audience that this is only a movie and all events and characters are fictional. In fact Roomai Noor introduces himself as an actor. I would have imagined a not-yet desensitised audience then, new to the movies, believing what they see in cinema to be true. Perhaps it was to discourage people from imitating the villains or taking matters into their own hands. As these are trained professionals he would say and our real officers are keeping the country safe. I love his shorts and high socks with the black bands by the way. The quote in italics above was in my notes so it was probably what Latiff/S. R. Noor said in the beginning in Malay. It is funny for an actor to break the fourth wall right at the beginning of a film, forewarning his audience not to believe what he sees. Besides New Wave films, Brechtian theatre and the Theatre of Cruelty, movies depended on the suspension of illusion and for the audience to not have a self-critical awareness and not be emotionally manipulated when watching a film. Although this is for a reason then, the best films I find now depend on an audience having a self-critical awareness as a kind of resistance towards mainstream media and cinema.

3:46 Nicely orchestrated impact and introduction: a body, I think, falls into the dark murky water, *splash!* the words 'Sumpitan Rachun' appear in a rachety pulp font to a heightened horn section refrain of a soundtrack by his frequent collaborator Yusof B. Ok I know what the fonts remind me of, the *Flintstones*, that cartoon about prehistoric cavemen. 'Crime' is synonymously spelled out loudly, darkly (and rather cartoony). This is all-out film noir with elements that Krishnan had been only experimenting with before. It is 1961, two years before Singapore joins Malaysia.

5:43 Latiff and his date arrive at the iconic Cathay Building at Dhoby Ghaut and head for the restaurant where a dinner and a performance were taking place. Until 1958, the building was the first and tallest skyscraper in Singapore and in Southeast Asia, at a height of 83.5 metres. In those days, it was known as Cathay Hotel and had at least 60 rooms which subsequently expanded to 170 rooms. It had a restaurant, nightclub, swimming pool and shopping arcade.

At the lift, there are advertisements displayed of the latest films and performances at Cathay's sister and flagship cinema called the Odeon. The Odeon closed in 1984, its last film screened was called *Breakdance*. Interestingly, it was a film that would introduce hip hop and breakdancing to the world (debuting Ice-T) and signal the death knell for cinema in Singapore caused by low cinema attendance and high property prices, accelerated by the emergence of videos and rampant video piracy. It was also the final Cannon film production released by MGM.

6:04 A magic show is about to take place by a queer-looking fellow with a pigtail called Chua Foo Ling. Latiff's glamorous date is an attractive *kebaya*-clad Chinese doctor. As they enter the restaurant in style, a band plays under an oyster-themed set, serenading couples on the dancefloor. A Malay-looking man at a bar whispers to his Chinese date, who is wearing a cheongsam:

Who is the woman that Latiff is with?
Oh, that's Dr. Tan Lai Peng!

6:50 Such was high society portrayed then—modern, cosmopolitan, interracial, glamorous amidst music, cocktails and intrigue.

Chua Foo Ling's show is about to begin.

26 July 2021

From my room, I like watching the shadows cast over the half-opened windows of my neighbours' apartments, maybe some seven to eight metres away. Four black boxes on the wall reacting to the light at different times. Black in the day, lit in the night. At 11am, their shadows are a quarter opaque. The top one has a long straight nose down like an elephant, the other has a high sharp nose like a French bellhop in a Wes Anderson movie. From the opposite end my neighbours would see faintly a half-naked man prostrate on his bed. Maybe that's why they usually draw their curtains.

Shortly after we opened to Phase 3 with looser restrictions of social distancing and people were able to return to their lifestyles, we were locked down again because of new clusters formed in the underbelly of Singapore's KTV nightlife. People are generally disheartened and are throwing all sorts of vitriolic at the *Hum Sup Lo* KTV Uncles and their *teekopek* brethren (dirty old uncles) together with their Vietnamese hostesses. Overnight, more clusters formed. But really, how are any of these uncles so different from us? They are just about resuming their normal social lives and fulfilling certain needs. The hostesses are just doing their jobs to earn a living no matter what else they have to do whether they enjoy it or not. Who are we to impose a morality and a social responsibility on others when it can happen to any of us doing other things in gatherings?

Tonight we are going to install the second iteration of *Slander!* at the Jurong Regional Library. I came early to recce the site. It was a pleasant long ride by train and bus to the west side of the island. I tried to read but fell asleep towards the end of the journey. I sat in a vast outdoor shelter, watching other denizens go about their lives and dinner while I ate. The hall was unlit and night was breaking, a certain mood of calm and ennui fell over us.

I realised I had forgotten my journal so I will end this entry without any timestamp.

29 July 2021

9:00 Chua Foo Ling makes the governor disappear. Ok I don't know if he's the governor but he looks like an old British guy in a high administrative position. And he did not disappear by Foo Ling's magic but through some film magic editing. It's ridiculous if audiences in the 50s actually *do believe what they saw.* Foo Ling also speaks in an unconvincing halting Chinese-accented Malay.

10:42 Another song-and-dance number about drinking in Mandarin by a female singer in a *cheongsam*. Afterwards, she breaks into the refrain in Malay: *Let us drink and be merry !*

12:35 A Mr. Penruber arrives and joins Latiff and Foo Ling at the table. Penruber is another British suit and wants a favour from Latiff and the police. I am trying to decipher the conversation between them without the aid of subtitles. A precious jewel worth a lot of money is arriving in a train and Penruber needs Latif to escort the crate safely to his apartment. I am watching the three of them: a Malay, a Chinese and a Caucasian conversing in Malay which is the *lingua franca* of this world. I am also observing these roles of the lead actor, the leading/supporting lady and the colonial Caucasian subject, who later would come to be more prominent in his role. Latiff gets interrupted by a phone call. A body has been found and he is needed at the mortuary together with Foo Ling, who is a forensic pathologist.

30 July 2021

At the 2021 Tokyo Olympics, Joseph Schooling fails to defend his gold medal from 2016 in the 100m fly. At 53.12 seconds, he is almost 3 seconds too slow to cut it even for the heats, coming in last. I do not care so much whether he is a national and world champion who did not bring glory this time, or pointing the finger to what might have failed: his fitness, his commitment, his form, his support or just pressure. I am intrigued by Schooling's fall from grace in five years and the possible psychological state of his mind and the public scrutiny of the spectacle we make of our athletes. And that makes him a fascinating yet identifiable human being.

15:50 *Ke tempat simpan dan mayat, mat.*

In the spirit of this film, while doing my research on the laptop, I feel like both an investigator and forensics specialist. It's a thoroughly fulfilling endeavour loaded with pangs of delight and excitement in any discovery. Let me first describe the noirish aspects of this engaging scene and then furnish it with psychogeographic elements later:

Inspector Latiff and Dr. Lai Peng get a cab from the Cathay Hotel to go to the morgue. Like straight out of a graphic novel, in the blackness of the night, the street lamps and headlights of the automobile burn bright halos onto the film. They arrive at a site of columns, blocks and archways and enter the long arc of the driveway, past the alabaster portico of the neoclassical-style mortuary and wind up at the side entrance where they are received by a reporter and a police officer.

What makes this short scene compelling is that it's the first real moody introduction to the noirish elements of the film (amplified by Yusof B. and Rahim Hamid's soundtrack), if you don't really count the introduction. *Sumpitan Rachun* probably borrowed elements from the film noir genre of American films in the 1940's and 1950's exploring the darker aspects of modernity. They are usually set in a criminal milieu of killers, corpses and doomed romance, or exploring the consequences of a criminal act. The pulse or affect of noir is not a bodily one but a psychological ghost that only manifests in the night. It is about the 'dark self' and the alienation of the city rampant in crime and paranoia. The genre was born of despair, which had more to do with the desperate loneliness of urban life in the aftermath of the Depression and World Wars and also to counter big budgeted, brightly lit American films. Colloquially and economically, film noir came about as low budget B films, generally filmed on studio sound stages, so the directors and cinematographers took advantage of effects borrowed from the German Expressionist movement of the 1920s. Many of these great European film noir directors from the movement also landed in Hollywood after fleeing fascism. While some of them had leftist views and the films they made were a response to existentialism, the response of others was an inclination to nihilism, and we can see many nihilist elements in classic noir films.

I had also discovered the father of both the film noir genre and pulp-fiction was an American novelist called Cornell Woolrich, who wrote many short stories about fear and the dark urban cities that were adapted by film directors such as Alfred Hitchcock, François Truffaut and Jacques Tourneur.

I realised then that for *Slander!* I was going for an aesthetic that was both 'pulp' and 'noir-rish', between day and night, black and white, inside and outside, between order and unruliness, between the whiteness and fog of my previous installation *A White, White Day* and the darkness and ambiguity of *Slander!*

Granted, Krishnan had adapted the genre from American and European cinema for local audiences; adapted for the values of the city's inhabitants then, and indirectly to the socio-political context of its time.

Inspector Latiff and Dr. Lai Peng get a cab from the Cathay Hotel to go to the morgue.

The automobile features most prominently in this film, and in this scene the modern metropolis cannot be imagined without the automobile. These symbols of social mobility and expanded identity, along with the skyscraper (The Cathay) and their inhabitants occupy the streets and define the noir city and their ambiguous spaces. Dark deeds, heists, escapes, kidnap and death all happen in and around cars.

I imagine we follow this one on its route as a ghost above the city of Singapore as it pulls out of the Cathay Hotel into Dhoby Ghaut, whose name literally means 'washing place' in Hindi, after the laundry services provided by Indian immigrants there. The black car then careens along Bras Basah Road, 'bras basah' a transliteration of the Malay words 'beras basah' which mean 'wet rice'. The name was given because of the 'decayed rice' from sailing vessels which had to be transported from ships to a site out of the city centre due to the abominable smell of saturated and rotten rice. It rounds right into New Bridge Road, which was built in 1842, after George Coleman's new bridge, Coleman Bridge, had been built in 1840 over the Singapore River. The bridge links Hill

Street to New Bridge Road on the north bank to the south bank of the Singapore river respectively. It makes another right into Outram road, formerly known as Cantonment Road followed by River Valley Road until 1858 when it was separated from Cantonment Road. It was then renamed Outram Road in honour of James Outram for his role in the 1857 Indian mutiny. The area of Cantonment Road was the site assigned by Stamford Raffles in 1819 for the East India Company's Sepoy troops as barracks. The contingent of Indian sepoys were asked to stay and stationed here when they accompanied Raffles to Singapore. One of Singapore's earliest prisons, Outram Prison, was located at the foot of Pearl's Hill in Outram. Originally known as Pearl's Hill Prison, and Outram Prison in its later decades, it was demolished in 1963 to make way for redevelopment. Finally, we reach the old morgue at the Singapore General Hospital. The first General Hospital was built around 1821 and began its life as a wooden shed in the British cantonment located near present-day Bras Basah Road and Stamford Road. It was rebuilt four times at different locations over the next four decades before its construction at the Sepoy Lines, where the above-mentioned barracks for sepoys were situated, in 1882. The hospital comprised three separate blocks—the Upper, Middle, and Lower Blocks. After the Second World War the blocks were renamed after the surnames of medical officers Bowyer, Stanley, and Norris Blocks respectively. The mortuary sits behind the Norris Block and is presently replaced by Block 9 at SGH. On my present-day navigational system

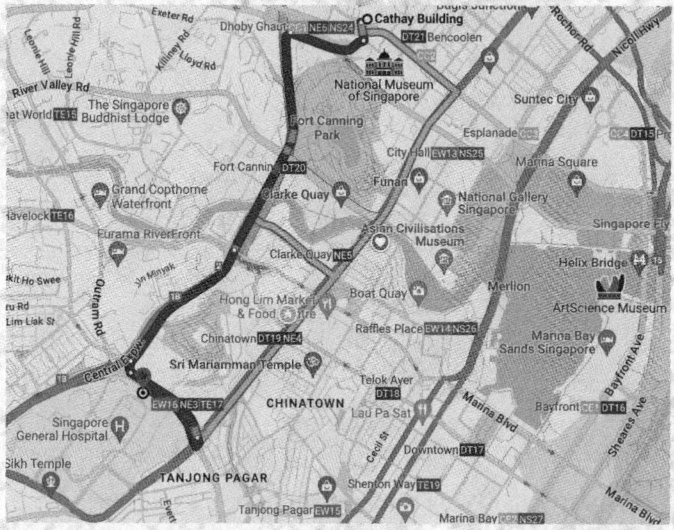

Block 9 is parallel to The Cathay (as it is called now), some three kilometres away. I also used an old site map and a current SGH road map to cross reference this.

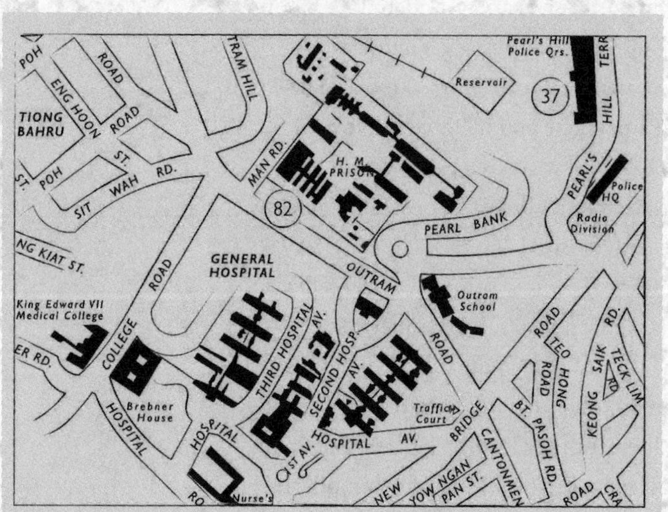

I will later come back again to this route in *Korban Fitnah* where its location history is more detailed but closely connected to *Sumpitan Rachun*.

They arrive at a site of columns, blocks and archways and enter the long arc of the driveway, past the alabaster portico of the neoclassical-style mortuary and wind up at the side entrance...

There must be something about the lighting and film which makes this scene very noir-rish and ripe for further de-construction. I don't know if it had something to do with the dark recesses of shadows, night and building. The cluster of medical blocks were designed with colonial features, perhaps the most famous and currently preserved building is the Bowyer Block, which features a prominent clock tower. The government architect Major Percy H. Keys, who also designed the former Fullerton Building, decorated the building with elegant Doric pilasters, mouldings of festoons and colossal Tuscan columns and some of these features may have influenced the other blocks. However in place of this neoclassical (colonial) magnificence and grandeur, is a gloomy presence of tomb-like buildings, suggesting a netherworld of borrowed Western elements of both a film genre and its architecture, making it a pastiche and metanarrative of postmodern elements. Not to say this is a postmodern film, but it is a film that is unaware and out of its own time, having modern elements that are borrowed as a pastiche to serve an audience for its context, to borrow some ideas of Frederic Jameson's essay on postmodernism and consumer society.

I believe Noir is the distant cousin of Goth, which must have influenced Noir in architecture and literature. If there is a lineage from Gothic literature to German Expressionism and then to film noir, then it must be some kind of postmodern pastiche when it arrives here. You can't really get Noir from Chinese shophouses. It needs to be closer to the remnants of colonial architecture like the many Art Deco buildings they leave behind. One hideous yet endearing pastiche of a piece of architecture has got to be Parkview Square, designed in a classic New York Art Deco style even though it was completed in 2002. It is affectionately called the Batman Building or Gotham Building to match its gargoyles. In coming back and exploring the themes of modernity in our local films, surely there was an element of decoloniality (consciously and unconsciously) in addressing colonial elements in a fresh way? When the black car entered the SGH medical cluster to go to the mortuary, what resembled was not a revival of Western classical antiquity in late 1950s Singapore, but one of a graveyard in the dark night. Surely neoclassicism is already a pastiche of something bygone in the West, which makes this a pastiche of a pastiche.

16:17 As the car pulls over, they are received by a journalist and a cop. The journalist is scooping for a story. The cop is a friend of the dead person. The journalist appears to be played by an actor, the cop seems to be played by a non-actor. This is because the person who plays the journalist has exaggerated mannerisms and expressions. He's not a bad actor. That is what actors do. And the reason his acting looks exaggerated is because he is standing next to the policeman whose body language is in stark contrast when Latiff approaches them individually. The policeman really behaves like a person you would naturally see on the street, wooden and natural; expressionless. It reminds me of Bresson's non-actors and their blank gazes, where Bresson only uses them as vehicles to convey emotion in the viewer and not the actor.

17:57 *A poisoned arrow tip.*

Dr. Tan Lai Peng, our pathologist, dramatically dislodges a poisoned arrow tip from the body of the corpse with a pair of forceps, just as inspector, cop and journalist walk in. From the corpse's lower vantage point of view on the clinical bench, Dr. Tan's eyebrows look as sharp as the daggers of Cathay Keris emblem, crossing at the beginning of every film. I cannot make out the Malay but it seems maybe the poisoned tip paralysed and tore something in the victim before killing him. The cop's sister from Kampung Terbakar, a singer in Happy World and girlfriend of the dead man, is their only link and clue now. 'Singer', 'Kampung' and 'Happy World' are enough tag words to suggest what is to come next in the plot. Not to mention the coming of a mysterious villain using a rather indigenous and archaic weapon with a 'poisoned arrow tip'.

I might have exaggerated a little and allowed my imagination to take over. After seeing the mortuary block in a dated picture online in the National Archives, in broad daylight, taken in a very mundane setting, it resembles nothing neoclassical but more a barracks-styled architecture.

4 August 2021

I never heard the ticking of my clock so loud as this morning when I switched off the airconditioner. It sounded like it was going to beat out of its own compartment. Usually I could barely make it out. But the deafening silence picks up everything—the snores of Horlicks, the remnant rain drops from the corners of rooftops, a constant generator hum outside—whirring to start and then it dies and then it comes back on again. It doesn't help that I'm right smack in an airwell of the building. Then I hear the first faint crows of the mynah.

19:05 *Happy World*

The painter Hilmi Johandi specialises in a kind of speculative imagining and throwback to the country's history and their lost utopian dreams. He paints certain scenes from the films of this golden era. I must have recalled some actresses looking like Latifah Omar in his paintings. I do know he has his amusement park series of Great World, Happy World and New World. On the fragmented splices and spaces in his paintings, he says, "My position is always to manipulate that sense of familiarity, to evoke a kind of estrangement, a tension." I would agree with him it is not really about a convenient nostalgia. In a way, this brought to mind what I said earlier about the 'uncanniness', this 'not-being-at-home' in the everyday world. *This sense of placeless-ness becomes a form of melancholia that is 'irre-placeable'.*

19:39 Latifah's character is gorgeous, a vision of delight here as the *femme fatale* of the film. If there was an ideal of a classic Malay beauty of our film world then it would have to be her or Maria Menado, with their broad faces, large limpid eyes, wide smile and dark bouncy locks and a curvaceous body to boot in a body-hugging kebaya. She also has an irresistible little mole at the corner of her lower lip. I certainly remembered her in *Che Mamat Parang Tumpol*, but she really comes into her own here as the introduction to the amusement and nightlife park in Kallang called Happy World. Before the advent of television or shopping malls, these 'worlds' were the only form of entertainment for the locals.

These amusement parks have all but vanished today, save for perhaps Beauty World and Great World City, which have just become shopping malls and symbols of *lost utopian dreams*. What once used to be a very eclectic mishmash of cultures, scenes, dances and stages that unravelled the layers of colonial society.

Where the Cathay Hotel catered to members of high society, Happy World entertained the locals. Nevertheless, Latiff is still dressed in a suit. I don't know about tropical Singapore in the 50s, were detectives required to wear a suit at work?

Also, what is a girl from Kampung Terbakar performing in a place like Happy World?

9 August 2021

National Day.
In the morning I was listening to Aldous Harding's *Imagining My Man*:

I'm going to answer, protecting
It can be so hard to forgive
It's not what I thought and it's not what I pictured
When I was imagining my man
You are so nervous all of the time
Giving the classics
I know that imagining my man
Imagining, imagining my man

From croon, whisper to wail, with every passing of the real through her wistful melismas, she crosses from imaginary to symbolic with lyric and a far-ranging voice. He is *not* what she imagined, does she stay? *I am in love. But what is this love? This is not what I imagined to be.* Perhaps love is an imagined reality in which the object of love is but beholden to the person's imagination. Perhaps one is never in love with a person, only with one's imagination. Pitchfork says it's a saxophone solo at the end, but I imagined it was just a melodica in the spirit of her weirdness.

21:02 We are back on the dance floor of Happy World. The cha cha seems popular for this time, remember *Che Mamat Parang Tumpol*? People in both traditional and modern garb doing the cha cha *joget* on the floor while Latifah's character serenades them. We get a glimpse of the small-time baddie who looks his part—skinny with a pencil moustache and brylcreem-slicked black hair with a handkerchief around his neck. He steals a menacing glance at Latiff and then back at the singer. He looks like a reject from the sailors' docks and kind of reminds me of a funny student who used to dress up as David Bowie. What's he doing here as a calefare in a Malay film? The camera beautifully roves through the various couples on the dance floor and then to the stage. Krishnan employed a lot of 'pin-up' cuts to the actress, caressing her face with his lens. Mind you, this is a club with a full-piece band and horn section.

22:00 This is an actual local dancehall setting back in the day of dance signal boards and musical chairs. Right now in this time, I live in an entirely mundane, isolated and alienated reality, cooped up on my computer, alone in the dark. When I was a kid, I had a perverse imagination about my dad and his kins and how they grew up in old Singapore. Whereas my biological mother's side is a complete void and absence, my culturally colourful side of my dad's family captured my imagination with their anecdotes and ridiculous family urban legends. Examples are like my father being bullied and whipped by his mother's notorious brothers. His mother being some sort of a child bride, when her husband died, she traded paper cash for a chest full of coins, like treasure. Or that my father was delivered by Dr. Benjamin Sheares, Singapore's second president, who was a colleague of my grandfather. Or how when they used to stay in Katong when it was just water, before it was reclaimed into Marine Parade. I would speculate that stories of a teenager like my father then being regaled by one of his hooligan young uncles, about going to one of them dances in Happy World. Much like the 'Greasers' and the upper class 'Socs' from the S.E. Hinton's novel *The Outsiders*. As always borrowing from American culture, the greasers are a youth subculture formed by working-class communities in 50s-early 60s America. My family were *greasers*, I'm metaphorically always one. I have no idea how my grandmother ended up with a doctor, but like the lacuna formed by my Chinese mother, there is absolutely no record of my Indian grandfather having existed.

So I imagine some greasers in the day telling a kid, what it was like at the dances. Meeting so and so, this girl and that. What song was playing. Who got drunk. Who got laid, shocking! Some fights with the Chinese boys and so on and so forth. Going to dances to meet girls.

On the dance board there are four labels:

TANGO
SLOW FOX
MALAY RHYTHM
CHA CHA

I have a nagging feeling our army, when they came into existence in 1967, adopted these as call signals for the recall of reservists in their mobilisation exercises. Think about it, both the dance board and the call signals mobilise people—one for entertainment, one for national service.

SLOW FOX lights up, and a piano sonata comes up. Latiff stubs his cigarette on the floor and grabs his chance to ask a bevy of dames sitting on the chairs for a dance. He goes to the attractive singer. Her name we now know is Rokiah. Were there community classes to learn the slow fox or the cha cha? Everyone seems to know how to.

Latiff asks Rokiah to join a singing competition at the Cathay Hotel after spotting a poster on the wall. Again, like the story-telling competition in *Che Mamat*, these notices are gateways to social mobility—making it and moving up in the city. Latiff also asks Rokiah to meet him after work.

I'm not that kind of woman, Rokiah says. *I'm not that kind of man*, he replies. It's about Bakar he says, and Rokiah is alarmed.

24:32 The little runt of a villain with the neckerchief walks away glum-faced from his seat in envy/jealousy/contempt and makes a call to an unrevealed character (enter Mastermind). seated on a Chinese antique chair, his back to the audience. He then draws a diagram to what seems like some symbolic arrangement and passes it to one of his cronies.

This unknown Mastermind operating from his chair is a crucial element in this film. I will return to this later with examples in the film noir genre, whose symbolic implication is pertinent in understanding the restlessness of the turn of the 60s.

12 August 2021

College is starting soon and I fear I will not have the energy nor the time to write.

I experienced a little of what it means to have climate change in the microcosm of my little refrigerator—the melting of glaciers as I dethawed my fridge. An icy continent had grown in the freezer compartment and taken over all frontiers and I wasn't able to use it to freeze any food. So it was time to play god and pull off the plug on Antarctica. The lockdown had come in useful—all those *dabao* meals had produced a surplus of plastic containers I could use to collect glacier water from the fridge. I dam-ed the bases of the compartments further with little dish towels and a pail at the foot of the fridge. I celebrated the clearing with three tubs of ice-cream.

Recently, I have taken up an old camera to record random scenes everyday. It is the last of the DV cameras of its time, ones that used digital tape. I had found it in my studio and was thrilled it was still working after I charged it. I must have left it there more than a decade ago. I should bring it out more often. Like now, it will be a good time to use it at the Without.U cafe. It's raining outside. Three loud Vietnamese women are at the table opposite me sharing a hotpot, skinning everything off the bones with their fingers. Someone's daughter is there too. All are wearing tiny denim shorts; the women are adorned with gold, imitation brand goods, clunky mobile phones and wireless earbuds.

29:13 Latiff divulges the news of Bakar's death to Rokiah. The camera gives her all 15 seconds to dramatise and mourn his death against a fence by dollying close to her while Latiff hails a cab.

30:06 Another scene of three cars in tandem following each other in the dark night of urbanising Singapore. Back in the day, you couldn't tell a taxi from a civilian car, perhaps the taxis themselves are not legal or metered (regulated) and so the identity of the automobile is ambivalent between civilian and passenger. Two of the Mastermind's unnamed hooligans are in a black car—let's call them Little Runt and Moustachioed Farid—following Latiff and Rokiah in a black cab while the reporter hailed another white one to trail from behind. They pass by Billboards and early neon signs of the city.

They enter a deserted road sign called 'GULEGA ROAD 16'. I look it up and find that it's related to the coastal kampung called Somapah Village, which does not exist anymore. This is the only clue besides the visual cue of where Kampung Terbakar, where Rokiah lived, was located. Somapah Village was named after Indian landowner Hunmah Somapah. Today it is now the industrial and commercial area comprising Changi Business Park as well as the Singapore Expo convention and exhibition centre.

In its heyday, Somapah Village at Changi served as the gateway to the coastal villages that lay to the southeast such as Mata Ikan. The village consisted of a bustling open-air market, medical clinic, police post, kindergarten and dairy farm. The area was redeveloped in the 1990s. Thinking back I am thinking of the beginning of *Orang Minyak* and the locale I mistook for the city. That is because I had a backward view of the *kampung* when they could actually be sophisticated quaint town centres.

Other notable villages in the area included Kampung Harvey (along Harvey Avenue), Gulega Village (along Gulega Road), Mata Ikan Village (at the junction of Somapah and Siak Kuan roads) and Padang Terbakar Village (along Siak Kuan Road). I assume the last village to be where Rokiah lives. These make up what used to be halcyon days of the southeast coastal villages dotted with holiday bungalows for colonial administrators and then later, for civil servants.

In this short historical journey of fictive nostalgia I undertook on the internet, I imagine these settings to be in the day and not the noir of the night and the dark urbanising city of clandestine dealings captured on this film.

We then come back to Fatimah (from *Che Mamat*) by the beach. Rokiah and Fatimah are played by the same actress but they are really of the same person. Fatimah represents an idyllic *kampung* girl free of worldly concern, whereas Rokiah is the same *kampung* lass that now has to work in the city where crime, vice and tragedy take place.

2 September 2021

Long, long break, but unwasted. I had been taking down a lot of notes and wanted to catch up on reading and watching films which I felt like I needed to do. Term has also started and I'm back at work.

Whose voice are you hearing when you read this? Mine? Yours? A stranger? Or do the words move silently over this page?

There are many strange denizens of loneliness in my street. When you have lived here long enough, these strangers become familiar. The elderly Chinese male drinking by himself is a common fixture. But women drinking by themselves are rare; if there are, none lonelier than this woman who frequents the coffee shop I always go to get my packed lunch. We know loneliness when we see one and I acknowledge my own loneliness yet I know for a fact I privilege a few relationships with people in my life who more or less are privy to my intimate dealings. But this woman, a slightly built, almost skeletal frame, exotic in ethnicity like maybe she's Indian or Middle Eastern, and with two deep large orbs for eyes that stare vacantly with a slight tilt of her head. Her being frozen in thought unnerves me. This is a quality that I would love to capture on photograph or film but to do that is almost violent so the only way to represent her is to write about her in the truest subjectivity. And I know for a fact she is alone and that something has happened in her life. She cuts a lone middle-aged figure with the deep dark features and hair caught in a high bun, reminiscent of the slender melancholic art nouveau figures of Gustave Klimt. She's also an inaccessible image of something you are privy to but cannot represent. I always catch her at the end of a meal staring vacantly into space and then she would mystically wander off slowly.

Then on the other end of the spectrum is my young neighbour. I don't know if she qualifies as a lonely woman but my only relationship with her is through the window. I see her at home through my window and hers. I've never seen her out of her apartment. Never. Petite and attractive, occasionally I catch her praying or coming out of the shower or walking in her spaghetti straps and we've exchanged the weird glances and smiles before we close our windows to each other. But it's strange I have never seen her in any other context, which makes me wonder if she ever exists. Once or twice I see a bronzed, bare-bodied young man in her place and I remembered it was different from the other man when she first moved in. Otherwise, the only details I get are filtered impressions through the gauze of her curtains.

On the way home in a Grab from a tour at the Print Institute, we passed by the National Gallery.

The driver asks "You come here before?"

I said "Ya".

"The place very nice especially the restaurants. But also very expensive ah."

And I just laughed. Laughed at our hopelessness.

Either our institutions and government did right by us, saw through us or that they turned us this way. Restaurants and capital over art. Essentially.

Though everything was redeemed by food and conversation on prawn mee afterwards.

Oh for the old film world of theme-obsessed Yasujirō Ozu and his rotation of actors, especially the splendid widow-playing Setsuko Hara. Filmmakers love their people, sometimes love and hate, like Fassbinder and his cast. L Krishnan used the same actors too, perhaps because they were in the stable of Cathay Keris.

I saw 'lonely woman' again at Katong Shopping Centre. If I am to choose the loneliest mall in Singapore, this would be it.

Noir belongs to the dark, together with listening and thinking, forms the most compound experience—cinema.

Film is already a meta medium. Watching a film is like watching memories of memories, thoughts of thoughts. It forms an assemblage for the viewer.

Return of the repressed—like the *Orang Minyak*. Something about film returns belatedly. I guess this fits right into my project. It is doubled—first with the *Orang Minyak* who returns to terrorise the city and second it returns again in the present through this film in the millennium. It returns as memory, it returns as reminder, it returns as artefact. If horror's potency depends on the metaphorical fears of its time, then its return signals the looking back and watching it happen again.

We passed the seventh ghost month as quickly as its memories of offerings, joss sticks, candles and burning paper in cages and bins fade away—not as quickly though as the smell and air of hungry ghosts, and the ashes at the bottom of the pool whenever I swam.

32:11 It's been a while since I last saw these two. Latiff and Rokiah reach Kampung Tebakar, their car pulls over at a stilted attap hut on sand, presumably near the sea. Rokiah, as a strange courtesy or perhaps formality that exempts Latiff from etiquette, tells him there's no need to remove his shoes upon entering her home. She lights up a kerosene lamp in her house. The camera opens up the modest interior of her home. I assume too there's water from a well somewhere and a bucket in an outhouse. I paid more attention to the *kampung* house because I remembered the scenes from U-Wei bin Haji Saari's film *Perempuan, Isteri & ...?* that featured a Malaysian *kampung*, and I also recalled the vernacular malay architecture work of talented young artist Farizi Noorfauzi's who in his art school studio, rebuilt the *kampung* house verandahs and windows out of scavenged wooden slats. We know from their conversation Bakar was a reformed *samseng* (gangster), who joined the police force and was laughed off by his former brethren. I am guessing from the patchy Malay that I understand, that Bakar might have tipped the police off about his former gang and they were unhappy.

33:15 The couple was followed by Little Runt and Moustachioed Farid who had also reached the scene. Little Runt passes his revolver to the stronger Moustachioed Farid who is lurking among coconut trees in his stylish disco clothes although he is some 20 years ahead of his time.

34:47 *Maybe in Hollywood!*

Rokiah explains that Bakar took matters into his own hands by not telling the police about the gang. Latiff stresses here that (perhaps to the audience too) that this is Singapore, *maybe in Hollywood* the concept of vigilante justice makes sense, but not here where people need to work with the police and the team. This signals the break away from conventional American film noir where the characters are more individualist and dimensional and conflicted in their existential ennui and morality, working against the state.

Moustachioed Farid startles Rokiah with the shadow of his gun through the curtain of the window. Krishnan places his actors well in the mise-en-scène but I wished he would have utilised the economy and the movement of his camera more with staging and blocking of his actors; it would have been perfect here to build suspense though it would have changed the tone of the drama. Instead, he uses a lot of cuts:

35:40 *Shadow of gun; Rokiah startled; Moustachioed Farid shows himself; Latiff throws his blazer; lands on the weapon as distraction; jumps out the window wrangling Moustachioed Farid; Little Runt looks on from his lookout point bewildered; two men wrestling quasi-erotically on the verandah.*

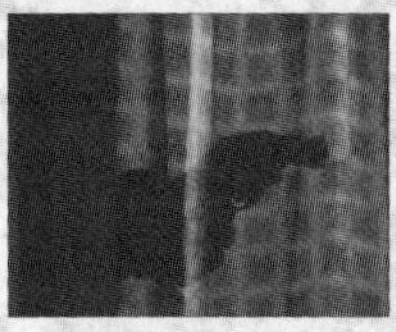

The couple rolls back into the *kampung* house under the damsel doe eyes of Rokiah. A fistfight ensues, the actors forgo stuntmen. At first equally matched, Moustachioed Farid seems to be losing steam so he awkwardly grabs a chair to swing it at Latiff, who dodges it to execute a swift karate chop to Moustachioed Farid's neck but he's too strong.

36:40 It is such a silly performance of machismo with Rokiah in the middle, biting her nails and watching like a frightened referee. Both men continue to struggle with the blameless chair. Moustachioed Farid blows out the kerosene

lamp with a swing of his furniture and they fight in the blackout and roll back out into the verandah. As they are wrangling, trying to subdue each other, Little Runt, anxious from afar, decides to help Moustachioed Farid by throwing his dagger at Latiff. He misses, and the fateful knife ends up lodged in the burly back of Moustachioed Farid instead. He crumples to the ground and that's that.

7 September 2021

Waiting for class to start right after lunch as I type this.

39:21 The police HQ operations room with its strange sounds and signals reminds one of the bizarre operations and war room in Stanley Kubrick's *Dr. Strangelove* (1964)—the police force is put on showcase again, however this time it is behind-the-scenes of the inner workings and machinations of the state seen in terms of a network of points on a map and census writ large. As Latiff makes the call to report to HQ about the new dead body of Moustachioed Farid, I am tabulating the body count since *Che Mamat Parang Tumpol*. There was one in the death of the triad leader but no ostensible body; a whopping five in the horror flick *Orang Minyak*; three in *Rasa Sayang*, which makes it a black comedy? And two so far at the one-third mark in *Sumpitan Rachun*. A total of eleven.

Since the dead cannot speak for themselves and hence the slander of silence, a film's task through my rewatching is perhaps to wake the dead again and save the vanquished in what Youssef Ishagpour calls "re-memorisation" in referring to Godard's films. I'm stealing with liberty here but what is cinema and theory without these seminal figures? So I would like to think (naively or not), I'm creating these fissures from these cultural artefacts, ruptures and crystals in time (film memory) and creating objects of counterpoint in my installation and a polyphonic simultaneity. Hiroshi has called them signals from the past whose images I think perform like signal boosters, unleashing in the viewer a network of further connections.

It demands on the contrary a history that rejects the idea of continuous development and uses a structure that accentuates fissures and jumps to liberate the unrealised forces contained in the past. Then the past assumes its true face...

This opposes a narrative based on a rupturing of history so as to create a national future based on the vision of official dominant forces. This is to dis-embody any national and economic goals, to refuse survival and competition in a capitalistic society.

40:59 Another cat burglar scene again: an unknown figure climbs to the top window of a walk-up apartment where a gentleman sits within reading the papers in the evening. The burglar remains on the outside and inserts a rodlike thing in between the curtains. Just as the gentleman looks up, wondering what it is peeking through the curtains, he gets hit with a poison dart from it, a blowpipe. Nothing is stealthier than a blowpipe, the indigenous weapon of the Orang Asli of the forest. Our short history here again consists of outsiders climbing into windows to steal, rape and murder.

Latiff and Ali (the reporter) arrive too late at the scene to find Mohammad, the gentleman, sprawled on the floor. Apparently he was a lead through his involvement with Bakar. Now, both of them are dead.

41:46 Body count: 12

43:22 Latiff tries to suck the poison out of Mohammad's neck in vain. From where did he learn this skill? From the army? The forest? His parents? He spits it out into a potted plant and asks the reporter to call for Dr. Lai Peng for an antidote. But really we should ask, what is this poison infecting this city, and what is the antidote?

44:41 Dr. Lai Peng dons a tight cheongsam that shows off her curvaceous figure, we know this through the generous views of the camera. She receives a call to hear that Mohammad is dead after all, so she is not needed anymore. Her date with Latiff is cancelled.

8 September 2021

Last week I was at Dino's place. I haven't seen him in eons and he had recently built himself a family. I video-ed his gorgeous young son, who is not even one year old yet and we spoke about times gone and missed like the true middle-aged men that we are. But really, I'm happy to be reborn as a 20-something again.

Two weeks ago, Dirk spoke against the sunset in an arresting view of the city while Siu Li and I listened on. He was in their veranda, cutting a silhouette in a German accent, recounting the impossible task of mounting an exhibition of artist works involving slide projectors.

A month ago, I watched Liao Jiekai's film *As You Were* (2014) on Mubi, an elliptical narrative of exquisite crepuscular shots in Singapore's southern islands that continue to haunt the mind long after the film ends, reminding one of its not too distant colonial past and its ill-at-ease, internally exiled characters who try to negotiate a sense of belonging. I am strangely reminded of the political prisoner Chia Thye Poh, who was bizarrely exiled to Sentosa island, a tourist resort island that was then developing into the mother of all amusement parks that we know today. Prior to this confinement, he was released from 23 years of imprisonment without charge or trial on the mainland for suspected communist activities. He has the dubious honour of being the longest-serving political prisoner in the world. He was detained in a one-room guardhouse in the colonial Fort Siloso, ordered to pay rent as a prisoner while also being offered a job as a curator.

Of the strange ultra-capitalist Disneylands and playgrounds of the world I also think Macau and Dubai meet ours on the list.

Who started writing in fragments? Nietzsche? Baudrillard? Benjamin? Barthes? Wittgenstein? St. Augustine? The composite self that breaks the great book, the great unchallenged narrative, the History, the Epic. Instead we now have multiple narratives, a rhizome of stories against history. What started it? The birth of the modern or the consciousness of a fragmented broken self? The century of the mundane? I know the answer—it is all of us, the diarist. Walter Benjamin attributes this to the birth of the novel in which its dissemination only became possible with the invention of printing, as opposed to the great stories orally passed down. *The birthplace of the novel is the solitary individual*, the uncounselled individual who has to deal with the difficult task of representing the incommensurability of human life. I call it the Great Mundanity in my context and the like. We don't sit around fires anymore listening to the storyteller. Godard has mentioned something similar for film, in that capitalism wanted to produce film for the individual and came out with video and television and killed film which is more of a communal experience and affair.

45:17 You know, Dr. Lai Peng's attractive Malay helper with the thick black hair looks suspiciously like Rokiah herself. Maybe that was the look. The standard of attractiveness for Malay women back in the day. Much like how sometimes Singaporean Chinese women *nowadays all got one kind of look*. It is half a joke here that needs to be articulated in Singlish or else *no impact*.

50:09 A wonderful scene of the richly ornamented, Art Deco-styled Tanjong Pagar Railway Station which has since been disused. It was decommissioned in 2011, where the land on which the station and the KTM (Keretapi Tanah

Melayu) railway tracks stood and which Malaysia had partial sovereignty was given back to Singapore. The main building of the railway station became a national monument in April 2011 as per agreed in the objectives of the new Points of Agreement between Malaysia and Singapore. It will be a future site and the sixth stage of Cantonment MRT station, one of the stations for the Circle MRT line.

10 September 2021

50:36 Latiff arrives at the train station in uniform. He is waiting to escort the arrival of Penruber's jewels to the bank.

Mata-cheng-deh-kor.

"Last time police wear shorts" is the colloquial phrase you would have heard from your parents or grandparents. It refers to the khaki uniform worn by police officers from the turn of the 20th century right up to 1969. *Mata refers to* 'eye' in Malay and that was the early local term we used to call policemen. It's telling how in the old days we had terms which were rather symbolic and critical of the police as 'eyes' of the state, ones that spoke of spying and surveillance. Who could forget the ill-fated and glamorous *Mata Hari*, the 'eye of the sun' who trained as an exotic dancer in Java, who became a spy because she wanted to see her lover, injured in one eye, in World War I and became a spy for France to gather information on the Germans by seducing an officer and was accused of treason thereafter, shot by firing-squad for double-spying for the Germans.

Coming back to our khaki shorts-clad policemen, I suggest they are a colonial remnant of the British army uniform with high socks (puttees) in the tropics, of dual function—to fight off humidity and for visuality—an obsession with legs (calves) as an extension of strength and power. You would have been fooled like I was in the black-and-white world of film that it was an all-over khaki uniform. From the post-WW2 period up until 1969, policemen wore khaki shorts with a grey flannel shirt. You obviously cannot see this in black and white where colour is neutralised in a filmic reality. The photographer Nobuyoshi Araki spoke about how black and white signify death, and adding colour signifies breathing life into work. Jean-Luc Godard said "Life is in colour, but reality is in black and white." I would say black and white is a constructed or produced reality. If black and white signals a reality masked in death, then colours are the rainbow of experience associated with life.

That the *mata* here relates to surveillance, it is ironic then that the Police Force in the present day, addressing robotics and unmanned systems capabilities, parodies itself in M.A.T.A.R—the acronym for the new 'Multi-purpose All Terrain Autonomous Robot'. It also champions itself when compared to its male-dominated history, as being inclusive and equal where "women stand shoulder to shoulder with their male counterparts, be it in rank or appointment" though I suspect another reason is to maximise human resources besides reassigning gender roles.

13 September 2021

My body aches really badly from all that exercise I had been trying to get myself into. It feels like either ailing form or age that everytime I get up it is as if a giant rubber band that stretches from my lower back to my hip is about to snap. I decided to get a massage. It was a toss-up between the traditional Chinese-uncle kind and the 'clean' spa. I chose the latter. Maybe because I wanted a female touch. In the darkened room, I was groaning with my posterior exposed and what was supposed to be a one-hour basic massage extended by price and time everytime the masseuse's hand slipped higher and harder into my nether regions. *How about a butt massage? I am not finished, do you wish to extend another half-hour?*

How did I end up with less pain and dignity at the same time?

53:17 Another conversation of flirting on the phone between Latiff and Lai Peng, under the excuse of enlisting the doctor's help to put Rokiah up in her place to keep her safe, while also asking her out for a dinner date.

53:09 A scene where the out-of-sight Mastermind is talking in Chinese-accented Malay to his right-hand person, an attractive Indian woman in a *sari* and high-pitched voice. Where does Krishnan find these actresses from every race? Telling her to finish the job—kill Rokiah and everything that stands in their way.

56:47 Bar at Stamford Road.

Latiff gets a tip-off on Marican, the jewel dealer who operates in this bar and has dealings with the Mastermind's gang. It's a diverse cosmopolitan crowd. We still have bars like this actually. The drinks and cocktails are the same, but the crowd has been replaced by many a white expat and his Asian partner, trendy professionals and hip young TikTokers.

58:00 *Selling to Americans*

Latiff tries to extract information from Marican, who claims he's just an honest jewel merchant who sells to the Americans who are willing to pay 30 times more for the stones. This seems to suggest the subtext of America's growing economic presence and cultural imperialism on the world stage and Southeast Asia at large.

India was well known as the only country to produce diamonds before the modern world. Closer to Malaya would be the more obscure presence of the diamond production in the alluvial mines of Borneo and Kalimatan, controlled by the Dutch. The script for *Sumpitan Rachun* was adapted from American film noir for local audiences and the screenplay was not written by a Malay producer or filmmaker, like in the previous films, but by the British writer Pelham Groom, a retired RAF group captain and former Fighter Command staff officer based in Singapore. So it would be safe to speculate that Groom's interest and investment comes from the side of British coloniality and empire. Even though the KTM rail runs from Western Malaysia to Singapore, I assume the geopolitical territories then were much more fluid so I'm striking out Kalimantan where these diamonds, carried by the Indian merchant Marican, come from. It has to be from British India, if anything, going by the Empire's desires for profit and production in colonial literature, of which part of the detective noir genre is born. One finds historical precedence in the novels of *The Sign of Four* (1890) the second novel featuring Sherlock Holmes written by Sir Arthur Conan Doyle and *The Moonstone* (1868) by Wilkie Collins of which Groom might have been influenced. In both stories, treasure stolen from India generates local crisis. In the case of *The Sign of Four*, there is a striking resemblance to the plot here: a steamboat chase in which the exotica of a poisonous blowpipe faces off with the modern revolver, and the treasure is sunk in the River Thames.

In resonance, Britain is facing growing criticisms to return 'looted' treasures from former colonial territories like the famed Koh-i-Noor Diamond from India which now belongs to the Crown jewels of the British monarchy and the Elgin Marbles taken from Athens in the early 1800s.

Coming back to the present and America's relationship to history in the tectonic shift of power, though the US produces almost no diamonds for commercial consumption it buys more than 40 percent of the world's gem quality diamonds—making it the world's largest diamond market.

Incidentally, *The Moonstone* is an example of an epistolary novel, a form written as a series of documents like letters, diary entries, newspaper clippings and other documents. Somewhat similar to this writer's experiment here.

17 Sept 2021

Today I made a trip back to the AFA to watch *Sumpitan Rachun* more clearly with subtitles. Michael, who had been assisting me with the footage, was there to receive me. There are many details that got lost in translation in my earlier interpretation. The most embarrassing and glaring error was that the deceased Bakar was actually Rokiah's brother and not her partner or lover. And Hussein, the other cop, is her lover—I got it the other way round. In the higher resolution and quality of the screen I went back to the beginning epilogue of S. Roomai/ASP Latiff's disclaimer and message to his viewers. Some peculiar details struck me. For example, I missed the picture frame of the first president Yusof Ishak and was wondering why his picture was hung in a 1961 film when he was not made President yet in 1965. Then after some Googling, I learnt he was Yang di-Pertuan Negara (head of state) after the PAP won the first election after our self-governance in 1959. I realised too that both the presidents Yusof Ishak and S. R. Nathan attended the same secondary school I did. In the first scene, S. Roomai Noor's character, in his office, had a rattan cabinet which reminded me of the rattan bar of my childhood home, and the window had a large beautiful arabesque grill. There was also a large map of Singapore on his left. Another peculiar thing that struck me was that we were using the Ringgit as our currency, as seen in Penruber proclaiming the worth of his diamonds as a million ringgit. This doesn't surprise me since we were still part of Malaya then. But it would be interesting to know that our history of currencies and legal tenders as being part of the Straits Settlements from pre-colonial to colonial times ranged from Chinese coins; the Indian and Javanese rupee; Dutch guilder and Spanish silver dollar; the Mexican dollar; Hong Kong, Spanish, Peruvian and Bolivian silver dollars to the Straits Dollar; the Malayan Dollar and the Japanese Military yen (nicknamed banana money). The Singapore Dollar arrived in 1967.

Also, just to elaborate: Marican's mysterious gem formations, as suspected, was a cryptic code from the Mastermind. The patterns of the diamonds were based on orders given. I guessed this was logical before the advent of encrypted messaging apps on mobile phones—objects that connected their animated human counterparts in a network of intimate dealings, in a flat ontological world so to speak. I guess in making sense of the plot, I cannot depend on a purely phenomenological reading of the scenes as this experiment progresses. But there could be two reasons why I needed to find out more: I'm really more interested in *Sumpitan Rachun* as a genre film and I became more inquisitive at deconstructing films as the project progressed.

Coming back to the last scene, I don't know how much liberty from realism Krishnan took in this film to portray the police here. While the message is clear in the last few films and this one that the police always maintain justice and order, they are certainly not above corruption to get things done. This is seen here when Latiff bribes Marican to obtain more information.

1:04:11 The man who recognises Marican's jewel formation code at the Bar looks suspiciously like Ming Wong, I am pretty sure it's his doppelgänger. Ironically Ming Wong is a pretty well-known contemporary Singaporean and Berlin-based artist who does like a Cindy Sherman of classic films by replaying the characters as himself. Over here, Ming responds to the code/order and proceeds to the Mastermind's lair, an elaborate shophouse I assume to be near Stamford Road. Unbeknownst to him, he is being followed by Latiff in a trendy incognito getup, wearing a neckerchief and a groovy patterned shirt no less.

1:05:00 I think Krishnan attempts a tiny bit of Hitchcockian psychology here by employing the metaphor of staircases, architecture and heights in this film à la *Vertigo*. We will come back to this again but over here we see Latiff following Ming up the ornamental staircase where the Mastermind resides.

1:05:38 The One that gives orders here. But instead, what he finds in lieu of a person is a machine, a tape recorder that self-erases upon dissemination to the receiver. Latiff manages to catch the distinct high-pitched voice of the sari-clad henchwoman who was acting as proxy for the Mastermind, before the message's destruction. These are excellent metaphors of memory devices, staircases, and the disembodied voice. Almost Kafkaesque in the chinoiserie-decorated abode of Chinese and Peranakan influences, where Latiff sees a meaningless device while trying to confront a higher menacing authority. This is organised crime at its most devious. We see traces of influence of Fritz Lang's crime thriller *The Testament of Dr. Mabuse* (1933) in the diabolic and telepathic Mabuse, an underworld boss hellbent on building a society of crime. Perhaps this agent of chaos or cunning, is best remembered again in Ho Tzu Nyen's *Pythagoras* (2013), an elaborate video installation of curtains, film footage and disembodied voices.

20 September 2021

A strong feeling of malaise and fatigue, a kind of fuck-all to everything. I am deeply appreciating the mundane nothingness and the peace of doing nothing except thinking, reading and watching films. Anything close to labour produces a slight reflex of aversion to outright rejection. It has to do with starting work and teaching for a living and not getting to do the nothings and the creative things you want to do. In the weekend, I watched Jia Zhangke's impressive debut film *Xia Wu (Pickpocket)* (1997), almost like a diary of a young delinquent in an authoritarian Chinese town, reminiscent of Scorsese's nihilist *Taxi Driver* (1976) and Bresson's own masterpiece *Pickpocket* (1959). Enjoyed the silly activity of drawing temporary zebra marker tattoos with XY that seemed to take the ills away. On Sunday, I caught up with Sophia after a long time and we had Mexican—margaritas, mezcals and ceviche were in order. She got sick right after. She also bought a couch, which is an indication of a longer stay and investment here.

1:06:00 RUMBA

The band plays a number. I'm paying great attention to the unusual editing style and camera movement of L. Krishnan and his DOP Han Kai Juan. The camera work is exquisite; a series of panning, dolly and zoom shots pivoting around the *femme fatale* character of Rokiah as the camera caresses her face in a jump cut and close-up while she sings (mid-interlude! Think of the time image!), perhaps ominously—*farewell to the beauty of the night*. The camera catches the cop who is watching over her, enthralled with a cigarette, *whatshisname*, is he not the love interest too? I must have replayed this scene ten times, writing does not do it justice here and it's hard to explain a cinematic order of time through camera movement and editing with the inadequacy of language. It is a complex set-up of wide overhead shots and the camera navigating through the dancing audience and interchanging shots between singer, band and audience, all suited to the bittersweet melody of the rumba piece.

Rumba Gembira

Selamat tinggal, malam dan keindahannya	*Farewell to the night and its beauty*
Dengan hiburan dendang dan tarinya.	*With its entertainment of rhythm and dance.*
Selamat tinggal, malam dan keindahannya	*Farewell to the night and its beauty*
Dengan hiburan dendang dan tarinya.	*With its entertainment of rhythm and dance.*
Selamat tinggal, kepada sekeliannya	*Farewell, everyone*
Datanglah lagi, menghiburkan hati.	*Please come again, amuse the heart.*
Selamat tinggal, sehingga berjumpa lagi	*Farewell, see you again*
(selamat pulang)	*(have a safe journey home)*
Selamat malam dan selamat pulang	*Goodnight, and have a safe journey home*
(dan selamat malam).	*(and good night).*
Selamat tinggal, malam dan keindahannya	*Farewell to the night and its beauty*
Dengan hiburan dendang dan tarinya.	*With its entertainment of rhythm and dance.*
Selamat tinggal, malam dan keindahannya	*Farewell to the night and its beauty*
Dengan hiburan dendang dan tarinya.	*With its entertainment of rhythm and dance.*
Selamat tinggal, kepada sekeliannya	*Farewell, everyone*
Datanglah lagi, menghiburkan hati.	*Please come again, amuse the heart.*
Selamat tinggal, sehingga berjumpa lagi	*Farewell, see you again*
(selamat pulang)	*(have a safe journey home)*
Selamat malam dan selamat pulang	*Goodnight, and have a safe journey home*
(dan selamat malam).	*(and good night).*

1:10:00 It is a kind of scene that will remain etched in memory; a moving image in the form of a *tableau vivant*—that mode of time, in the words of Roland Barthes, "whose mythic prototype is the princess falling asleep in *Sleeping Beauty*," quite contrary to a photograph, in itself a near-perfect metonymy and juxtaposition of the actual *Sleeping Beauty*, shown as a billboard on the Cathay Building just minutes later in this film. As if Rokiah meant to say to us, on that very stage with her band and her dancing audience and their invisible stage hands (remember Hilmi Johandi's painting of amusement parks and stages), *Goodnight my love, I will see you soon*, before going into the deep freeze of time.

Cinema is not dead here, it's merely asleep.

1:10:38 Latiff goes for a second date with Dr. Lai Peng at the Cathay Restaurant while the police are on patrol outside the building. Penruber is housed in one of the rooms with the diamonds. It's daytime and a *mata mata* patrols back and forth at the junction from a viewpoint above. As he comes towards the camera, the signs behind him read 'NATIONAL' and PARIS RESTAURANT & BAR'. This is somewhat peculiar to me, as I realise this must be the junction of Handy Road, that now leads up to the School of The Arts building. This junction, to me, provides the *punctum* of intensity that is Time, of the *that-has-been*, repeated in another scene at exactly the same spot with another policeman on shift in the night (again minutes later in the film). Both viewpoints are unbeknownst to the policeman on guard—a tactical viewpoint from above, one whose final repetition is the difference of the absent policeman on guard, who represents the 'NATIONAL', not necessarily the restaurant and bar as they disappear in the night. That final repetition is me having remembered being in that spot, my own body absent, but looking down onto Handy Road years before I chanced upon this particular scene in a film. It is a *punctum* I would have missed if I had not happened to go back and forth in the video, and frozen the scene to produce stills in order to study them. There is no *punctum* in a moving, fleeting image, according to Barthes and I would agree here. But also this scene of the policeman walking has its repetition (inadvertently or not) in the earlier Robert Bresson masterpiece, *A Man Escaped* (1956), where the French Resistance prisoner in WW2 has a similar viewpoint from his cell above, studying the guards on patrol, while planning his escape. Bresson must have repeated that again in the prison scene of his last film *L'Argent* in 1983.

It is a viewpoint that is done stealthily. It is a survey, a sweep of what is at stake on the ground, the present that *would be* past. There are two historical images I have been obsessed and enthralled with for some years now, almost like my own *Camera Lucida*, I come back to them from time to time. Like Barthe's concept of the *punctum*, they only exist that way for me and might not necessarily hold the same value for others, though scholarly, there must be so much that can be said about them in the phenomenological sense. Anyway, one of them is a photograph shot and developed in secret by an Australian POW (at Changi) during the Japanese occupation in Malaya Singapore of a group of prisoners bathing and doing nothing/ laundry by a water body. The main dialectics of the picture is this: a photograph shot in secret by a colonial-by-proxy prisoner, capturing Asia yet holding me captive himself with this particular image. There is something about what *has happened* in the past recorded by a memory machine that fascinates me. Even the English title of Bresson's film *A Man Escaped* (1956) is in the Greek aorist tense 'he escaped' in the pure past, amplified by the austerity of his black-and-white reality. But this is only the icing of the cake that would not fit here. I also feel it has something to do with the camera being an instrument of power for the weak or captive, but not as a weapon.

During the long pandemic, I had been reading voraciously, a habit that has intensified with age and I have a few recent key books to attribute my keen interest in reading images: the invaluable *Images in Spite of All: Four Photographs from Auschwitz* by Georges Didi-Huberman, the experimental and diaristic *Sight of Death* by T.J. Clark and the incomparable *Camera Lucida*, which I am re-reading rewardingly again (no longer the clueless student) by Roland Barthes.

21 September 2021

I was woken by an incessant handphone alarm ringing in the wee hours of the morning. But I knew it wasn't from my phone next to my bed. It was very faint. It just kept me up. At first I thought it was my sons' phone that they left in one of my cabinets. But I eliminated that possibility. It was somewhere in the distance, maybe it's my neighbour, but it was also quite impossible to hear something like that from my nearest neighbour. Then I thought about Lacan's *objet petit a*, which I read about the night before. The object that is the cause of desire for the Other, but also the void that is a nothingness you cannot understand but drives you to desire. This incessant, enigmatic ringing is it. As much as the diamonds that Penruber is delivering, which you never see, only as something that drives the plot of the whole film. Žižek compares the *objet petit a* to the MacGuffin, the Hitchcockian object, the pure pretext whose sole role is to set the story in motion but which is in itself 'nothing at all', and is present only in a series of effects. You would recall earlier that I wrote in *Rasa Sayang* of another Hitchcockian object—the unused and unturned faucet. The symbol of anxiety that would unleash the flow of all modern trappings.

L. Krishan owes much to the Bangsawan theatre and equally as much as to Hitchcock as compared to the next two directors of films to come later in this writing.

I am socially tired from a long day and this feeling of meaninglessness is something I should learn to enjoy (not even accept) and not see it negatively.

I think over here we live in a weather that makes us hate ourselves and lose our souls. Thought about this as I walked with my groceries back home. I call it *cuss*ory weather—hot and humid as fuck, that only favours the privileged who get to work in the comforts of their air-conditioned abodes. We should be given to complete indolence in this climate but instead we slave away in our anxious bubbles. The colonials knew this, the natives knew this and the post-colonials knew this, that heat is hell if heat gives to labour. So I never got the tropics and its exotic imaginings. We suffer from the lack of seasons, of understanding change and time and rhythms and spaces and our body clocks run on a relentless clock of heat and numbers. One should not walk in this heat. Think of our migrant workers who work in this heat everyday. The heat that drives our modern machinery. Cherian George wrote about the politics of comfort and control in *The Air-Conditioned Nation* (2000) about how Singaporeans are kept away from the heat to increase productivity, that we appear willing to forgo political autonomy and civil liberties for prosaic material comforts. He claims air-conditioning (which Lee Kuan Yew declares as the greatest modern invention) is a selfish technology—where its net effect is an increase in heat—not only does it contribute significantly to global warming through energy consumption but it works basically by transferring heat from inside the building to the outside. I think it's quite an ingenious short paper that covers both sociopolitics, history and the environment at the same time. Henry Miller wrote his memoirs of America called *The Air-Conditioned Nightmare* (1945), after living a decade in Paris, and describes his disenchantment in his roadtrip across US of a cruel, sterile and monotonous culture-scape. The American artist Sam Lewitt displaces light in spaces and reroutes their electrical circuits to produce heat for heaters instead that also spell out text from industrial vocabulary. In it he employs the concept of utility as a mode of standardisation through the division of labour; standards as units of quantification and commodity (think electricity bills) of which pleasure and happiness are accounted for in the data derived by the behaviour of consumers. The artist-curator Kent Chan explores heat's relationship with art in his films and practice through tropical imaginaries as a result of colonialism and modernity and its consequential developments to ethnicity and culture. The poet Euginia Tan writes in the last stanzas of *Calculated City*:

Frozen into my seat
From the same air-conditioning
Depleting my metabolism
For free will;
I wonder where the hell I am.
Am I one stop away, or
Did I ask that

Ten minutes ago.

Psychically, I don't know how much of all of this bears down on our human relationships which have also become standards—transactional and mercenary.

In the evening after meetings at home on Zoom, I hastened down to the National Library to get my hands on the reserved copy of *Latiff Investigates*, Pelham Groom's detective pulp fiction from which *Sumpitan Rachun* derived its content. Groom, as screenwriter, adapted Latiiff for the silver screen. Worn and softened with time, this gorgeous vintage little publication is the closest I've ever gotten to both local pulp fiction and detective noir for the entire time of my research. By Federal Publications and dedicated to a *Sadar Singh*, the back cover synopsis describes Latiff bin Ismail as from a very good Malay family in Kelantan. "Tough as steel. Joined up with a party in the jungle during the war, then came into the Police force. Educated at Raffles Institution and just back from the Police course at Ryton. He's very bright."

...no ordinary detective...razor-sharp intuition...loveable Chinese girl assistant Dr. Tan Lai Peng...

In the short stories, none of them were about *Sumpitan Rachun*, though there were glimpses of characters like *Rokiah* in them. The first story tells of when Latiff' first arrived in Singapore and was assigned his first case—a murder in the *kampung* of a beautiful Malay lass in the forest. She was going to marry a white administrator. Her killer turned out to be the married and lecherous old Malay servant of the white guy, whom she spurned. Already the colonial desires and exotic imaginings were well put in place.

On the front cover, ASP Latiff is seen staring resolutely at something above in the distance while clutching the sleeveless shoulder of a cheongsam-clad woman who seems both perplexed and lost at the same time, staring at another object to her left. I imagine the woman to be the Lai Peng character (Mary Lim in the film) even though here on the cover, it's Malay actress Umi Khaltom.

1:12:29 *Right under the Police's nose*

And so Penruber's diamonds are stolen from his hotel suite; the colonial looks especially distressed to have lost his jewels and he is literally ashen, or unusually pale, maybe too much foundation applied on his face or maybe Krishnan's camera is not flattering on paler skin. He is mad for trusting the police. Who here would not remember the whole farce of the Mas Selamat incident in 2008 where the limping suspected Islamist extremist/fugitive fled while being in police custody, much to the amusement of the public and embarrassment of the government, where security lapses are virtually unheard of.

Here literally on our shores, *A man escaped.*

5 October 2021

On the news, 3,486 new Covid-19 infections were reported and the death toll reached 130.

So what is happening is this: work at the college started and also I'm going down the various rabbit holes in this writing project that I can't climb back in. Another metaphor is I'm getting lost in the labyrinth and I can't seem to find Ariadne's thread. And I've been confronting minotaurs in my dreams. Minotaurs I can't see.

I had a dream that woke me up, and kept me up. Maybe it's what you would call a bad dream. For once, since my life turned, it felt more than a tinge of regret. I had returned to my matrimonial home in a bizarre event, not that we were in love again but that it was for the better—the practical reason of commitment and familiarity and the in-laws, and my sons. I think it's the familiarity I've been lacking all my life that I've sought the touch of strangers and the unfamiliar as I had always been, unhomely. But it's a dream, I thought I was looking for as the last shred of familiarity and for some reason I thought of my time climbing the knoll during my time in the army on the second ATEC in Australia. We had completed an arduous mission. I was a signaller with a heavy-ass signal set on my back accompanying my officer. To this day, it is my most vivid out-of-body experience in the mother of all exhaustions when I crashed on top of the knoll. I felt that I left my fatigues and saw the whole section on that hill at dawn.

A week ago, Chris Ho, punk rebel pioneer and DJ/musician passed away from stomach cancer. I never knew him as a person but my two fondest memories come in 2004, where my punk band Cupcake opened for his Zircon Gov. Pawn Starz on the Theatre Stage of the Esplanade. We brought the house down in a raucous night of camp and rock and roll. Two years later, he interviewed me on the now defunct LUSH 99.5 station on his alternative programme for my first solo album *Atom Nations*. It was a real honour but I was nervous as fuck and I must have blipped like an idiot on the air. His calm raspy voice always came first for me, before the icon with the tattoos.

1:16:05 *Mak Inang* Musical

Or the grand singing competition at the Cathay Restaurant, the lead-up to the climatic finale.

But wait. Let's rewind a few seconds before where I happen to pause at this moment:

1:16:00 Latiff and Rokiah are framed under both the circular archway in the vestibule and the vertical rectangle doorway whose grilles are peculiarly shaped in 6s and 9s. The couple are splendidly matched in white (in the black-and-white film). Rokiah, a step forward, is escorted by Latiff on the left. He is positioned perfectly under the front door lamp when he happens to be blocking Lai Peng who is in a black dress walking a few steps in front.

There are three frames of spaces here in this order: First Lai Peng's house framed by the cinematic aspect ratio and then the vestibule in a circle frame and its accordion-folding grilles, two rattan seats flank the sides, followed by the vertical rectangle of the door and its own ornamental grilles that leads to the porch and just ahead in the distance—trees, clouds and the black night of the exterior outdoors. It's a fantastic frame in flattened space by L. Krishnan, if only for that split second and I don't know if this was conscious or not, though it's too beautifully composed not to be. It's even choreographed to lead to this moment—as Lai Peng emerges from her room while Latiff and Rokiah were waiting at the doorway, Rokiah realises she's forgotten her clutch bag after seeing Lai Peng with one (with the gentlest of rivalry), she goes to retrieve it from the helper, and comes back into the frame so that she is side by side with Lai Peng, as Latiff steps back to exit after the two ladies, just behind Lai Peng.

And this leads perfectly to the next scene at the Cathay Restaurant, in a repetition where the resident band is framed by the circular oyster shell-themed proscenium.

1:16:05 Here we go again. *Mak Inang* Musical.

Mak Inang is a traditional Malay dance that originated from the time of the Malacca Sultanate. This nostalgic ditty belies the strong and complex historical reference to the origin of Malay identity during the golden era of intellectual, spiritual and cultural developments of the Malay Sultanates. Its pre-modern lineage to Singapore is one of kings, from the island's first rulers of Sang Nila Utama and Parameswara to the Shahs of the Malacca Sultanate. It was also a time where geography made Malacca an excellent port for trade which led to relationships and influence from the Chinese and Portuguese. Hang Tuah, the great Malay warrior-figure and Malaysia's nationalist icon, lived at the end of the Sultanate.

The *Mak Inang* is accompanied by music which is believed to have been composed by the order of Sultan Mahmud Shah of Malacca. Here, Rokiah relives its royal function and past through graceful song and movements.

Mak Inang Musical

Mak Inang lenggang, Mak Inang	*Sway to the dance of Mak Inang*
Tangan melenggang diatur langkah	*Hands swaying to the steps of the dance*
Mak Inang lenggang, Mak Inang	*Sway to the dance of Mak Inang*
Tangan melenggang diatur langkah	*Hands swaying to the steps of the dance*
Tarian asli putra dan putri	*The true dance of princes and princesses*
Ciptaan orang di zaman Hang Tuah	*From the time of Hang Tuah*
Tarian asli putra dan putri	*The true dance of princes and princesses*
Ciptaan orang di zaman Hang Tuah	*From the time of Hang Tuah*
Mak Inang lenggang, bergaya	*Sway with style to the dance of Mak Inang*
Melenggang tari berjiwa Timur	*A dance true to its Eastern spirit*
Mak Inang lenggang, bergaya	*Sway with style to the dance of Mak Inang*
Melenggang tari berjiwa Timur	*A dance true to its Eastern spirit*
Walau ada samba dan rumba	*Although there is samba and rumba*
Tari Mak Inang lagi teratur	*The Mak Inang is more appropriate*
Walau ada samba dan rumba	*Although there is samba and rumba*
Tari Mak Inang lagi teratur	*The Mak Inang is more appropriate*
Mak Inang tarian lama	*Mak Inang is our traditional dance*
Tari yang asli di dalam kota	*A dance that originates from the city*
Mak Inang tarian lama	*Mak Inang is our traditional dance*
Tari yang asli di dalam kota	*A dance that originates from the city*
Tarian sopan bila di pesta	*A graceful dance for a celebration*
Sesuai untuk zaman merdeka	*Appropriate for this era of independence*
Tarian sopan bila di pesta	*A graceful dance for a celebration*
Sesuai untuk zaman merdeka	*Appropriate for this era of independence*
Hidupkan tarian Mak Inang	*Keep the Mak Inang alive*
Majukan seni budaya lama	*Onwards with our traditional arts and culture*
Hidupkan tarian Mak Inang	*Keep the Mak Inang alive*
Majukan seni budaya lama	*Onwards with our traditional arts and culture*

Kerana seni nilai bangsa	*Because the worth of a nation is in its arts*
Hidup seni, hiduplah bangsa	*When its arts is kept alive, the nation continues to live*
Kerana seni nilai bangsa	*Because the worth of a nation is in its arts*
Hidup seni, hiduplah bangsa	*When its arts is kept alive, the nation continues to live*

1:19:36 Master Chua Foo Ling the magician returns.

"I still don't know how he does it," Dr. Lai Peng remarks when Foo Ling makes his assistant appear from thin air. Again camera editing was used to perform the 'magic' of Foo Ling's trick which makes it hard to believe it's an illusion performed in *reel* life. L. Krishnan breaks the fourth wall to assist Foo Ling by employing the magic of editing instead to produce the illusion of a magic trick, if so to enchant the real audience (the movie-goer in 1961). The assistant appears to be the *sari*-clad woman from the gang.

Pelham Groom and Krishnan had devised an ingenious setup of scenes that leads to the finale. I do believe *Sumpitan Rachun* is a much more complex and sophisticated hybrid film of comedy and film noir than the previous three films of Krishnan I had watched (maybe with the exception of the psychologically-edged *Orang Minyak*). However this could be due to the more tumultuous turn of events in film that seem to reflect the anxieties of a burgeoning nation.

1:21:56 Krishnan, through his own sleight of hand, weaves in three concurrent plot devices for this in a brilliant synthesis of time in the form of two parallel events and a flashback (another reason to call this Hitchcockian). The first is Ali the journalist snooping around the dressing room of Foo Ling, presumably in the underbelly of the same Cathay building. Ali applies foundation cream to his face in the dressing mirror, as if about to perform himself, when all of a sudden he gets ambushed by Ming from behind the changing curtain. Ali loses and becomes incapacitated in the struggle. Next, Latiff becomes distracted in thought during Foo Ling's magic show, when he recognises a prop, the trunk, as the one used to transport Penruber's cargo in the train carriage. Foo Ling then invites Rokiah to the stage to be part of his disappearing act. They wrap her head in a *sarong* and place her in the trunk before locking it.

1:24:25 The puzzle is pieced together when he recognises the voice of Lotus (*Sari* Woman) from the tape recorder in the Mastermind's shophouse. This is where for the first time, Krishan employs the element of a noirish flashback only privy to the viewer: in the black of the night, the train is chugging down the track, it cuts to the interior of one of its cabins where Lotus emerges out of the trunk to replace the box containing the diamond with a replica. She then returns back to the trunk to smuggle herself with the rest of the cargo back to Singapore.

1:26:17 In a truly remarkable and absurd end of the scene, both Lotus and Foo Ling disappear under smoke and curtain, and Krishnan's *dissolve* editing respectively. Latiff, made a fool again, is seen clutching stupidly at the air, hoping to find a trace of the criminals. He opens the trunk, removes the *sarong* to reveal Ali instead who stands and looks dumbly at the audience. This is the closest resemblance of Krishnan's earlier slapstick fare and Ali here, with foundation on, is the unwitting Wahid Satay of this scene. His performance is complete and replete with bathos and the audience is in stitches.

1:27:04 *Those who know buy National*

Foo Ling's plan is underway now and his cronies Lotus and Ming kidnap Rokiah and lead her out of the Cathay building, but the multiracial outfit is obstructed by a policeman on guard at the Handy Road exit.

It is now night, the end is near, but not before a series of unravelling. Let me remind you again that it's the second repetition of the policeman on guard at the junction, the first was during the day. At night, the NATIONAL sign Is ominously revealed to be with the extension THOSE WHO KNOW BUY NATIONAL with a huge logo of a lightning bolt above. Let me elaborate on the semiotics here, surrounding it are two more road signs that signal 'No Exit'. I see four deterrents in the form of the policeman, the huge NATIONAL sign and the 'No Exit' signs. I don't know how much of this is intentional, and it could very well be advertising for an electrical product company (like Panasonic's old name) but the logo strangely represents the lightning bolt logo of the ruling party, the People's Action Party, albeit upside down.

This is around the first years of the The PAP government, which had won the 1959 general election, the first one to produce a fully elected parliament and a cabinet wielding powers of full internal self-government. However came 1961 and major disagreements over the proposed plan to form Malaysia and an internal power struggle within the party caused it to split into two factions—the left-wing Chinese-educated group and the English-educated moderates led by Lee Kuan Yew's faction, who remained in the ruling PAP. By 1965, Singapore was out of Malaysia, Lee Kuan Yew had consolidated power, with many in his opposition branded and imprisoned as communists, and since then, the party has won the majority of seats in every general election.

I am of course reading this symbolically to say they are more than deterrents of authority to crime—they are deterrents of power to opposition. What's this really have to do with this scene of three bodies trying to escape the police? Isn't all art open to all sorts of hermeneutics?

12 October 2021

I dreamt I was swallowing coins for some kind of wellness routine. I think it's a recurring dream so I looked it up and there were so many interpretations like ones that describe trying to save money, while others talked about having unfinished business. Thought about it for a while when I remembered XY talking about a mythical Chinese character with no anus called a *Pixiu*. This 'fortune beast', one of the five auspicious animals, has the head of a dragon, the body of a horse and the legs of a *kylin*. Mythology has it that one day it ate too much gold, silver and jewels (its staple food) and defecated in the Jade Emperor's palace, thus provoking the incensed Emperor to remove its anus. Today people use it as an amulet to trap wealth, power and protect homes but they are quite harmful if not placed properly. Pregnant women and children should also avoid it as it may 'eat' the bad stuff as well. Actually if anything, it feels more like a punishment, or a repression (constipation).

1:29:58 *The Atmosphere of Crime (or deviance)*

Lotus distracts the policeman and they lug Rokiah out to a getaway automobile. Meanwhile, Latiff confronts Foo Ling in the dressing room. After some interrogation, Foo Ling shoots at Latiff with a blowpipe while he wasn't looking. But the detective's reflexes were deft enough to catch the dart with a handkerchief. Must have been his jungle training. He handcuffs the magician.

The getaway car careens towards its destination in the middle of the night until it runs into a police roadblock.

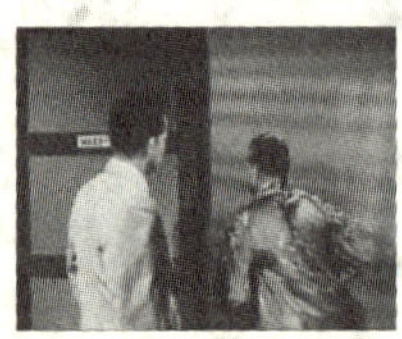

1:30:00 Latiff comes to know about Foo Ling and his cronies' plan to use Rokiah as ransom for their escape by means of the harbour and disposing of her body afterwards into the water. Latiff convinces the slippery criminal that he has marine police sealing off that area. To which Foo Ling remarks:

Rokiah won't be killed unless the Cathay lights go out.

Revealing his cue to Latiff arrogantly before doing another trick to uncuff himself, declaring *the lights will go out* and escape from the dressing room. A man chase ensues.

Rokiah won't be killed unless the Cathay lights go out.

This line is so symbolic that it's like the first nail of the coffin for the film industry.

1:31:56 I wanted to write how Krishnan juxtaposes an elaborate car chase scene with the man chase scene but upon several viewings, I realise it's not elaborate at all. It's fairly tame, minimal and realistic. The only thing that is making it dramatic is the theme music on overdrive, which I am starting to find annoying. I don't mean the scene is tame in a negative way. I think what is working for it are the camera angles and the mood and atmosphere of crime or in a way, deviance, which implies a path that breaks from the law, signified by this car chase scene.

I think what is working for it are the camera angles and the mood and atmosphere of crime or in a way, deviance, which implies a path that breaks from the law, signified by this car chase scene

I think it's the way the cars make their presence one last time, not as vehicles but as actors too. A local economy of careless destination and drift. One more fix, the last heist. What do criminals/cars feel? Treachery? Evil? Misplaced loyalty? Courage? Regret? Freedom. Choice. Or just adrenaline and thrill? The true noir—*the denizens of a nether world trafficking in sordid magic and lurid hopes.* But actually what I feel here in these characters, except the hysterical Foo Ling, is nonchalance, obedience and resignation in the way that feels more real of 'criminals' that may be you or me. It's all affect and mood and you can replace the soundtrack with a shoegaze number and it will fit just right in. Especially Lotus in the backseat with Rokiah and Ming and something about her turning back to look at the screen of the rear window while the car careens and turns, and then looking forward, with Rokiah in the middle, unconscious and Ming being passive. They get chased over Sheares Bridge , make a detour and the cops lose their tail, while they hide under another bridge. Then they head for the pier.

The *mata mata* communicate on 'Special 37' to radio HQ, telling them they lost the suspects. Do you know who still calls the police *mata mata*? Hokkien-speaking gangsters, ex-gangsters and uncles. The term has been relegated to a socioeconomic demographic within a particular dialect-vernacular in everyday parlance.

1:33:48 A ferryman receives them at a timber jetty, and the boat glides across the pitch black of night, even the horizon line to differentiate water from sky is banished, like Charon escorting the dead to Hades.

1:34:22 Latiff chases Foo Ling to the top of the building, in an exquisite display of stairways and corridors. Midway, Foo Ling realises the switchroom is locked. Guess he has to turn off the huge lights himself then. Lotus and Ming bring Rokiah atop a cargo ship waiting for the cue. I'm wondering about the realism and logistics of this. If the Cathay was at Handy Road, which water body could they have been in? The Singapore river at Boat Quay? Don't think the ship could fit. The mouth of the not-yet-conceived Marina Bay ? It kind of makes sense Charon ferried them from Boat Quay then.

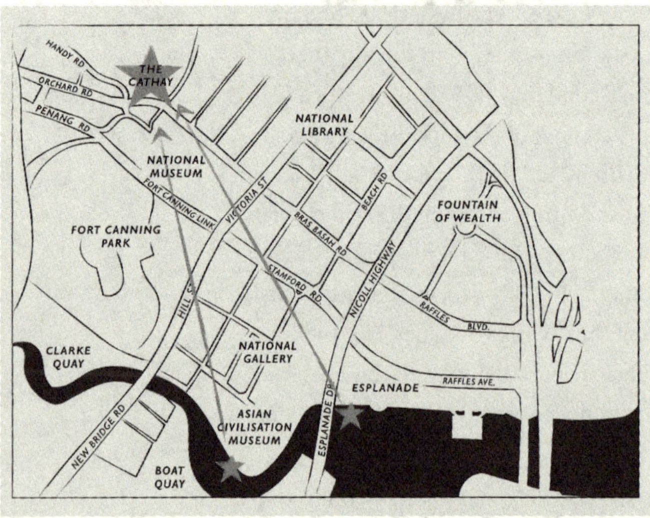

Anyway the cue was for the lights to go off and for them to weigh Rokiah down and sink her to the bottom of the sea.

1:36:04 *Man on the pole. The fall.*

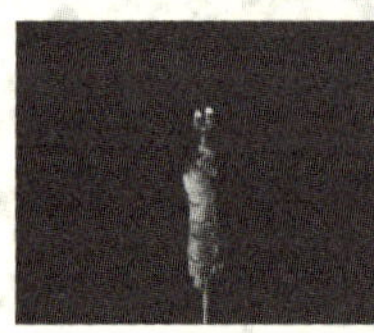

In the last symbolic scene here, Foo Ling dramatically climbs a pole in a feeble attempt to put out the lights at the top.

For such an exaggerated display of cues and signals, it is a shame they did not have mobile phones then, but it sure made for great cinema. Two marine policemen climb overboard the cargo ship and put out Ming instead. Lotus flees the scene (bless that sweet devil) and they rescue Rokiah. Predictably, Foo Ling falls to his death, but falls not the whole 90 metres of one of the tallest skyscrapers in Southeast Asia to land on the ground, but on one of the floors between the towers. An enigmatic scene shows the silhouetted figure falling from a low perspective (probably a dummy thrown out), and onlookers from the hotel staring out their windows at the commotion on the top floors of the skyscraper. They all come out to see what just happened and congregate around the body. Latiff and Lai Peng also arrive at the scene and wade through the crowd. Latiff picks out something familiar from the dead man's face, then removes his hat and wig, then his eyebrows, moustache and beard to reveal—Penruber! Great, a white man in a period Chinese costume doing a daredevil parkour stunt on a skyscraper, then falling to his demise.

I bring to your attention both the tragi-comic Manchu villain of *Che Mama*t and *Sumpitan Rachun* employed by L. Krishnan for Malay Cinema. Perhaps it's a coincidence but some of us in the older generations might remember *Dr. Fu Manchu*, a fictional villain introduced in a series of novels by the English writer Sax Rohmer in the first half of the 20th century. The portrait of Fu Manchu was based on the popular music hall magician Chung Ling Soo, "a white man in costume who had shaved off his Victorian moustache and donned a Mandarin costume and pigtail" and Fritz Lang's Dr. Mabuse was created in the vein of a Fu Manchu-like character with the exception of Rohmer's pseudo theories concerning "Eastern devilry" and "the unemotional cruelty of the Chinese." On the psychic level, these could be anxieties projected on the Other, but if there is any signal more ambiguous that Foo Ling made with his death, then it is definitely not the death of the magic of cinema.

Television Singapura was officially inaugurated on 15 February 1963 and on the 2nd of April 1963, President Yusof Ishak officially inaugurated the regular service of Television Singapura. Singapore became part of Malaysia (together with North Borneo and Sarawak) with the signing of the Proclamation by the then Prime Minister Lee Kuan Yew on 16 September 1963.

Chapter 5:

Lion City (1960)

Moving in, movie out

Recently, parliament passed a new law aimed at preventing foreign interference in domestic politics called FICA, another to add to our acronyms. This means that authorities may compel internet service providers and social media platforms to provide user information, block content and remove applications used to spread content they deem hostile. Suspected individuals are required to disclose foreign funding sources and be subjected to other 'countermeasures' to reduce the risk of overseas meddling.

Already the opposition and activists have criticised it as a tool to crush dissent in yet another piece of draconian measures by the city-state to curb civil liberties.

My face mask smells like a pub in the morning. I think I'm done with cigarettes even though I smoke very little. My asthma is not letting up. Someone said it's just the body breaking down. I feel it. I felt it. Everything changed when I went past 40. It's not the permanent midlife crisis that I'm having but, maybe this is related, that my body is heading for its eventual demise. I'm wearing bifocals. My lower body aches and groans everyday, I'm attracted to younger women. I scrapped my car and picked up skateboarding. My hair is past my shoulders. I'm strength-training in the community gym. I want to throw my old clothes away. My sons treat me like a dude. I can't pee the full strong stream like I used to.

I am going to miss *Sumpitan Rachun* and it feels my 'noir' limit climaxed with the American neo-noir films of *Crash* by David Cronenberg and David Lynch's *Mulholland Drive*, both of which explores the logical, extreme end of the culturally-imported genre. The Americans remain masters of a cinematic form in a Hollywood I find otherwise increasingly irrelevant to me. Both auteurs are self-critical of the industry. Where Cronenberg explores the body-horror relationship of man and machine, Lynch digs deep into the recesses of the mind in a fable of guilt and rejection. You find all the elements of noir in heightened modern-day modulations—dark lonely lugubrious human beings, desolate non-places, insidious/disconnected/

morally ambiguous villain-like characters, and yes, apocalyptic automobiles that spearhead the narratives. Lynch's great mind-altering film is at the bleeding edge of a twisted erotic dream hell worth rewatching for redeemless clues ten times over. Whereas Cronenberg's audacious film ending is almost a nod to Antonioni's *Zabriskie Point* mountain orgy scene but at the perverse remains and ends of culture in the lonely assemblage of automobile and human. Even Howard Shore's guitar is a minimalist deconstruction of the soundtrack. Loveless.

Also a note about L. Krishnan since the next two films are not helmed by him. Back in the day, a peculiar thing happened with the studios. They hired mostly South Indian directors, with Chinese financiers, British scriptwriters and Malay actors! I find this dynamic and social relationships quite telling and I will leave it to you to read further into it. Anyway, Krishnan, like most directors then, was influenced by *bangsawan* theatre, a kind of traditional multimedia theatre that used stage, song and dance. In these four films, I found his stamp and touch to be uniquely his: deft camera work and exquisite timing, equally adept at comedy, action and horror and innovative song-and-dance routines. That the India-born, Malaysia-raised and British Army-served director was regarded as the father of the Malay film industry is no overstatement, considering how he was not only responsible for launching the careers of P. Ramlee, Wahid Satay, Maria Menado and Roomai Noor, he also laid the foundation for the modern film industry in Malaysia.

Stephen Teo writes on "Malay cinema's legacy of cultural materialism" that "had Singapore remained in Malaysia, it might have continued to function as the base of Malay film production. Malay films gave Singapore an identity when it was still an integral part of the Malay world. When Malay film production ceased, it lost not just an identity, but a whole industry." Alfian Sa'at mentions that Malay cinema is "peripheral to the consciousness of not only Singaporean audiences, but filmmakers as well." As Sonny Liew illustrates in his wonderful *The Art of Charlie Chan Hock Chye* where the comedians Wang Sha and Ye Fong narrate in a part that spoofs the 'Singapore Story':

> *Which is, of course, why we had to leave Malaysia! We simply couldn't accept a society in which any one race would be given special treatment, as this chart so clearly illustrates!*

We then enter a new phase with the next film, in a genre closest to the social realist drama in *Lion City*, Cathay-Keris' first postwar Chinese Language film.

Lion City 狮子城 (1960)

> *Legend has it that once, an Indian prince called Raja Chulan set himself out to sea, in the hopes of conquering China. He encamps on an island on the peninsula and comes across a ship of old men, with a cargo of trees and needles. The men informed him that they had started their journey from China as young men, with a shipload full of seeds and iron bars for trade. By the time they reached this island, they had grown old, the seeds had sprouted into trees; the iron bars rusted and disintegrated into needles. Seeing that China was so far away, the prince was hence discouraged and decided not to pursue his mission. Little did he know that the Emperor of China had sent these envoys to trick him. Many years later, he had a son named Sang Nila Utama, who one day, as a young man, was caught in a terrible storm at sea, which was only abated after he threw his crown into the waves. He reached an island, where he encountered a peculiar beast—black head, red body and white breast—that he mistook for a lion (singa), thus naming the island 'Singapura' (Lion City) thereafter.*

17 November 2021

Let me update you on what has happened. My exhibition ended and my work was invited to be installed at a university college library for the next six months, which I'm stoked about. It feels like it will have a younger, more critical audience there in a liberal arts background, considering they will close their doors in 2025.

I suffered a knee sprain two weeks ago when I fell off a skateboard while trying to descend a ramp. I picked it up again at the grand old age of 43, and I cannot account for the impulse (not even on my own kids for whom I bought penny boards) except for a kind of death drive which hopefully I will expound on some day. I suffered a previous injury recently on the same bad knee; I don't know if this is due to my slowly declining efficiency of my physical body or the other sport I picked up—weight training. I'm kind of serious, I think it gives me discipline and satisfies my other drive—self-preservation.

It's funny, I'm watching a restored print by the AFA, scanned from the sole surviving 35mm print loaned from the Hong Kong Film Archive at 4k resolution and restored at 2k. The opening credits in the original print were missing so the AFA had to fill them in from the available publicity materials. We know that this film is helmed by a director who goes by the two-character stage name of Yi Sui (易水).

1:35 Almost like a returning character in this film, a glorious view of the old Cathay Hotel in the night with the heading *Cathay's Organisation's Dedication to Malayan Cinema*, followed by the logo's two *keris* (daggers) stabbing into cross formation as if to emphasise Cathay's dedication.

2:00 *Lion City*

This city is located at the crossroad of the Far East
and people called it the Lion City.
This city is where I was born.

We see the back of a young Chinese woman in a *samfu* blouse on top of a hill, as she narrates and points dramatically at the skyline. First of all it is strange to refer to Singapore as the Lion City (unless you are translating *Singapura* or you work in URA or Tourism), so it must be put upon you to say it in a script. Secondly, we are not in the Far East in the strictest sense; the area typically denoting China, Taiwan, Hong Kong, Korean and Japan, and maybe bits of Russia and Mongolia. We are, as part of a geographical landscape, in Southeast Asia, but I'm not splitting hairs here.

2:02 A short whirlwind tunnelly transition and then the Merdeka bridge makes an appearance again. The restoration is one of the best I've seen. And then a wonderful flyover of the city. The soundtrack, an operatic, communist-styled anthem rises above the city in a chorus of voices, to the height of the camera mounted on the plane (or helicopter) flying overhead the city:

This is Lion City

Lion City is our lovely home.

This is the meeting point of the Eastern and Southern China Seas,

Where the Indian Ocean lies to the west.

She is nourished by the monsoon seasons.

She enjoys the equatorial sun.

Lion City is the gateway to Malaya.

Malaya watches over our well-being.

Rubber plantations stretch over thousands of miles.

Tin mines are our treasures.

We call Malays and Indians our fellow brothers.

We work hard together to develop Malaya.

We create a new culture with our wits.

We develop new pieces of land with our hard work.

We call Malays and Indians our fellow brothers.

We work hard together to develop Malaya.

We create a new culture with our wits.

We develop new pieces of land with our hard work.

She will be great and spectacular.

Majulah (Onward), Singapore.

Merdeka (Towards Independence), Singapore.

As I'm reversing the scenes in Quicktime, it's like a lifetime (mine, yours and ours) has passed by in black and white. Time is the greatest yet most mysterious variable in our insignificant existence. I don't mean to be nihilist here, but I'm talking in the essence of deep time we truly become insignificant and video and film must be the greatest technical human wonder ever to be invented, that it has managed to counter the laws of physics and thermodynamics and entropy and all that is that. We can rewind scenes over and over again to see how it's done, and see if we had missed a detail or two. That's something we cannot do and are powerless against our fated wretched lives.

Because I see these scenes in hindsight, I understand what a piece of work and propaganda this is, echoing the political conditions of the time, but beautifully shot and I assume the budget to be higher than the usual Malay production. It was shot for $100,000, equivalent to over $900,000 today but also considering production and materials were more modest then, compared to today's Hollywood's excessive CGI and stage-sets bonanza.

The emphasis via the lyrics and symbolic imagery like the lion and an ongoing road reiterate values of independence and progress, which are counter-played by a documented reality of a nation-in-the-making *created from our wits*.

2 December 2021

It's been a long absence again and I find it incredibly hard to sustain this project as I've reached a real low in my life. I'm depressed and I find it very hard to cope in this world. I've said it. For a long time as long as I can remember. As I write this at 6.51am in the morning, I feel like I need to bang all this out and get it off my chest. It's an accumulation of many things that weigh upon the soul: my recent obsession with skateboarding and suffering a nasty knee sprain on top of an already bad knee that has put me out for weeks. I don't think I can skate anymore for a long time, I'm barely walking. I don't attribute this to a mid-life crisis. I attribute this to the earlier death drive to fill up some void again. I made a purchase on a resale flat and I am going to wipe out my savings and possibly go into debt. This is mostly due to the cash over valuation scheme, a typical Singaporean practice in a sellers' market where they jack the prices way over the state valuation of their property. This I attribute completely to a materialistic and mechanistic society, of which it has no place for people like me. Divorce, rent, child support and an elderly parent have taken the beans out of me.

Next, I've been unceremoniously dropped by my Berlin gallery. It feels like another long-distance and cold relationship, made worse by the pandemic, that led to another divorce. I attribute this to different expectations and ultimately to my difficult and absolute idealism, made worse by socioeconomic conditions.

Finally, my intense alienation and trouble forming stable relationships, my deep lack and loneliness and repressed and uncontrolled desires that lead to addiction, self-destruction and sabotage. I attribute this really to my shitty family for years of silence, secrets and dysfunctionality. The more I try to be a buddha for it, the more I doubt and slide. This denial that nothing exists and my own Catholic guilt and self-punishment make bad bedfellows. Two hours before this I was on the verge of a mental breakdown and considered calling a hotline, or admitting myself to an institution. I was out of breath, my feet were sweaty and I felt a faint release at the top of my head. I'd like to watch the sun rise now and head to the beach. I purchased the property as close to the east coast as what I could barely afford. As close to the water as I could get.

The thing with productivity is that you have to work in spurts or sprints that take you further everyday and you have to set something up for the next day so that you can return to it. It's funny I'm talking about productivity when I can barely lift any spirit up. But I simply have to get this writing done so I can set it up for the next passage and therefore be able to continue its life.

4:35 *SIT Flats*

You will never find again, except for this period of time and nation-building and less cynical citizens (because they are newly born and anxious), films that were also a way of public announcement for what the government has done.

To the mellow piano soundtrack of Debussy's *Clair de lune*, over here, we have a neat piece of documented history. We see public housing flats built by the Singapore Improvement Trust (SIT). It would be remiss and also a misconception, because of the film's perspective, to assume that these are the first SIT flats built. Ironically, they were one of the last as SIT closed shop in 1960 to give way to the newly formed HDB (Housing Development Board). In common parlance today, SIT flats, known with the hip and trendy as gentrified and conserved Art Deco-styled apartments in Tiong Bahru, with the post-war apartments going at a cool million a pop, even with half a century left on the lease. As the narrator says, "This is the backdrop where our story begins," our protagonist opens her window in a flat to another one, which then cuts to a ridiculous view of the majestic Singapore River, her girth wide as a grand lake. If I studied the image of the SIT flats on that film negative, the closest resemblance would be the ones at Dakota Crescent. At most, some would have faced a dirty Geylang river. I am betting on Dakota because they were also featured in earlier Cathay films like *Satay* (1958) and *Che Mamat Parang Tumpul*, which I wrote about earlier. I was looking for HP's research to corroborate with my speculation, but nothing on the *Lion City*.

And then after it cuts to Feng Ling (our protagonist) being called by her mother in theatre Mandarin (equivalent to clipped English) to help out with preparing breakfast, pulling her away from the window frame, through which you see a painted backdrop of boats by the river or a sea port of some sort. I might return to the art of the painted backdrop later but first, why was this kind of idyllic utopia that audiences were supposed to believe?

Also, there was a sense already of a strong Confucian work ethic established. Second brother has to raise money to go buy a taxi, the older brother has to rush to the docks for work. The young daughter, the next generation, is already in her pinafore about to go to school. Everyone has no time for breakfast and the matriarch is left on her own at the table.

10 January 2022

So the New Year came and went and it took me so long to get back to this impossible task of writing again. Novak Djokovic, tennis champion World Number One who tested positive for Covid last month, has just won a legal battle in Melbourne after being detained Down Under for a week for not having been vaccinated for the Australian Open. I find him smug as hell, as in with all talents at the supreme top of their game, like Nyjah Huston for contest skateboarding. They are often cocky and choose to do whatever they want, but hey maybe it's lonely at the top.

Two months back I finally got to catch Apichatpong's *Memoria*, and it is as sleepy and brilliant as any he has done. It is a lonely film as well for Tilda Swinton's character going after a pile of bones and following a sound halfway across the world in the southern hemisphere wearing a constant worrisome frown. After all that has happened, I still do not have a plot to tell you about except there was a spaceship in the end and it was about sonic collective memories in the airwaves and the images they conjure.

As my double Jeremy Sharma is writing, this character who thinks, feels and writes as Remy is recalling how the 'genre' of filmmaking adapts or responds to changing mores and identities in flux through the ongoing process of nation-building. Malaysian film scholar Norman Yusoff writes about two different realities—"an 'everyday-defined' or 'authority-defined' social reality. The former refers to the reality experienced by ordinary people in their everyday lives while the latter refers to that which is defined by those who are part of the dominant power structure."

He is also thinking of the Cronenberg film *Crash* again. Jeremy, my double, contemplates the other literal double of the death drive at the end of the film, *Crash*! Two doubles in perfect combustion of thought.

7:09 Feng Ling and Second Brother dash across the road—ah—I see it now and recognise the road that Che Mamat was riding his scooter on—and as a confirmation to my guess, the Dakota SIT flats, recently demolished. They wait at a 1960 bus-stop, where shortly a pre-SBS bus arrives and ferries them to their destination. I believe some parts of the world and Southeast Asia still look like this, maybe parts of Vietnam or Myanmar or North Korea or Cuba, but considering the present—that's a sixty-year gap. And I don't mean it as a condescending thing where a country is way behind what progress should look like. I mean it in the sense of a loss in time and a mood of nostalgia to someone from the 'future'.

14 January 2022

8:11 In the bus Feng Ling tells her friend sitting beside her that Second Brother has bought a new car in which he will take them for a ride later. Second Brother laments he is still a taxi driver but he does not have to worry about car rental anymore. Today, we have the much cursed Certificate of Entitlement, a kind of tax that costs as much as a car to reduce traffic jams on the tarmac in a land-scarce country. You don't know how much we love our cars until you scratch one or not so much as bump lightly onto one, you will almost certainly suffer the stinkiest of dagger stares which is quintessentially a Singaporean gesture. When I drove a couple of years back, it was probably my third or fourth accident that I decided to just fuck the claims and insurance and just drive about my car with silver duct tape on the hood for a few months. Cars are ridiculous here. Period.

And even today, Grab (our premier transport app) drivers struggle to make ends meet to break rental, even if it's still supplementary income.

8:42 *Women at the factory*

This has got to be one of the most striking scenes ever to be captured on a Singaporean film, the direction is simply exquisite. But what is particularly striking and personally serendipitous for me in the time of images is that of a particular frame which I froze just as the women were about to enter the factory and start work: my attention was caught by the company signboard at the head of the entrance that read 'CHIN HOCK RUBBER CO.LTD'. Many years ago, probably around 2005, I shot an image of a man walking past the entrance of a tyre shop, on medium format with a Holga toy camera. On the signboard, it said 'CHIN HOCK TYRES'. This may just be mere coincidence, but I am pretty sure these two images are separated by a time frame of 45 years, linking the local automotive tyre industry to the early rubber industries and perhaps even earlier to their plantations.

As I'm typing this in Al Fahah coffee shop, serendipitously again in Joo Chiat, I catch hold of two minor local Indian celebrities. One is the notorious and flamboyant lawyer M. Ravi, well known for championing and defending political dissidents. He is in an all-black ensemble of a tank top and tights with a pink glittering sequin cap and aviator sunglasses. Everyone in the coffee shop recognises him, from the stall assistants to the customers who ask if he remembers them. Clearly he is either relishing in, or he is oblivious to the attention his presence attracted: loud, jovial, singing and joking with everyone, giving personal and political anecdotes, while having his tea-time meal.

A few minutes later, preeminent Art Historian T.K. Sabapathy walks by in shorts, his Caucasian or Eurasian wife a few steps behind with a walker. In my writing here, this layout of merging text with images on margins is inspired by his seminal publication *Road to Nowhere: The Quick Rise and the Long Fall of Art History in Singapore.*

Coming back to the women entering the factory again—four years ago at MOMA in New York, I caught the superb exhibition of conceptual photographer Christopher Williams, who constructs images not taken by him, called *The Production Line of Happiness.* The title refers to a line taken from a documentary by Godard in which an amateur filmmaker describes his work editing his films of the Swiss countryside as "the production line of happiness". The advent of cinema and film coincided with the second industrial revolution and mechanical reproduction. Henry Ford got the idea from pigs in the slaughterhouse, where they hung from conveyor belts and each butcher performed only a part of the task of butchering the animal. This death machine and the division of labour called the 'assembly line production' was brought over to automobile production and drastically altered it in the process at a much lower cost. In 1895, the Lumière brothers debuted the first ever film *Workers Leaving the Lumière Factory* and forever sealed cinema to industrial reproduction.

The development of the division of labour increases production capacity and results in the provision of many manufactured goods, thus increasing a society's wealth. However, Akira Kurosawa said something uncanny about the dissolution of the human structure during the decline of Japanese film. Their golden period mirrors ours—from the 1950s to 1960. The years 1960–63 saw a rapid decline, the same period of Singapore's rising nationalism. It also coincided with the rise of television. Kurosawa saw the human structure as the cooperative of talent surrounding film production, much like Krishnan and his trusted team. This dissolution gave way to the division of labour and the breakup of film and the fall of attendance. 'Film' gave way to 'data' and 'media content'. Once colour television became a common fixture in

Japanese households, film was relegated to the back burner. Marx had something to add to this equation through human alienation—Walter Benjamin wrote how the social mechanism blunts an individual's need and dependence on others. Like Cherian George's air-conditioner, comfort isolates and bring those enjoying it closer to mechanisation. "Of the countless movements of switching, inserting, pressing, and the like, the 'snapping' of the photographer has had the greatest of consequences. A touch of the finger now sufficed to fix an event for an unlimited period of time."[1] Amazingly, Benjamin links the rhythm of production on a conveyor belt as the basis of the rhythm of reception in the film. This connection first appears to the factory worker on an assembly line in an independent, objectified form.

9:00 In the factory these women receive, shear, and pack these rubber sheets in a line; the moving images of domestic and feminine labour reflected on the nascent stage of the country's nationalist identity captured and fixed on film, received first by its local audience in an analogous rhythm of the film reel in 1960, and like the "delayed rays of a star," again by this writer. I would like to stress there are no heavy machinery but a mechanised choreography of manual movements by these women shearing and packing these sheets, such that workers learn to co-ordinate "their own movements with the uniformly constant movements of an automaton" through practice and repetition.[2]

10:54 Later on, the men do the heavy lifting and transportation of these packs.

Fine motor labour had been separated from skilled handicraft in the assembly line and even in the division of labour—there is further division of workers into skilled and the unskilled, with the unskilled worker most degraded by the drill of the machines. "His work has been sealed off from experience; practice counts for nothing here."[3]

Societies are formed on a technical base that serves as the bedrock of the economy and this domestic scene of Chinese women coaxing, working and gossiping over rubber sheets must form some part of the base in that period. Ninety percent of all global production of natural rubber comes from Southeast Asia, China and India. Rubber exudes Asia and is quintessentially Asian, embodying qualities of flexibility, resilience and weather-hardiness. We end this study and anecdote with this country's own remarkable story with rubber. It was said that our time as a rubber-trading hub started in 1877 with 22 rubber plants gracing the island from Sri Lanka. Other disputes put it to 22 rubber seedlings smuggled from Brazil and then germinated in London's Kew Gardens before coming here.

Twelve of these were then planted by the Botanic Gardens in Singapore. During some 20 years, important data was collected about their cultivation. Of these sprung botanical director Henry Ridley's pioneering scientific contributions to commercial production in Malaya. Later, the island developed into an important rubber-packing as well as a rubber-milling centre to serve the plantations in Malaysia and Indonesia for the next 80 years. Rubber produced by these estates was then processed, packed and transported to Singapore for shipment to London to be sold and distributed to rubber manufacturers in Europe and the USA.

As a commodity, it was the Singapore Chinese entrepreneurs and dealers that turned Singapore from a rubber hub to a bona fide international financial and trading service centre, against colonial ownership interests. The volume produced through the buying and holding of processed rubber for shipment grew, making a huge financial impact that was able to support a capital base of banking, shipping and law, which in turn led industry groups such as the RTAS (Rubber Trade Association Singapore) and the Singapore International Chamber of Commerce Rubber Association (SICCRA) to create an organised market with good liquidity and technology. This also meant providing the pricing standard for the rubber industry globally, attracting leading rubber producers and traders to participate in this industry and major tyre companies locating their rubber procurement offices in Singapore. With great wealth comes great patronship, as exemplified by one of the richest man in Southeast Asia during that period, rubber tycoon Lee Kong Chian, if you look at all the institutions named or benefitted in his honour. These pioneers contribute widely to social and economic development in Southeast Asia. But overzealous production has its perils and impacts directly on our environment, such as the burning of regional peatlands to prepare the land for crops and plantations. Peatlands can simmer and burn forever and a direct consequence of this is the suffocating haze from Indonesia we encounter every year. Wealth and capitalism are great bedfellows and no discussion of rubber is complete without mentioning China.

China is the largest producer and exporter of automobile tyres but is heavily dependent on rubber imports. The industrial monster, while devouring its rubber supply, has already begun its Belt and Road Initiative (BRI) and will invest in tyre manufacturing facilities along a contentious network of overland and maritime routes with Singapore, being one of its strongest allies, citing a '33-85' figure to illustrate 33 per cent of all outward investments relating to initiative flows through Singapore, while 85 percent of inbound investment flowing to China through the city-state. But until flying cars become a reality, we gonna be burning lots of rubber on the roads and lots of forests to go with it too.

If the logical conclusion to money from commerce is art—think again patronship and art fairs and million- and billion-aires finding galleries to park their wealth, many artists like myself think on the contrary. Art is not the conclusion of wealth but the first act of life. How to think, how to live, how do we learn about things and materials and engage with our environment. You talk about new digital technologies and

NFTs, but again they go the way of the former, which is a kind of foregone conclusion. The future is a forgone conclusion. If we come back to the technical base, these women touching these sheets that somehow like the push of the button, generate our economy, then the best artists want to know where the rubber comes from. They want to touch and feel its pulse, its texture, its weight. You can own something with money, but you can't touch it.

In her installation *sft crsh ctrl*, the artist WeiXin Quek Chong engages with the imaginative possibilities of touch. Her huge top-hung latex sheets are a throwback to her family history—her paternal grandparents tapped rubber trees in Malaysia and her grandmother used to describe pouring out huge heavy containers of the tapped liquid sap to make sheets of latex, which would then be sold to a middleman. As she began to source natural latex sheeting for her own work, she discovered that a lot of it were still produced in Malaysia and sold through a British company, a living legacy of anachronistic relationships built on the extracting and exporting of natural resources. Quek Chong aptly describes touch as one of "the material languages in which we sense and communicate what's around us, and as with all nonverbal languages," and is something we need in order to survive, communicate and grow, but today, the element of touch in society has been de-prioritised.

19 January 2022

Art Week. I hope it goes away quickly.

Yesterday I went back to my studio to look for the album with the medium format photo. Eagerly, I found it, but what I can confirm now did not match my earlier suspicion, and anticipation turned to disappointment. The photograph of a dingy and darkly-lit car battery shop had a sign above that spelt 'CHIN LEE' not 'CHIN HOCK'. This only proves one thing—people believe what they want to believe to suit a narrative. And memory must not be trusted.

24 January 2022

Monday. For some reason, very Kafkaesque today. I couldn't really sleep, got up early to go to the Stadium skatepark to practice skateboarding, only to find a posse of experienced skaters already there at 8.45am. I was too intimidated to practice in front of them so I headed down to the huge basement car park to practice riding and carving and then the next two hours just trying to drop down a curb. I was never gonna get it right, I was much too afraid. That's what I learnt about myself, I am physically quite timid and it takes a lot out of me to summon courage. I finally took a video of myself to see what's wrong and I realised it's been my shit balance again all along. After spraining my knee quite badly weeks ago, I popped a shoulder ligament last week going down a transition ramp. Coach Henry said I was bending at the hip too forward and not using my knees. I think I was over-compensating for the fall before so I was bending too much to the other side and it was the same awkward pose on video. After correcting my posture and another 7 to 10 minutes, I must have gotten one acid drop right, just in time for lunch.

Later in the afternoon, I took a bus to Tanjong Pagar to collect another pair of skate shoes. It was a subdued day and after what seemed like a pleasant ride, I reached the Lumiere, an upmarket highrise block of boutique apartments in the heart of the downtown district. I noticed a few women impeccably dressed in designer wear. You never know who you're gonna meet on Carousell, and all this while I thought I was chatting with a bloke when the message came:

Sorry could you go into the residential building and buzz 2705? My boyfriend will let you in and hand over the shoes

I was 90 percent sure this was a Singaporean Chinese woman with a Caucasian boyfriend (it's just a hunch).
I proceeded to the lobby to press on the intercom <27><05><bell>, a foreign male voice answered and there was a buzz. Then I pressed the lift button and waited for one of the four lifts to open. I went into one and pressed 27, but the button wouldn't light up. But it was going up anyway and I ended up on the 29th. A resident entered the lift to go down to the ground floor. I asked him how do I get to the 27th? He tried with his card but it wouldn't light up as well so he shrugged. Back on the ground floor, I intercom-ed 2705 again, this time I asked how do I get to your unit, and the male voice said I could only take the lift beside the intercom.

Finally on the 27th, a white man opened the door. I can't make out the accent but it's probably UK or Australian. Buff in a tank top with arms sleeved in tattoos, he also wore a cap and glasses. He looks like a banker on his day off. I saw a maplewood Landyachtz cruiser without grip tape, and a typical photorealist portrait drawing of some celebrity as the requisite artwork. The studio apartment was otherwise quite bare, a room door was closed. Either the girlfriend was inside or she was out.

"I bought them a month ago, but they were too small," the white bloke said. I didn't even bother to try them on, they looked new and unworn. After a lacklustre inspection, I put them in my knapsack.

"Cheers mate." He greeted me out.

And I departed the building. A few minutes later, I found another message from the girlfriend on the Carousell chat. I must have missed it while I was trying to ascend the tower.

Hey just so you know you have to use the first elevator right by the buzzer. It's the 27th floor :)

'Lumière' meaning light in French, the name of this posh residential building and also the surname of the brothers who invented film, in an excellent example of nominative determinism.

Let there be light.

30 January 2022

The writing is fairly embarrassing but I'm chugging on. I've started to observe myself in social situations and it's really helped with the anxiety but I am such a stranger—the terrible, terrible outsider, the incorrigible loner—if you have doubted this then I must have projected an image. And through no fault of others who attempt to love me, my problems with intimacy are my own, being lonely and awkward with others is a connection resolved in making art that connects the attention back to my own indulgence that can be empathised through anyone's subject without my own. What has kept me alive, figuratively or literally are things that I am most at ease with: a guitar loop on repetition, pouring paint, writing, realising through any attempt that is part of a philosophical conceit etc, I put it in the castle of purity I call art, the remnant that would be there after I'm gone. Ego without ego, thought without the body. Many artists want to be loved without the attention on them because they loathe themselves. I am sceptical of the de-humanising aspects that art is becoming, I think the ultimate goal of art is human connection.

Memories are not sticky. Words are the stickiest things and we underestimate the power words have over us. Sometimes words try to replace what objects or materials are doing but they are a bad imitation but all art to some form are copies and imitations and we live in a world where originals are myths. I don't mean originals do not exist but rather, they create myths. So we live in a world of myths and copies. But words are something else on their own and the English language for me is a code that unlocks the immaterialities of deep ideas, feelings and emotions. Words are a craft that have textures, tactility and sound encrypted in the alphabet. These letters mean nothing but are keys to deep wells of meaning for anyone who masters the language. It feels funny even now for me to think, feel and speak English. English is my first language but it's still like a form of minor literature for me in the postcolonial sense, it's the language of my colonial past, not my heritage. But I own it like my universe the way Deleuze wrote about Kafka writing in German or Sebald writing about Joseph Conrad, whom we think is the quintessential English novelist, but is instead really a Polish émigré who is actually writing in his third or fourth language! And that's why their prose is so unique and peculiar. I used to hate the Singaporean accent for its flatness and hybridity of borrowed languages and idioms, but it was worse for me for people to adopt a generic Americanised accent. Lately, I have been stressing my Singaporean accent and my natural cadence of speech. I have begun to accept being in the colour of my skin, the reality of my un-privilege and the impediments of my speech. But only because to master a language is not to master its idioms but to master honesty, the way before a dancer relinquishes to true movement in grace, she has to admit her clumsiness, her imposed consciousness and awkwardness.

1 February 2022

I don't know how I ended up in Telok Blangah but I did. It always happens when I'm in some mental block and social exhaustion and in need of a headspace for zoning out. I had taken the wrong bus while attempting to go to the skate park and had gotten lost. The PSA Port looks really cool to skate in, its dark industrial exterior beckoning at the entrance but I had been forewarned by a security officer. The path back to the bus stop leads to a very long banyan root just along the edge of the path, as if the tree was extending a long arm on the ground. I would respectfully grind on that if I had the right skills for it must have been there for a century at least. Across the road is a church with a banner running across. I'm trying to remember what it said in the bus:

Be at peace and trust in God even when things are going wrong.

Or something to this effect. It had been a human preoccupation to fixate on a consolidated presence to take the place of a huge nothingness, prescribing a being at its worst spiritual caricature—an old bearded white man with a flowing robe. I much prefer attribution instead to benevolent forces or energy.

Today, science renews its theories on quantum forces of causality, we are none the wiser for faith except to know that knowing is not enough and breeds insecurity while believing takes a lot more gumption and courage.

Telok Blangah feels like what it is whenever I stumble upon it, a quiet old hilly land near the mouth of the sea. It smells and sounds like it.

I took another bus thinking it would bring me to the stadium, but it bypassed it in a roundabout way and I ended up home. I cannot fight the forces of nothingness; I will only feel like a loser. The more I observe my thoughts and behaviour the more it helps to cope but it doesn't alleviate the pain of existing. Jean said the everyday things are a burden for me, like it's so hard to pass through daily life and she was right.

It's Chinese New Year's eve, and I like the break but it is a holiday that does the worst to emphasise my otherness, that I'm not part of the dominant narrative, that I'm a part Chinese person with no kin and roots to a culture of which I remain a perpetual outsider. As I sit alone having dinner in Al Fahah—I continue to shut people out just as when I thought I let them in. I continue to feel most comfortable on my own, I can't trust anyone with that comfort and frustration but myself. I see how this leads to depression, self-destructive and self-sabotaging habits but at least I have the distance to perceive this now.

This is something people of privilege will not experience, and I'm saying in relation to others and myself as someone who could be more or less privileged. But at the worst in your life, you could fall back on some privilege—money, education, status, networks and property. But if you are at the bottom of the rungs, if you fall you fall hard and alone. So I will always be on the side of the less privileged, the underrepresented, the minority, the punk, the loser, the downtrodden, the misunderstood, the devil and the cat—those furthest and most sensitive to the centres of power.

But even within the underprivileged among us there are the wicked and the rotten. This could be the logic of recalcitrance or a cynicism bred over a lifetime of victimhood. And you pray you don't become one or have to deal with one.

The minority is not given to expressing himself cosmically, only given a small room with a view of his own to express only his own otherness, to express himself minoritarianly, or how he would be perceived as such; he's not allowed a chance to walk on the rings of his own Saturn, to be his own conqueror and explorer and tell his own stories. He is never the philosopher but the victim, the other.

We celebrate both the excellence at the lonely top and the camaraderie of losers down at the bottom but having to choose sides is the great predicament of life, and where the whole gamut of philosophy and politics fall between.

11:46 An old moving black-and-white postcard, but geographically, the editing is suspect. A motor boat tugging a bumboat filled with rubber goods I assume to be leaving the southern shores for the Singapore Strait towards Indonesia, chugging down the Marina Bay. You catch a glimpse of Clifford Pier, the Fullerton Hotel and past the Anderson Bridge but then it cuts to Boat Quay; to the unassuming eye that's fine but it's like literally going back in a circle to the godowns again by the river channel. It's funny because it feels like we are looking at this scene from the coloured future, the opposing view of Marina Bay's sci-fi metropolis.

I searched for Chin Hock Rubber Factory on Google and got a listed CHIN HOCK RUBBER COMPANY (PRIVATE) LIMITED, established on 10 May 1954 but recently struck off operations on 16 July 2020, right to the hair of the present. Timeline-wise, it seems legitimate, and its principal activity now is in banking and finance as expounded in my short rubber history earlier. Its head office was in Raffles Place so its godowns and factories had to be near which made perfect sense to this scene.

A mosquito bit me on the underside of my left knee. I would too if I loved moist dark places.

3 February 2021

The Queen of Italian cinema Monica Vitti dies at 90. I cannot remember if I fell in love watching the actress or Antonioni's devastatingly bare and elegant film *La Notte* (1961) more than a decade ago. I remembered her beautiful gaze, aloof and soulful in her scenes, where it's about the lives of two alienated people in the span of a night, and Vitti's character at some point entering them. So on the very same day I borrowed *La Notte* from the library and watched it at night again. Maybe it's because I'm older, experienced and more knowledgeable now but it was a much more rewarding experience to rewatch it. There was so much I wanted to say here while watching the film but I lost it all to the dismembering of the cinematic experience as I went back to the keyboards to type this. Watching it in Blu-ray was quite unnerving and uncanny as the resolution seemed to be unmatched in its hyperreality to that period of black-and-white grain in which it was shot. That film must have influenced me tremendously in my moving image work on a subconscious level. As I am drawn to capturing and documenting real time passing without any much plot, and also films informed by writing, *La Notte* feels like a novella unfolding in a span of one night. In my notes, I made it a point to rewatch it for an idea that has been spanning and evolving for years called *The Stranger*, initially inspired by Camus in the first person perspective but has since developed into a more filmic representation and *La Notte* seems very much in that moment and vibe I want, even if that film fictionalised the lives of the Italian bourgeoisie in the early sixties. Antonioni paid very much attention to navigating space and architecture in relation to film, as much to impressions and atmosphere. However, I wanted to talk about two particular scenes that stood out to me, not because they were stronger than others, but because they are scenes that are not best remembered for association of the film. The first is the othering of the two black bodies—that of the couple who were dancing and performing for the protagonist couple in a bar with the live band (that's the other thing—live bands and live music in the film too). The scenes of the woman dancer balancing a filled wine glass on her head and various parts of her body as she is stripped by her partner is peculiar in the least, disturbing at most, but definitely the erotic centre and allegory of the film. As Giovanni watches the black woman in boredom and intrigue at the same time, Lidia is distracted and humours herself instead. Antonioni captured both couples in a state of ennui, the only difference is that the *performed* repetition is much more obvious in the black couple. The other scene, and the director makes it so unplanned and serendipitous, is a bunch of working-class men launching homemade rockets in the field. Lidia chances upon them while drifting in one of her walks and there are many drifts and walks in the film. *-It can fly up to 10000 ft in the sky! -Do you think it can fly to the moon?* Then I was thinking of that period in 1961, and it would be another eight years before the Americans would actually land on the moon. I was just thinking of the Italian aspiration then was much more modest but no less ambitious at the peak of European modernism, that apex just as it declined, just as cinema was being critiqued and the French New Wave came about in all its deconstructed, post-modern stylings. Antonioni not only depicted the disintegration of a relationship and the disintegration of society (the ennui before the moral panic) but the disintegration of cinema itself before it became self-reflexive. So this plot-less breath of a film is an absolute gem, like Benjamin's Baudelaire wandering into the Parisian street, the *troubadour*, the *flaneur* as opposed to the film I watched just before—Michael Haneke's debut *The Seventh Continent* and what a treat to a contrast of styles! That film made just at the turn of the nineties, was totally dehumanising and cruel, the way Haneke likes his films. That is a strong evidence of the death machine through the camera, scenes precisely cut, humans coolly objectified with other machines and objects and the repetition of routines, of a suburban Austrian family systematically planning their suicide. All the perspectives and shots remind me of Christopher Williams's constructed frames, shot tight semi close-up on a tele-lens that makes the viewer seem distant or alienated. For Haneke is not a *flaneur*, he is a surgeon. I might be coloured here but I think there is a very strong Austro-Euro post-war sensibility and aesthetic to Haneke's vision—a continent and civilisation at the brink of a collapse and unable to cope with historical trauma.

On a side note, which can only be done in writing, and also as a homage to Haneke's wry intelligence and my love of connections and happenstance, in *The Seventh Continent*, is a mysterious and recurring scene of waves breaking upon a sun-glinted shore, a weird screensaver. I interpret this as the continent of Australia, what the title refers to, and where the family told everyone they are emigrating to. Of course, they never made it to the shores of the continent. In the scene, it is timeless, it could be any epoch in history or even prehistory.

More than a decade ago too, I wrote lyrics to a song called *Australia*. This was way before I knew the work of Haneke. In the lyrics, I spoke of a couple, in a hope of sailing to Australia, a continent yet to be discovered. Of course, it's a metaphor and it really was about doom and depression, and I imagined a scenario of a woman lying in bed unable to get up, and her frustrated or similarly depressed partner. She could also very well be dead already.

I believe very much in reverberations in the world and the emotional depths and similarities of the human psyche and the human condition and the environment we inflict ourselves upon.

Oh Jenna, don't stay in bed now
C'mon stop throwing a fit
Oh Jenna can you please put the knife down
C'mon don't you look at me like that
Oh Jenna, why can't I please you
We can sail around Australia
Oh Jenna, go put your red shoes on
You don't look too bad
Not in a thousand years

What do you want me to do now
Why are you being like this
When will you start to reason with me
We can't go on like this anymore
Do you remember Australia
No one's touched it for
42 000 years
But we're still groping in the wilderness

9 February 2022

What a delightful walk I had last night as I went to pick up XY. It seems the monsoons have made an about-turn and returned to cleanse us once more. As the sun set, the sound of a light pitter-patter of the rain enhanced by the membrane of my umbrella, so much so that I brought it closer to my ears as I strolled slowly to listen under this makeshift bowled speaker, and attune myself to my surroundings, and everything came alive in 4D—this must be art! Then I caught myself and said no this is life and it passes—I don't want to reproduce it, I don't want to record it. I am just content enough to have just experienced it and to have remembered it.

13:02 Back at the factory again, two women go beyond the domestic gossiping and engage in some shit-talking and bitch-fighting, drama ensues and it's a riot! This is sparked from some jealousy between a senior supervisor and her youthful worker receiving an extra wad of cash from a male employee. Disorder among the female workers halts the production. Feng Ling goes to stop the fight where the foreman failed, with gentle steadiness, catches the eye of Young Master/Boss/Scion (*Shào Ye*).

15:28 The foreman, having been put down by Shào Ye for being useless (well what is wrong with them Shào Ye queries), claims that "They're emotional." Would he rather they just remain automatons? Again, like Puteh in *Che Mamat*, Young Master is dressed in all white—the colonial get-up of power and authority.

16:02 Second Brother (Zhi Xiong) pulls over in a beautiful Austin Cambridge with Feng Ling in the front seat to pick up Father (Ah Cai) who works in the same factory. Young Master or Shào Ye happens to chance upon the connection in the relationships.

16:42 A Pegasus Oil truck in the distance while Young Master is talking to Uncle Tian. The flying horse logo would have been an increasingly familiar presence in the Lion City, being known as a high performance engine oil just as the oil industry began to take off in tandem with industrial modernity happening all around in the postwar world. Under the Exxon Mobil Corporation, one of the world's largest

Big Oil companies, the American multinational oil and gas corporation is the largest direct descendant of John D. Rockefeller's Standard Oil. It first established its presence on these shores in 1893 selling mainly kerosene and lubricants under the Mobil Oil brand name.

Mobil went into refining in 1963, producing its first refinery with a 18,000 barrel-per-day (bpd) capacity in 1966 at Pioneer Road in Jurong. Its capacity increased by 10-fold to 180,000 bpd by the late 1970s. Today, an entire artificial island in the west reclaimed through the amalgamation of seven smaller islands is dedicated to the modern facility that produces more than 300,000 bpd.

17:14 Almost like the precursor to the BTO (built-to-order flats)-before-marriage rite of passage for many young Singaporeans today, a young Chinese man proposes to his girlfriend within the staircase and the corridor of the SIT block of flats. Architecture of the flats feature quite prominently here as opposed to the *kampungs* in the earlier Malay films.

17:51 Which brings us to this splendid scene of the *kopi tiam* (coffee shop). I assume it's built around the flats, but it's not like the local coffee shops you see now, it's got a bit of a bar/diner vibe meets our *kopi tiam*. It's also a pit stop for taxi drivers. What I am drawn to in this scene is the way the camera moves, a linear unfolding of scenes like a moving painting framed by the windows, vertical pillars and shutters in the architecture, and I know they must have set up an elaborate track-and-dolly system to capture a passing moment of youth in a more rebellious environment, in states of idle consumption: drinking, smoking, playing the pinball, listening to music, chatting up women and dating, the opposite of being productive. The female server provides an excellent example of scene blocking as the camera follows her from frame to frame until she disappears into the back store. What I like about it too is the use of diegetic music in the background: a salsa/rhumbainfused number with just the right tinge of rock-and-roll and erotics that breaks the idle chatter just as the gentleman slots a token into the jukebox, providing some entertainment. This scene was set up for Zhi Xiong's (Second Brother) entrance in his Austin Cambridge while his friends were waiting, and as an introduction to a bachelor life of vice (booze, gambling and women) that Zhi Xiong might succumb to because of friendly influence.

22:30 What looks like Young Master having a friendly race with one of his employees on his motorbike while also leading him to where Feng Ling lives.

Everyone stares out the window to see what the din of roaring engines are about. The way they film the residents staring out of the high rise building is the same as when L. Krishnan, in *Sumpitan Rachun*, filmed the hotel guests peering out of the hotel after Penruber fell to his death. In *Korban Fitnah*, the next film I will be talking about, there will be a scene in the reverse where bystanders are looking up into the building at a commotion instead. Whatever the case, I think architecture is never given the short shrift in any of the films I have watched and can even be considered as actors vital to the plot too.

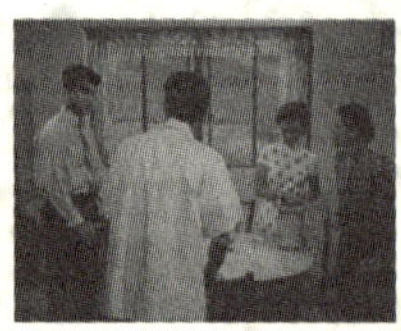

24:05 Young Master comes and leaves after five minutes on the pretext of visiting Ah Cai when he is really following Feng Ling and wants to visit where she lives. I assume Feng Ling to be older as she attends a night secondary school while she works in the factory during the day. Anyway, pursuing or grooming a secondary school girl seems wrong even in the sixties, was it not uncommon because of different education standards? Young Master is impressed by this working class diligence as much as I am impressed by the painted backdrop of boats outside the window. I no longer think it's a silly contraption, but a vital artifice of stage and set making. Very little credit goes to the craft and labour of the artisans that created the backdrops and movie posters of yore. I think they went hand-in-hand with the technology of the time and the visual reality of black and white. It was also a time where studio sets of interiors, which I assumed what this flat was, complemented on-location shots of exteriors (of which they will have less control of the elements like sound production). But still films like *Orang Minyak* employed painted backdrops for the outdoors especially for their musical interludes.

15 February 2022

The roots of organised Abrahamic religions laid in the foundations of its original radicalism and spread of its beliefs through evangelists and missionaries. The first fall through archangel Lucifer's pride and then again through Adam's exile for disobedience is certainly mystical and thought-provoking though spiritually antiquated with a kind of tribalist thinking not compatible with the conditions of our time. What I mean to say is that the bases of these early religions served to condition mediaeval minds, which may not be compatible with the modern mind.

It is in fact through the pre-modern Greeks and the story of Prometheus that we relate to, which is far more symbolic and ahead of its time (in a vicious time cycle) and therefore metaphorically compatible with modernity. The first fall actually is our knowledge of fire and our attempts to use technology to conquer forces of nature. It is our fate in the Heideggerian sense to be condemned to practical beings—our inherent relationship to nature is one of utility.

In the Rings of Saturn, Sebald spoke of our relationship with fire through carbon and its many uses, vital to all livelihood, and similarly the clearing of lands through burning, as the beginning of industries, as earlier too I spoke too of the burning of peatlands in Southeast Asia to grow new crops.

But for me the greatest fall or the start of our modern descent is the invention of the camera and from then on it became a narcissistic obsession to imprison the world in images with the trigger of every button pushed. Sontag wrote that to photograph is to appropriate the thing photographed, and compared photography more treacherous than the printed word, alienating and habituating people to abstract the world further for consumption, knowledge and power.

So the first technologies were really heating, cooking and warding off wild animals but early sapiens must have foretold after seeing the shadows that they could perhaps one day capture images too. 300,000 years later the pioneer media artist Nam June Paik, creates a work called *One Candle (Candle Projection)*, a development from a previous work *Candle TV*, where video projectors repeat the image of a burning candle across the gallery walls from a CCTV camera. This subject of both light and our reflection, is echoed in Gerhard Richter's *Candle*, itself appropriated from images, which again was culled by Sonic Youth for the cover of their seminal album *Daydream Nation*.

The supreme trickster Prometheus, who stole fire to give to humans after fooling the gods time and again, was punished by being bound to a rock, where an eagle would fly to him to eat his liver, which grew back overnight, only to be eaten by the eagle again the next day. The liver was thought to be the seat of human emotions, and it was Baudelaire again, modernist poet of the streets, who dedicated a collection of poems to the *spleen*, anatomically connected to the liver, which in the French sense plays on the double meaning of the word that refers to 'melancholy with no apparent cause, characterised by a disgust with everything'. In this modern sense, the gods have punished us with the spleen of melancholy, some of us feel it more, others bury it in the humdrum of their daily lives. The Greeks understood eternal agony through the anti-heroes of Sissyphus and Prometheus, at some point in the evolution of civilization eastwards, in all its cultural, economic and political export, humans must have thought necessary to think of redemption and sin too to add to the mix.

In the first part of *Thus Spake Zarathustra*, Nietzsche wrote the parable of Zarathustra who descended the mountains to preach to a cynical village about the *overman*—Man is a rope between beast and overman and must be overcome, and who will truly be the meaning of the earth. However, humanity has become too tame and domesticated and can only produce the last man, who like herd animals, are docile and not conditioned to danger and extremity, and have invented *happiness*. Just then a tightrope walker starts walking between two towers, only to be mocked and taunted by a jester behind him, who jumps over the tightrope walker, causing him to fall to his death. Zarathustra comforts the dying man, to tell him that his death has not been in vain but that he had chosen danger as his vocation.

We can never trick fate, but fate can trick us into death. We can never rewind back to our past to redo our mistakes, see where we've gone wrong but we can return and recur in other lives, or we have the power to record images that our bodies can leave behind. From fire to quantum physics, we are heading towards a nothingness between two thoughts of nihilism and sublime divinity. Which do you walk towards? Modernity is really the endless return, the forever loop, the in-between of existence and this has certainly been captured on film and tape ad infinitum, and *boredom*.

1 March 2022

It's been five days since Russia first invaded Ukraine and anxiety is felt even here. Putin's decision to attack a smaller sovereign nation next door with a thousand-year history, which he does not recognise, which he wants to reclaim and restore a new order from the dissatisfied ashes of the Cold War, rejecting American and NATO influence, this senseless defiance has provoked an avalanche of condemnation from world leaders and people in the streets alike, of a swashbuckling tyrant misled by a false bygone history of power and grandeur. But this could also be furthest from the truth from a Russian perspective, in which this has been brewing and calculated upon since the Soviet Era. The Ukrainians however, have proved to be just as defiant to their invaders (who call this a Special Operation), or even more so. It's unfathomable to think of war in the present, only distant and mirrored in social and news media, but it's also plausible to accept that we have always been the remainders of some previous war.

24:53 *National Geographic Class*

This is yet another spectacular dolly scene of a classroom filled with co-ed students about to start lessons. Again filmed in a set, with painted backdrops of the busting city vista by the windows. As the camera scans from right to left of some forty teenagers in white uniforms, a kooky bespectacled teacher walks in with a world globe in her hand.

起立! *qǐ lì*
行礼! *xíng lǐ*

The requisite classroom etiquette came in the form of a greeting in Mandarin, as a mark of respect for the teacher, everyone stood and bowed, led by the class monitor. When I first saw this scene I immediately thought of Chua Mia Tee's iconic painting *National Language Class*, completed a year ahead of this film, of which a group of Chinese students are learning Malay, the newly-designated national language of Singapore. Before I mention how this ideological formality has been lost to Singapore's practical winds of time (eighty percent of students would not know this now)—ironically this is a setting of a Chinese Ed school, which itself is a thing of the past—I wish to mention that Yi Sui sought to document a constructed reality on camera the way Mia Tee effectively captured another in painting—that of a classroom during a lesson, and in a larger sense that of national education. The roaming camera in *Lion City* afforded the expanse of a large classroom unfolding in time, this is contrasted with Chua's framed (almost claustrophobic) static representation of eight students huddled in a tight space around a table with their older darker-skinned teacher looking on. Chua modelled them after his own friends and wife, and I think the teacher was inspired by an Indonesian acquaintance he knew. I had to visit Chua Mia Tee's exhibition at the National Gallery especially after this and I sum up his remarkable oeuvre with not one iconic painting but a few more. This is where the Gallery gets it right in their titling his show *Directing The Real* because Chua certainly was 'after the real' (as opposed to reality) in his paintings. His striking fidelity can be stifling and rigid at first and claustrophobic as *Language Class* especially to modern and contemporary art viewers, for his is a classicism whose filmic equivalent is perhaps the *cinéma vérité*. But I doubt Chua would have been interested even remotely in filmmaking or giving agency to the camera as a device for documenting the real—that seems too fleeting and experimental compared to the immortalising and humanist craft of realistic painting. His are works that have survived better as iconic images rather than paintings, because in the flesh they look like artefacts hosting these deceptively detailed pictures. For example, one of the most striking things for me on seeing Chua's paintings before me, is in noticing the lifelike fly on the bare shoulder of the singlet-wearing Chinese male closest to the foreground of another iconic painting *Epic Poem of Malaya*. This is something you would not have noticed in an image on your laptop. In *What Painting Is,* James Elkins wrote about the legend of the great mediaeval painter Giotto, who apprenticing under Cimabue in Florence, painted a fly so real on the nose of a portrait that his master was tricked into attempting to brush the fly away.

As I type this in the freezing airconditioned staff office at the campus, a light rain precipitates over the building and greenery outside. This is perfect for being caught indoors in darkness watching a film. A film that I would want to make.

23 March 2022

It must be close to a year since I started this project and I don't know if it's my need to complete this or it's my fear or failing to finish what I had started again.

I have been going through some personal changes again and the biggest is that I have to move house again—to the flat I just bought. I'm quite chuffed. It's a nice little apartment very close to the beach. I always had that dream as a kid. But I'm not excited at all about the things I have to do to move like looking for furniture and appliances, getting fixtures done and the whole house repainted, though I think that I really got away without doing much renovation. I really did. A good deal it was. But why am I always so dissatisfied? It's a good thing XY is helping me with the move.

I had located a rotator cuff injury since my last fall skateboarding and it doesn't seem to be healing. I am ok with normal daily movements but I won't be able to hurl a ball or play badminton or anything that requires me to extend the full range of my arm movements via my left shoulder. So I decided to do some research on YouTube to do some self-rehabilitation. I am trying to avoid going to professional physiotherapy as the last one with my knee was so expensive but I have since recovered almost fully. Almost because it's not quite the same anymore, I still feel it tingling somewhere. I decided to give skateboarding a break to focus on my move though somewhere in my brain it's telling me that I loathe it as it has revealed how inept I am at it. That's sad.

I managed to go out with Sophia again after what feels like forever. I felt that I owed it to her to explain why I disappeared for so long. It's hard enough getting involved with people but harder when you are caught in the middle of something. And it was difficult because I like her and we were genuinely dating and starting to get to know each other. It was a nice fantasy imagining a relationship with a foreigner, with an exciting profession, but at the end of the day I got caught up with what felt like a more intimate and familiar relationship with another person. But it was always warm to talk to her anyway, it's always romantic, and I felt obligated to foot the hefty bill when she went away to the toilet, but I wouldn't attribute it to guilt but more to the knowledge that I have to be a gentleman. *I did ask her out.* After that I replayed the song that I sent her ages ago on my airpods which she said she always listened to, again and again. I felt stupid after telling her that it was actually sent to me by another woman I met on Tinder. That it was a kind of emotional connection developed through messaging and that she pulled out from meeting because she had to go back to Australia and she did not want to risk feelings and a relationship and that's that. What did I get myself into again and again? I do not know if I'm going to see her again.

I'm not suicidal like my mother but I'm sick of living every day. Everything bores the shit out of me, all forms of maintenance of the body, relationships and the apartment are all in bad faith, keeping up appearances and that the perfunctory chatter and talk you have to engage with. I'm cursing either in the shower or when doing the dishes. I am sick of it all. I can understand why some humans completely retreat from the world into genuine solitude without a care for the world. That takes a lot of guts, but also a lot of privilege too.

To be an artist, one really has to move mountains, because if there is anything authority and rules hate, it is the complete freedom of expression by an individual, the rebellion against the full onslaught and weight of life upon the wretched soul and body, the complete rage against the drudgery of administered modern life. And the most contemporary contraption to ever be invented are the airpods in my ears because no one can ever hear what you feel. You do not need Edvard Munch's *The Scream* to articulate an alienated existence anymore.

25:20 *Chapter 7 on Singapore*

- Population: 1.5 million
- The Chinese make up 80% of the population.
- In the Federation of Malaya, Malays are the majority race.
- The Federation of Malaya is made up of three major races: The Malays, the Chinese and the Indians

27 March 2022

Brabantia in the wilderness

It was good that I decided to get out of the house. Light seems to be godforsaken in my apartment, even my plants are dying. That or I haven't been paying enough attention to them. Watching a season of a Netflix drama serial was not the healthiest but it was comforting. In the series, the protagonist was a brilliant lawyer that hid a secret, with time, the secret became a burden for others to bear for him, and despite his good intentions, he seemed to have lost his way. And I began to identify with this character and others who all had a secret and past to keep. And I realised my family lived like that without talking, no one ever wanted to have difficult conversations.

As I was walking in the sweltering sun with a branded waste bin purchased from Carousell in a plastic bag, looking for the tent, I began to appreciate my walk towards the beach. Before that, I must have cried three times, thinking while listening to music, my Cancer rising more out of its tide than usual. A group of people were looking into the trees with their cameras and tele lenses but I was more interested in them. A father and his kids were playing football on a little patch of grass, and the cyclists were decked in their helmets, tights and shades. I contemplated having lunch first but I was too lazy and I wasn't that hungry. The dropped pin was easy to find on Google Maps, another 300m and I recognised the tents, one had a blue cap on it. I was looking forward to finding artwork in a tent by the beach.

26:55 In the same coffee shop before, one of the buddies tells Zhi Xiong that the Trade Union is recruiting and that he should do his part.

A quick historical background check reveals that there were an increased number of labour strikes from late 1961 onwards due to the split of political factions (leftwing Barisan Socialis from the PAP) which also led to the split of unions; the de-establishment of the Singapore Trades Union Congress (TUC) into the 'non-Communist Socialist' Trade Union Centre and SATU, a conglomerate of unions including a working committee for the communist unions.

Seven SATU unions were served notices by the Registrar of Trade Unions for displaying anti-Malaysia banners and placards during a mass rally on 25 August 1963.

28:00 *Paris Bar Scene*

The set piece here and tracking cameras are reminiscent of early Fassbinder films where he would get his theatre friends to rehearse in a bar scene setup in a theatre-like space. Fassbinder worked in the theatre. So did Yi Sui, the director for *Lion City.*

Zhi Xiong is accompanied by a voluptuous woman in a *cheongsam* who drinks with him in an 'indecent' place, somewhat accosting him later after several 'last drinks'.

15 April 2022

Good Friday.

I saw a need to bring myself back to writing before I lose it. As it is, I am preparing for a reading and talk about my work on Monday at Yale-NUS Library and I had just requested for a four-minute clip from the AFA to accompany my reading. It is uncanny how the newfound details from a high-resolution clip would have changed the way I would have written this manuscript: things I haven't noticed before after being so used to the poor images on YouTube.

To bring the reader up to speed, two things are pressing against my life that are underpinning my deeper anxieties, my future commitments and my own mortality. First, it is my shoulder injury from my skateboarding fall that is proving to be more serious than I thought. The physiotherapist had suspected a rotator cuff tear and now he's referring me to a specialist to have my shoulder scanned and potentially surgically repaired. The second is my house move that is happening in two weeks and all the other types of operations I have to undertake to make it home-ready, and not just for myself. I am doing away with the interior designer and the 60k renovation price tag. The bigger reason, other than it's fucking expensive, is that it is an intentional resistance towards all ridiculously Singaporean materialistic behaviour, like breaking my bank to break walls to make an old corridor flat look like a loft or a condo, so that it will look like all other flats that have the same stupid 'reno' showflat look, so that I rack up more in instalment plants to or loans to add up next to the mortgage. I would like to do things myself and work with the integrity of the apartment and source out my own furniture and fixtures, so to hell with IKEA.

Recently I have been comforted by four ways of being, maybe it was a little inspired by Bukowski, and it probably goes against everything we are taught to be here:

Give up—Yes, just give up. Give up your dreams and vanities and just live for god's sakes! This whole thing about chasing your dream and whatever you want in life must be the most selfish and stupid thing to impose on everybody. If everyone thought this, we would be even more wretched and miserable. So what about those who succeed? Then what? You would spend the rest of your life protecting what you have succeeded in achieving…unless you can release the fish when you catch it.

Lose—So when you win, it's not that big a deal either. Does winning define you? When you can lose, you will definitely be the greater for it. Be a great loser.

Don't try—This is definitely from Bukowski. Do not try so hard to be what you aren't meant to be, that makes you insufferable and pretentious. It makes you such an anxious piece of shit. Why oh why do we put ourselves through all that trouble for these false images that goad us way from our true authenticity?

Let it go—This is so fucking hard. Just let it go. Don't let it consume you, let yourself go light and free. How many other lives do you own other than the one you have?

And in place of all this, the reward is true acceptance and your mental freedom, free from the shackles of years and years of indoctrination and ideologies. Your belief systems will be shaken and broken, but you will have to decide whether it is worth it.

31:24 *Hotel Scene*

I have some sympathy for the hostess here, painted as someone with lax morals, seducing Zhi Xiong, the errant but otherwise good second son. They have been feeding us this load since time immemorial. Noone puts a gun to Zhi Xiong's head to go to a bar, nor to get himself drunk. And whatever the circumstances this woman had for her to live by herself in a hotel—*your house has so many keys*—it is a decent living she's making for herself. Everyone deserves to be loved and no woman should be lonely like this. The director has obviously put this poor lass to be judged by the viewer as an unsavoury character in a hotel that deals in some shady business. He hasn't given her dimension nor empathy.

Men have not reached the depths of honesty as women have here and that's why we are all suffering, we are still plagued by an insufferable masculinity.

34:11 Daisy, oh Daisy, you in the white negligee, a woman of the rain, lightning enters your window, strikes the depths of your tired aching heart, to only find love in stray men is not a crime, I would take a cigarette off you if you would share one with me and drag on the crimes of time.

23 April 2022

Pain is unjust but as it turns out I was spared the agony of not having to deal with a full-on rotator cuff tear but an impending frozen shoulder as illustrated by the MRI diagrams. Scar tissue and fluids have built up and inflamed the area where I was injured and produced the pain and limited my movement in my left arm. I guess my body was trying to protect me as it healed. The doctor said it can take up to between 18 and 24 months of physiotherapy for complete recovery, if I don't opt for the more instant, expensive and aggressive approach of a keyhole surgery to remove the tissue. Pain discriminates against the poor and underprivileged as I pass the hordes of rich Indonesian patients who come here for treatment. As I walked the affluent streets, past Napier Road and Nasim Drive towards Orchard Road, I realised I once had a short-lived, ill-fated affair with Nadya who I used to drive back home up and down these hills in the middle of the night. A procedure such as an MRI scan is such an intrusive procedure to the body, let alone surgery. But the truth and irony is, as much as we are intimately connected to our own bodies, we hardly know what's going on inside. We are slowly imagining a future when we can collect our own bodily data and be statistically closer yet distant to both life and death.

On the overhead bridge going to my new flat I caught a most tender but heartbreaking scene. An old Malay (or possibly Eurasian) elderly couple were sleeping by the corner just before the steps. They had their shoes and bags parked to the side and they were in an embrace. I told XY about it and she said she once bought coffee for a similar couple in Melbourne.

Immediately, I felt ashamed I didn't think about that, seeing how XY's heart is more attuned to care than myself. I cared not to disturb them and to snap a picture from a faraway distance, as a record, but never to post online.

As the country opens up and loosens its regulations against the pandemic, I had been happy to catch up with Mum and relatives during Easter and with Dino over drinks two days later. Just yesterday I was with Richard in Joo Chiat. I consider Richard to be one of the best abstract painters on the planet and chasing abstraction is both a luxury and an intellectual pursuit. Richard had the fortune to spend most of his life abroad, studying in some of the best art schools. I brought him to the *Sider Bar* but it's not the same since Carl left and the whole vibe had changed: my usual Aspall wasn't available on tap and the Weston Reserve tasted flat like a day-old pee; his grumpy, socially awkward English boss had taken over the bar, no more small talks and fist bumps, instead of local indie music in the air, it's early industrial with Nine Inch Nails. "This is so classic!" I acknowledged it to the boss but he didn't so much as give me a response but a quick shrug. I know that along with Carl, the tides of change are coming again, more shops are turning over in this street, tenants like myself are replaced and wars are shifting the world order. After an Indonesian dinner, we were walking the food off. I told Richard for every five metres we walked, you find one Asian woman for every Caucasian man. What you don't see very often still is an Asian man and a Caucasian woman he quipped and even when he is in the UK, he faces the same discriminations. Asian men are just not sexy, thanks to geeks and kungfu. But white women like Indian men he remarked, and he was right I have seen quite a few here. I think it's the 'exotic other' he said. I thought briefly of my relationship with Sophia and both of us don't really qualify. A few steps later, I saw the porkchop seller from the food centre with a Vietnameses hostess, he's half drunk and smoking a cigarette. I hailed Richard a cab home. Got to love Joo Chiat.

At night I thought about all my wants, wishes and desires. But I realised one thing: nobody taught us about what you would have to give up for things that you want and desire. You don't always get what you want and if everybody got what they wanted, the world will be annihilated.

35:45 Mike the scoundrel has made the neighbour's daughter pregnant and now wants to shirk his responsibility. Of course this is a caricature of someone everyone would have known that has done it to one's sister, one's daughter or one's friend's sister or daughter. The very same corridor of a block of flats that a marriage proposal takes place doesn't discriminate against other news to happen.

36:54 Young Master waits outside his own factory for Feng Ling to finish work. We have no idea why he is pursuing a woman still in secondary school other than he has a Lolita complex or he is simply in love. Feng Ling, at first playing hard-to-get, brings him up to her favourite haunt on Mount Faber on foot, trodding on the then unpaved road, and at the top we are treated to a lovely view of Singapore in 1960.

25 April 2022

My mind is a prison, I haven't unlocked the key to its freedom. I'm painfully intelligible of all that goes around it and yet only I am helpless and privy to its own suffering.

The moment we start to see colours, we start to discriminate. Homo Sapiens, the only species capable of hypocrisy, can't seem to wrap this around their skulls for 200,000 years.

Xenophobia and racism definitely exist here, but to say that I am exempt from this is absolutely pretentious and hypocritical. The best we can do is observe our own shortcomings. The rate at which we import PRC families here is alarming, I do not have statistical proof but my own conjecture and speculation. But you cannot go ten steps anymore without hearing a Chinese accent. I do not have a problem with this, as Richard said, Singapore, like America, is a land of immigrants but what I am alarmed about is how much we are changing and being foreign to it. In the most positive example perhaps, you find a Chinese female worker assisting and cleaning in a *prata* shop like Al Fahah and in more alienating ones, spa shops have crept up all over the island whose predominantly Chinese masseuses sometimes masquerade as sex providers. Yesterday when I was having lunch in a ramen place, what looked like a typical Singaporean Chinese family at first, turned out to be PRC migrants the minute they opened their mouths. I did not look close enough. But the features now were telling. The father's arm was in a sling and the mother was not very fashionable, especially her hairstyle. But the son was the dead giveaway. He had one of those current BTS mop top hairstyles and a cool white jumper. It wasn't so much his appearance but his gaze. It was one of complete ennui, disinterest and alienation like that from a much bigger town or city. When he stood up, he was much taller. I imagined they were from Northern China and that he was into basketball even without seeing his Jordans. To be fair, many kids have this look nowadays, but his is a kind I have observed before huddled in groups around Peace Centre and places many PRC kids go to. Like something that they were tasked to do like study here but other than this place being the most techno-friendly with a Chinese dominant population, they can't connect any more to this tropical island anymore than chalk to cheese. My bias would also think that the first example is a positive one and not the latter examples.

Other changes are happening in the virtual realm. You have Netflix and HBO still promoting traditional family values, where everyone is straight and everyone is looking for salvation but the real changes are happening on social media which the present generation is turning to in all its LBGTQ++ and other social justice manifestations. In one of the Netflix series I'm bingeing on, akin to a soap opera, a character claims 'Family is foundation', and they are often pinching at our tear ducts and all is good and uplifting until reality tells you that not everyone has been blessed with foundation, and many are raised by wolves on the internet. In other news, as in sealing film's coffin further down under, Marvel has taken over the cinematic universe in another gigantic globalised yawn. I am out of touch but there's nothing to touch.

37:28 *Nan Yang*

Again, who calls Singapore the Lion City casually? Unless it's the branding in the eponymous film.

Feng Ling says she comes here to get a clear view of the *Lion City*. She likes the Lion City in the east, whereas he likes the Strait of Malacca in the west, which could mean a few things: that he grew up with connections between Malaysia and Indonesia, maybe he is the son of a rich Indonesian businessman. Or that it's the shortest shipping route between the Far East and the Indian Ocean where ships have passed through for centuries, sprouting bygone famous trading posts. But I have a far more interesting interpretation. You see this is a clever, interesting scene by the director. At the tip of Mount Faber, there are opposing views. Feng Ling takes the view to the East—that of the void between the Java Sea and the South China Sea facing the Riau Islands and Kalimantan—towards romance, raw passion and primal forces. Whereas Young Master takes the view of Sumatra and beyond to the West—towards commerce, education and science. Both of them love the sea: Young Master because of his interest in fishing, swimming and sailing, and Feng Ling, when she recites a poem, because of its emotive qualities. You see Feng Ling used to go to Katong Park and watch the ships dock and depart Pasir Panjang Port and Young Master used to visit the locally-inhabited surrounding islands on his motor boat. It is at this revelation, facing the Keppel Bay that Young Masters cops a feel and puts his arm around Feng Ling's shoulder and invites her to sea on Sunday on his motor boat.

27 April 2022

I had a strange thought about wealth and intelligence; ultimately they are burdens. If you had all the wealth and intelligence in the world, imagine what a total waste it would be if you do not put it to good use. Great power comes with great responsibility they say and if all you do is sit on your ass all day and indulge in corporeal pleasures all the time, then that decadence is not attractive at all. So you are never satisfied even if you are rich and smart, you can afford to look beautiful but the way human conscience is built and wired into us such as that you are ultimately obligated to help your kind, and at the minimum give back, because the resources you have now are not earned but inherited and distributed unfairly. Unless you are a socio- or psychopath which makes you neurologically different, we are inherently troubled and unsatisfied and faced with decisions and choices all the time, which governs our moral clock. Which makes it all the more remarkable that when someone poor and intelligent helps beyond her means, she is a pillar of goodness. That couldn't be said about someone poor and dumb because that would be considered pure but naive and foolish. As if both intelligence and wealth taint and corrupt. You can be happy when you are poor and ignorant. Knowing and having ultimately comes down to power.

When, in disgrace with fortune and men's eyes,
I all alone beweep my outcast state,
And trouble deaf heaven with my bootless cries,
And look upon myself and curse my fate,
Wishing me like to one more rich in hope,
Featured like him, like him with friends possessed,
Desiring this man's art and that man's scope,

With what I most enjoy contented least;
Yet in these thoughts myself almost despising,
Haply I think on thee, and then my state,
(Like to the lark at break of day arising
From sullen earth) sings hymns at heaven's gate;
For thy sweet love remembered such wealth brings
That then I scorn to change my state with kings.

William Shakespeare wrote *Sonnet 29* in his late twenties in 1592, during the Bubonic Plague at the height of his financial troubles. The melancholic poem addressed his anxieties and self-worth and questioned his genius while also being sneered at and criticised by known critics in the bitchy London theatre world. He also addressed his own shortcomings and impending risk of failure through his own vulnerability. I have always thought that's the hardest level to be in as an artist, to risk being ridiculed and nobodied and eventually sidelined into obscurity. But this is beyond fame and recognition, fortune and respect. It is about having no other way to be and it is also about courage to do what you are afraid of. It is about speaking honestly in the face of not being heard at all.

Yesterday when I bumped into Gary at MOS Burger, he told me his boyfriend loathes me and says I'm too conceptual. I supervise his boyfriend, a third-year art student in college. I have never thought about myself as a conceptual artist as I thought it's pretentious for me after using that tag for a short bit before. But the thing is, I would have resisted a person like me too. Gary says it's not that I'm conceptual, it's just the way my mind is. I am grateful for that quip. You see I pride myself in knowing what art is even though I might not know more than nothing at all. It's just that I have lived it very intensely and sporadically. But even if I wanted to 'quit' and give up 'art', it continues to live rent free in my head. I'm making work as we speak and in my head the way Picasso said it took him a lifetime to draw like a kid. I might not be in the studio actively making but I am making art or thinking about it all the time and I cannot run away from it. I know how to make a painting work, produce and sell them; I have seen what works for years. I also know how to put the right research to sell and promote myself academically and none of them have ultimately interested me. And that is why I am drawn to ideas. But I am more drawn to my personal discovery and truths. Hopelessly indulgent. I am drawn to conceptual art's legacy of political resistance to commodity and world events but I am more drawn to the philosophy of what can be deemed as art if I give value to anything. And I know for a fact this is not currency here and eventually I might be obscured, but if that gives me the time and space to think and do and make, it really is the ultimate freedom, pleasure and privilege to be given the chance to be an artist at all.

Notes

Chapter 5: Lion City (1960)
Moving in, movie out

1. *On Some Motifs in Baudelaire*
   by Walter Benjamin (1939).

2. Ibid.

3. Ibid.

PART 2

SILENCE

In the still of night, tears fall, grieving—I seize my brush to banish my loneliness

Chapter 5:

(cont'd) Lion City (1960)

Rubber rebellion

21 July 2022

Sticky humid summer heat.

There is a work by Zoe Leonard called *Strange Fruit*. It consists of some three hundred peels of oranges, grapefruits and bananas strewn across the floor, sewn with buttons, zippers and stitching after their consumption. I first came across her work while researching for a lecture a couple of years back. Martha Buskirk writes about the "multiple references of the title—to the Billie Holiday song with its powerful image of lynched bodies, to Leonard's friend David Wojnarowicz, who died of AIDS in 1992, and to the pejorative use of the term 'fruit' as slang for gay—suggest specific associations that support a general sense of loss." I started my class playing the Holiday song off YouTube as way of introduction to Leonard's work, stating that it was a protest song against black lynched bodies just as the online research told me. A couple of months back I finished a book by James Baldwin called *The Devil Finds Work*, which was about his time growing up as a black person watching Hollywood films. Towards the last few chapters, he was reminiscing about the film *Lady Sings the Blues*, a kind of whitewashed biopic on Billie Holiday starring Diana Ross. In his elegant fashion, he censured the script for taking liberties and being inauthentic to Holiday's legacy and tragic life, as compared to her own biography. Here he clarifies the origins of her famed protest song:

> In the book, her father is a jazz musician, mainly on the road, who, eventually, leaves home, divorces, and re-marries. But, when he was in town, Billie was able to blackmail him into giving her the rent money for her mother and herself. And she cared about him: "it wasn't the pneumonia that killed him, it was Dallas, Texas. That's where he was, and where he walked around, going from hospital to hospital, trying to get help. But none of them

> would even so much as take his temperature, or let him in [but] because he had been in the Army, had ruined his lungs and had records to prove it, they finally let him in the Jim Crow ward. By that time, it was too late." And later: "a song was born which became my personal protest—'Strange Fruit'—when [Lewis Allen] showed me that poem, I dug it right off. It seemed to spell out all the things that killed Pop."
>
> This is quite forthright, and even contains, if one dares say so, a certain dramatic force. In the film, on the southern road, Billie leaves the bus to go relieve herself in the bushes. Wandering along the countryside, Billie suddenly sees, on the road just before her, grieving black people, and a black body hanging from a tree. The best that one can say for this moment is that it is mistaken, and the worst that it is callously false and self-serving—which may be a rude way of saying the same things: luckily, it is brief. The scene operates to resolve, at one stroke, several problems, and without in the least involving or intimidating the spectator. The lynch scene is as remote as an Indian massacre, occurring in the same landscape, and eliciting the same response: a mixture of pious horror, and gratified reassurance.

Baldwin's great example illustrates this gross discrepancy between film and book—institutionalised reading and personal anecdote, that is the stuff of nuance and complexity much lacking in the binary of fact and fiction that encompasses all our lives, some more famous than others, but all relatable once activated by their hidden stories. I was only half right, Holiday sang *Strange Fruit* for her father.

After a long absence, I am suddenly so aware of Yi Sui's many cuts and truncations in what could have otherwise been a seamless scene. Is it a style of the past? I've noticed it distinctly in Michelangelo Antonioni's *Blowup*. I thought it wasn't that necessary to cut a scene up so much with the camera like that.

41:10 *The large colonial home of the rubber tycoon.*

We arrive here at the large building which, to me, at first glance, looks like a building built somewhere in the mid-century styles—Art Deco, Bauhaus and Brutalist. It's a splendid piece of architecture, a longish block with a large cylindrical facade at its centre, in which the long driveway would lead into the main receiving hall. A white marble Grecian statue greets them on the right towards the large open meadows. It's a house too big for a typical family, unless you have many guests for business and parties. Shao Ming (Young Master) guides Feng Ling to the living room and chides her for returning him the swimming costume, still boxed, that he bought her. *I can't swim. It's ugly to wear that. Didn't you say we're just sitting down on the motorboat to view the islands?* The petulant lass rebuts, like she really wanted a passive vacation. The tycoon (Shao Ming's dad) comes down the stairs, a porky figure of a dead ringer for Kim Jung Un (I guess that's the period the North Korean leader gets his style inspiration from) and dismisses them on ceremony to carry on. He is about to go out. *She is the daughter of Uncle Cai, the machinery supervisor in the factory*, Shao Ming says. Dad doesn't say a word to Feng Ling but steals back an inspectory glance before leaving the building.

A quick whatsapp to the ever reliable and resourceful HP, after my online searches turned up nil, reveals that the mansion was owned by Dr. Tan Tsze Chor 陈之初 named Xiang Xue Zhuang 香雪庄 (the fragrance of plum blossoms), where his art collection was housed. It used to be located along Upper East Coast Road after moving from Pasir Panjang but has since moved again to Bournemouth Road (the last time I checked, the address is a condo development). Dr. Tan was a heavyweight influence on the local art and literati from 1930s Singapore and Malaya. Way before our national museums and galleries, Dr. Tan had the earliest, largest and most exquisite private collection. At its peak, the main collection amounted to a thousand pieces, including calligraphy and painting, ceramics, inkstones, seals, bronze ware, purple sand ware, jade carvings and bamboo carvings. Dr. Tan's favourites were the ink paintings and Tibetan paintings that formed the core of the Xiang Xue Zhuang collection.

Sometime in one of those dinner parties that the businessman-connoisseur hosted in his East Coast mansion near the sea, where the distinguished literati assembled, he must have met Yi Sui, the director, who was looking for a large house to shoot in, who pitched his new film as a way to forge an identity with the values and culture of the Nanyang heroes, to set a standard.

We have to link up some earlier fragments here—the earlier social realist paintings of Mia Tee, Zhi Hai's (older brother) union meetings and Zhi Xiong's 'decadent' behaviour—what do they have in common with each other?

A little back story:

The literati consisted of members of the China Society and the Singapore Art Society, both inaugurated in 1949 to foster social cohesion and both with members tied to the colonial regime. The Singapore Art Society was consciously formed along ethnic lines with their various representatives—Liu Kang, of Society of Chinese Artists, C. Mahat of the Malay Art Class and Gibson-Hill, a British colonial official and its first chairman. Its mission was to marry the Eastern and Western style of painting, so that a distinct Singapore style would emerge. In contrast, the anti-colonial Chinese Middle Schools' Graduates Arts Association of 1953 sprouted the Social Realist art movement, "prepared to commit all our efforts to help Malaya gain her independence."

The names of a typical guest list from Dr. Tan's gathering will include: first generation Nanyang painters like Liu Kang, Chen Chong Swee, Chen Wen Hsi and Huang Pao Fang; British colonials Commissioner-General Malcolm MacDonald and Art Superintendent Richard Walker.

We have still not set up an art museum.

So what the Xiang Xue Zhuang Collection actually represented then to this cultured circle was an art museum for archaeologists, poets and artists. Liu Kang believed art appreciation to be the antidote to 'yellow culture' (the term is a direct translation of the Chinese phrase *huangse wenhua*, which refers to decadent behaviour such as gambling, opium-smoking, pornography, prostitution and corruption against which a government campaign was launched in 1959 and lasted right up to the 80s) and the perennial fear that Singapore and Malaya was culture-less. Chen Chong Swee wrote an afterword to Dr. Tan's ink painting catalogue, himself an accomplished calligrapher, where he flourishes: "How amazing it is to have such a corpus of great art in this remote, uncultured region of ours! Is this not a case of how, as people say, divine items receive the care and protection of the gods and spirits?," thereby ignoring centuries of indigenous and Straits-born craft, textiles and literature.

I don't know if Yi Sui hid a subtext to this film but I am going to speculate here—I suspect Dr. Tan Tsze Chor the elegant pepper magnate, who worked his way to the top, was the model not for Shao Ming's rotund dad the rubber tycoon, not even Shao Ming himself—he must have slyly finessed a parallel counterpart in the young feisty and feminine protagonist of Feng Ling, who is the most literate and artistic-inclined here. In this cinematic universe of Malayan film, she would go on to marry Shao Ming and inherit his wealth and build the first national collection. She would be the first Lady of this inspiring architecture, a museum and an institution, blessed by the gods and spirits, that would cure yellow culture, unite the anti-colonials and the loyalists, and save this cultural desert once and for all.

9 August 2022

National Day.

44:29 Over the next few minutes, Shao Ming quickly and casually establishes to the audience that he's a playboy who is not interested in current girlfriend Jasmine (because she's too westernised after studying in Australia), scoots around the undeveloped islands on his motor boat in the weekends (even after 60 years since the film, I have not had that luxury), and dresses way ahead of his time in his tiny boat shorts (that heralds the retro fashion of today with our young men), skimpier than the conservative Feng Ling. It's the beach scene of the elite class where the outsider Feng Ling gets a glimpse into what it's like to be affluent on a Malayan weekend.

46:29 I am struck by a particular scene on a remote island by the rocks, where Shao Ming is serenading a prostrate Feng Ling and proclaiming that they are lying in the Strait of Malacca (in Hollywood, it would surely end up as a passionate first kiss) , that reminded me of some found images of Elizabeth Choy, our war heroine, in the college library about a decade back.[1] She was by the beach and then by the rocks in what seemed to me like an image of repetition and therefore particularly interesting to paint on.

During World War II, Choy and her husband supplied medicine, money and messages to prisoners-of-war interned by Japanese soldiers at Changi Prison. I had reproduced the black-and-white images of her robust figure by the sea on aluminium composite panels and applied zinc white oil paint on the images, such as that some point in the process (which was quick) the paint had taken on the appearance of features in the landscape like cliffs, clouds, sand and rocks, both representationally and reflexively as paint and landscape. The one by the sea is almost obscured and had turned Elizabeth into a ghostly apparition of time and the one by the rocks had paint literally cracking as part of the geological feature. Two years back, when I rediscovered these paintings in my studio as part of my larger set of overpainted images and postcards, I had observed that the paint had oxidised and yellowed quite badly. I roped in XY to help me restore and touch them up because of her excellent skills as a painter and her attention to detail. It took her weeks to months of procrastinating and being involved with other tasks but when she finally presented them back to me, I couldn't tell what was done, they were as good as day.

Elizabeth by the sea and rocks

47:29 And as if representations of the virtuous woman couldn't be topped after being beautiful, filial and cultured, for all her wilful dispositions, Feng Ling has to be a chanteuse as well and croon operatically like a lark like when Shao Ming asks her to sing alongside the sea (the song is called *The Song of The Sea* no less), she gladly climbs atop a rock and belts out one to music accompaniment. Of course this is Malayan cinema, and this being the equivalent of the musical interlude of the earlier Malay films save for some differences:

I am struck by a particular scene on a remote island by the rocks, where Shao Ming is serenading a prostrate Feng Ling and proclaiming that they are lying in the Strait of Malacca

Firstly, the scene is static and stage-like, like a play/ performance of your daughter or colleague singing a rehearsed song. It lacks the vibrant camera movement in the mise-en-scène of the song-and-dance *bangsawan* style of their Malay counterparts. And though they have adopted the popular ronggeng style in the accompaniment, giving it a touch of local tradition, the scene is fixated on propaganda and not the art form. The camera cuts to the Singapore flag, just inaugurated the year before, and the peaceful harbour, portraying a future of tranquil harmony in the tropics.

Even in leisurely pursuit, the modern subjects here are under the auspices of national fortune, where the sea is the life-giving force surrounding the island state that prospers in some kind of *nanyang* harmony. In this sense, the cinema here does not capture or portray subjects of true modernity but subjects as actors or spokespersons for nationalism (bestowed by Nature).

The blue seawater.
The green seaweed.
She's the cradle of the people.
And the swathe of the fishes.
She surrounds the Lion City.
This beautiful island.
The sea is quiet, calm and still.
The swallows fly gently over her.
The sea is misty in the rain.
And bright in the sun.
We sing of the greatness of the sea.
We praise her magnificence.

It is unlike say the films of Eric Rohmer, where the beach is set as a background for a literary trope—the restless bourgeois dilettante with ambiguous morality or the novels of Camus set in the sea or beach—the site of both banal leisure and existential threat in the face of a great nothingness—people go there to rest, escape, convalesce, watch films, make love, kill (with the same indifference) and have nothing to do with labour or industry. And if someone were to rebut here and say it has nothing to do with national values but Asian ones, then they (or I) would have to stand corrected. Modernity comes to us all, whatever the colour and orientation.

17 August 2022

Yesterday was strange. The first day of socialising with colleagues first at lunch (and a catchup with an erstwhile colleague who has since gotten married and relocated to the Middle East), and then with students at the college. And then some text message exchanges first with Jean, who I believe is coming to terms with my need as a co-parent but nonetheless, often, un-cooperative with my requests, producing a lot of exasperation on my part. Then another exchange with a friend (not close), who is asking for another friend also, and her concerns for my relationship with another person. Today I thought back about this and it sounded like an ambush on me, where I totally misread the signals and cues—that was enough to ruffle my night (I needed two beers), but back in the studio priming my canvases felt therapeutic.

I had returned to painting not too long ago and I have been afflicted with a newfound obsession again with painting images. I felt free yet insecure that this world is pulling and withdrawing me back into a lost cause/medium. But right now it seems that these canvases waited 20 years for this to happen. I have almost settled in my flat and gotten used to the rhythm of things; I very much still go into Joo Chiat (into town) for the gym, groceries, to drink, eat, any excuse. I love Marine Parade, but it's getting too close for comfort sometimes with fellow artists living there. I feel like I'm spied upon or that I'm obligated to form some connections there. Things are slowly easing out of the pandemic and social rituals are resuming all over again.

But back to strange, and anxious at the beginning of the week of all the socialising I have to do in seven days: colleagues, curator, a friend I haven't seen in years who needs to clear up something with me, and my stepmother on the weekend. Slander is not silence but silence aids falsity. And I understand now why it's hard to write and be personal and put your writing on the line. I read Maggie Nelson's *The Argonauts* not too long ago and I am impressed by her guile, ease, vulnerability and her care and finesse in crafting theory, philosophy with her day to day relationship with her transgender partner, with whom they share two kids (the second being her own with the current partner). And I've gotten to know this term called 'Auto-theory', which is a hybrid form of writing with roots in intersectional writing and feminism. We have some similarities, Miss Nelson and I—both of us are academics, interested in art and have partners who are in the spectrum (well, I might have), and we are experimenting in writing. But everything stops here. The famed writer is an established and accomplished beacon in her scene and is contributing to a genuine discourse, whereas sometimes I feel like an impostor doing something akin to Sunday painting. It's weird how this project even started and I thought it would end in a few months. To claim some allyship in feminist theory and intersectional writing might seem disingenous for me, in spite of my unbridled support and alignment. I am of the dying breed of straight indulgent male—I was accused of being hyper-masculine during relationships with both proclaimed Deleuzian feminists and social anarchists, the tag that was slapped on my shoulder which I hardly defended. A colleague at the same lunch remarked that this is currency and ripe for the picking and I should play the minority card, to which I said jokingly I should why didn't I. Perhaps I am slipping the card into this project here. Me as an unreliable narrator, whom you would not know fiction from fact here, as earlier I thought I was writing autofiction. I might just be simply experimenting with form.

But I remember one thing Nelson said about being a "traitor to writing" in which she quoted from the conversations of Gilles Deleuze and Claire Parnet:

> *What other reason is there for writing than to be traitor to one's own reign, traitor to one's own sex, to one's class, to one's majority? And to be traitor to writing.*

By this time, in the morning I would have listened to some exquisite organ music, Antonio de Cabezon's *In The Organs of Covarrubias and Daroca* on my vinyl player, that brought along with chills, the memories and recordings of Torcello island when I visited the Venice Biennale in '06 and chanced upon an organ practice in a church, in which I recorded and sampled it for the song named *Air* on my first album. The idea of recording, certainly, has coincided with photography as a need to archive an anthology of the world according to Sontag. Today the world has been reduced to an inventory of data and information—my sons' world—the modern project has ended and now we are approaching as they say, the singularity, of one flattened space that will be brought out by artificial intelligence.

I would have also thought about my own wheelchair-bound father in a home, his last stage of institutionalisation, of geriatric and assisted care as I have no means, and no desire, to care for him on my own. The father who brought me nothing but grief and denial, which incidentally are qualities you might find in my work. I'm annoyed he's happy without a care in the world, in a faceless new building that my sister and I are helping pay for. He has church, physiotherapy, food and recreational activities served to him before he beds at 10pm. The life.

I would have thought about Carl, who loved playing *November 91* by The Padres (*damn shiok la* he would say nostalgically), leaving the Sider Bar, and Buen getting hit by a motorcycle two weeks later in a hit-and-run just as he was about to take his shift, and hasn't been back since, and I losing the slightest urge to drink.

By the end of the night, I would have taken a 45-minute personality test that XY made me take and coming up as an INFJ, the so-called rarest personality in the world, especially in men, but I would have subscribed to it only with a pinch of salt.

49:50 A brief conversation at the table of Feng Ling's residence, as she prepares to go for evening school prepares us for the dynamics of the characters in the film, the society then, and the larger region at large. Zi Hai has returned early from work because Indonesia is facing a rebellion again and the ships are stuck at the port.

18 February 2023

Oh my god, it's been six months since I've written. It is so damn hard to sustain a writing life amidst all other commitments and distractions. I have a body that has its own rhythm and time but it is not compatible with the society I am conditioned in. We do not have time to reflect and think and wonder and imagine. We are doomed the minute we do that. Doomed to the fringes of society which only cares about numbers, progress and production. The real tragedy is that we are made up of clocks and money here.

Jean Genet, the son of a sex worker, who sought beauty even in crime, in cruelty and violence. His muscular writing is poetry in prose personified, at times devastating, whose potent virility must have been the father of yet many more writers to come. His magnum opus *The Thief's Journal* inspires the thief in me, and I steal a passage from his lovely devastating book:

> This journal is not a mere literary diversion. The further I progress, reducing to order what my past life suggests, and the more I persist in the rigour of composition—of the chapters, of the sentences, of the book itself—the more do

I feel myself hardening in my will to utilise, for virtuous ends, my former hardships. I feel their power.

This journal too, the one I'm writing, owes to Foucault and his archaeological conception of history, the belief that the present can only be understood if we continue to keep the past in view.

50:33 Speaking of production, Feng Ling's Mother is dismayed at her daughter-in-law's child production—her belly has not been rising. To this, the elderly woman, whose terrible theatre make-up to make her artificially aged is starting to look ridiculous, also disparages about the trouble between the rich-poor divide and the issue of Feng Ling dating Shao Ming. One has to be mindful, she says to her daughter, to which the young lass pouts petulantly and puts the blame squarely on the wealthy scion for initiating the romance. Then the lad in question shows up just in time to witness her long petulant face. He presents her yet another boxed gift containing a dress for her to wear to his 'simple dinner party.' Mrs Zhang sarcastically says *There's even a need to wear something new for a simple dinner.*

52:10 *The Dinner Party*

Shao Ming's 'simple dinner' ends up being a ball, we didn't expect anything less really. People decked out to the nines and come in chauffeur-driven cars. It makes me think of Antonioni's penetrating study on the idle bourgeois class in his films. Shao Ming's apparently going-to-be former girlfriend is welcoming the guests in velvet gloves, and she chides Shao Ming for being distracted and reluctant to toast along her champagne glass, when really, he is waiting for his new love to arrive.

And then she does: Zhi Xiong drops her off in his taxi and offers to pick her at midnight. She dons a beautiful dark cheongsam under a 'Mondrian-inspired' blazer. As perfunctory as it seems, it is nice to see a Malay couple and a Sikh couple get invited to the party as a show of racial diversity in the film, not to say that Shao Ming would not have minority friends, but I think they are just associates. Actually I do believe there was a higher chance before for natural diversity since many spoke the local language of Malay then, in a very different political time. Jasmine, I just remembered her name, the soon-to-be ex-flame, who comes from the same social class as Shao Ming, plies him with yet more drinks, as a pretext for the lad to introduce his new squeeze to her. As the two young women exchange dagger stares, I observe that the casting is indeed spot-on with compliments to Yi Sui the director. Feng Ling is slight-built and petite, aloof and petulant with narrow penetrating eyes, but very sweet and alluring. Whereas Jasmine is athletic and doe-eyed, tall, brash, impetuous and seemingly vacant. Another gentleman comes to raise a toast with Shao Ming and Jasmine, and ignores Feng Ling, who does not have a drink with her. He then grabs Jasmine, who is reluctant, away for a dance. I don't know where Shao Ming got the idea that Feng Ling cannot drink, unless she's really underaged (and that would be a problem), as he offers to get her some water. I would have offered her a glass of red wine to go with that cheongsam.

He returns with the glass of H2O and a stalk of daisies for her.

60:00 Shao Ming invites a Miss Yang Yu, a singer, and a Mr. Ma, a pianist, to perform for his guests. Against the foliage-themed grey wallpaper, Yang Yu sings a bittersweet rendition of the classical 父亲我求求你 *(Fu Qin Wo Qiu Qiu Ni, I beg you, Father)*, and for the life of me, I cannot find another version online, but it is like a precursive version of Madonna's 1986 pop number *Papa Don't Preach*. A piano aficionado would recognise the familiar motif. Maybe a Chopinesque motif played by Vladimir Horowitz.

My most beloved Father.
Will you understand me?
Let me follow him.
Let me follow him.
Please don't hesitate anymore.
If you remain insistent
And he's to go without me
My heart will be broken.
He's the one, his endless love
Is absolutely clear.
I beg you, Father.

I like how the camera at the beginning of this sequence draws out from a top view of the piano, and then scans the audience clockwise, giving a sense of how the hall fills out in space and then follows a man as a target that leads it further to the right of the performer.

59:24 This scene is one where Feng Ling is clearly seen as the outsider, out of place in a high society party. Her mother's words ring through here, and the glass slipper in this Cinderella story is turning out to be this huge mansion where she cannot fit in and is shut out, her back to the sheer gridded divider, a lantern veneer, separating her from the rest of them who are dancing.

Feng Ling doesn't dance, and maybe she doesn't want to dance to this crowd. Dances are social events that originated for the Gods and evolved in the classes between court, courtesans and peasants. Everyone has their own dance, like the dancers celebrating the harvest in *Orang Minyak*. Here in the mansion, everyone is of some status, or at least by proxy of invitation and affiliation.

I arrived slightly past nine. I had waited nearby, my guesthouse was just across the main road. Travelling alone liberates me. I think it has something to do with being a stranger to a place when you are already so estranged from all other things. The one thing I am not estranged from is my gift for imagination. It's not something that is trained but is really part of my being. But I don't want to use the word 'being'; I'm insufficiently inadequate to its historical discourse. I much prefer 'rhythm'. We are rhythms. She is a different rhythm, so are they, and so is my cat. And that banana too. Rhythm and time. A rave is a dance too, it has its own rhythm. When you are one with it, you are no longer a body but an event. Raves are rituals of rebellion and de-territorialisation.

On the 18th floor of the warehouse, I heard the rumbling drone of Zai's guitar from the elevator and I knew I was near. As soon as Mei saw me, she handed me a ticket band and told me not to close the door behind me. She is not one for small-talk, all intensity and a force of nature. I was told not to openly disclose the venue on Telegram two hours before the show. I had a pint just before coming and I tipped the brim of my hat lower. Zai was getting into his rhythm: a delayed bass staccato with siren-like swooshes sweeping over it. *Not much of a crowd yet.* I found a pillar to lean on and shield me from the back, hiding in the fog of the smoke-machine.

By the time I hit the bus at 2pm the next day, I had cleared my bowels three times and peed twice as much. I was ready for my bus ride, to write on my laptop and to read a book. My line of flight goes by many names: rebellion, rejection, resistance, retreat. Retreat. How do we retreat and re-consider?

> *He wondered again for whom he was writing the diary. For the future, for the past—for an age that might be imaginary. And in front of him there lay not death but annihilation. The diary would be reduced to ashes and himself to vapour. Only the Thought Police would read what he had written, before they wiped it out of existence and out of memory. How could you make appeal to the future when not a trace of you, not even an anonymous word scribbled on a piece of paper, could physically survive?* [2]

1:01:25 I am drawn to Yi Sui's particular attention to Feng Ling's agency as a woman and her need to contemplate either her future or simply her being/existence. Here, you have her thinking about her place in front of an almost life-sized Carrara marble statue of a naked nymph bathing in the fountain, before Shao Ming interrupts her thoughts. Shao Ming asks her what's wrong, it's nothing she says, before Jasmine interrupts them and drags the torn, well-mannered playboy away from a meaningful conversation that could have taken place in the quiet of the night. Feng Ling pries herself out of this equation, chooses to leave the scene, and return home, without her brother's care of fetching a sibling, to return home earlier than expected with Shao Ming's driver. She contemplates yet again in the void-ness of the flat corridor; the stark walls complementing, perfectly, the elegant mosaics of her jacket (and I would kill for this piece of garment), just as her brother walks in and tells her: *He doesn't know how to love you.*

1:05:00 Shao Ming returns to the empty mansion after all the guests leave, just as his parents return home. His mother strangely does not say a word to him but his father holds out a telegram to him, saying he has to leave for Jakarta first thing in the morning. He has to settle 3000 tonnes of rubber due to the rebellion.

An Interlude:

Indonesia was abuzz in the 1950s. My slapdash attempt at history here looks at the very diverse territories of the archipelago of that period. Kalimantan—the Indonesian territories on the island of Borneo—had been under the very loose control of the central government in Jakarta. Jakarta could not control Kalimantan the way it did with Sumatra or Sulawesi. This had to do with the powerful Chinese in Kalimantan who had the economic advantages to maintain their autonomy, while completely disregarding the authority of the Indonesian state. Originally arriving as gold miners in West Kalimantan, they had already created self-governing *kongsis* independent from both the local Sultans and the Dutch. After the gold mines dried up, they shifted to agriculture and later became dominant in rubber production. Although there had been Chinese settlements for centuries and the greater part of the Chinese population was locally born, the Chinese in West Kalimantan remained overwhelmingly Chinese-speaking. This population did not understand the reality of the Indonesian government's jurisdiction nor did they acknowledge it, and behaved as if they were living in part of China.

Rubber was key to China's industrialisation efforts and military capability in the 1950s, where it was placed high on the international embargo list by the US. Indonesia's seemingly neutral stance at the UN towards the embargo against the People's Republic of China (PRC) did not disprove Beijing's suspicion of the Sukarno-Hatta inclination towards the West. Not only a major exporter of rubber, it was also an adherent of market principles, Indonesia sold the larger part of its annual crop to their highest bidders: the United States and Western Europe.

PRC's strategy to break through the American embargo was to take advantage of the expertise and labour of the Chinese from Indonesia, and contributing to the development of tropical agriculture on Hainan Island. Ethnic Chinese businessmen in Indonesia were identified as part of the "comprador class," and were lured with monetary benefits and high rewards and served as outposts. The Indonesian government had difficulty detecting these dealings given the long history of Chinese commercial activities. Even returning Chinese students were recruited into the smuggling networks and would discreetly distribute mysterious small packages wrapped in handkerchiefs containing seeds of rubber and tropical produce such as coffee, coconuts, and pepper.

Around the same time, regional rebellions in Sumatra and Sulawesi reached a new high. Supported mainly by the US and the Chinese Nationalists in Taiwan (Republic of China or ROC), they threatened to tear Indonesia apart. These insurgences originated in the economic disparities between Java and the Outer Islands of Indonesia. This was the same period the Great Leap Forward reached its height. Mao Tse Tung sparked the Second Taiwan Strait Crisis by ordering the People's Liberation Army to shell Jinmen. In response, the Eisenhower administration dispatched the Seventh Fleet to the Taiwan Strait, in support of the ROC. Regions outside Java like Sumatra and Sulawesi accused Java, as the authoritarian centre, of exploiting the Outer Islands, and taking in the larger share of the state revenue, even though the regions were rich in natural resources like rubber, copra and petroleum and produced nearly three-fourths of the nation's foreign exchange income. This led to dissenting groups, led by regional commanders from these parts of the archipelago to smuggle rubber and dried coconuts via Singapore and Manila for barter trade. President Sukarno, as an alternative, allied with supporters of the small national-communist Murba party. He instead blamed the prevailing dissatisfactions on liberalism and the political parties, and argued that the ills of the political order originated in the existing party system, and particularly in Indonesia's version of an imported brand of democracy rather than a democracy built on its own traditions. The regionalists controlled the political initiative in 1956 and much of 1957. Their initial challenge unfolded between May and July 1956, when army commanders in the rich exporting regions of North Sulawesi and North Sumatra organised large-scale smuggling of copra and rubber, claiming that this was necessary because of Jakarta's neglect of their areas and the welfare of their troops.

Their next challenge consisted of a series of bloodless coups in which army-led councils took power out of the hands of civilian governors in Central, North and South Sumatra in December 1956 and in East Indonesia (Sulawesi, the Moluccas and the Lesser Sundas) in March 1957. Jakarta only managed to succeed in undoing the seizure of power in North Sumatra by organising a successful counter-coup within the area's military command. With the exception of these territories, outside Central and East Java, home to the ethnic Javanese, all the other areas remain vehement supporters of the anti-Jakarta administrations. This is largely due to the sympathy and support received by the military and civilian groups alike. A deadlock persisted for the rest of 1957, while the Jakarta government and the regionalist councils with their military heads negotiated. The councils declared to return power on the condition that Mohammad Hatta return to the post of Prime Minister to re-establish the Sukarno-Hatta duumvirate.

In February 1957, Sukarno introduced his conception of Guided Democracy which he then put to the various parties. This consists of a cabinet consisting of the four major parties: the Communists as well as the three parties of the current coalition (Nationalists, Masjumi and the conservative Moslem Nahdatul Ulama). Next, a National Council was to be established, based not on parties but on functional groups-workers, peasants, national businessmen, artists and so on. This council would be led by the President himself and would make decisions by unanimous agreement, and give advice to the cabinet, solicited or unsolicited, therefore serving as a bridge between the government and society. Jakarta also issued an ultimatum to end the barter trade by February 1958. What ensued was an anti-government revolt and the establishment of the Pemerintah Revolusioner Republik Indonesia, an organisation formed in opposition to the Sukarno's government in Jakarta.

3 May 2023

Borneo is a mystery like all islands are. I have been stuck here for the last six years, accompanying my husband who was seconded here to take up the post of chief administrator. A dilapidated building served as office, courthouse, and living quarters. The only steam launch belonging to their government was not at our disposal. When Jack took a rowboat on inspection trips to the villages, I was left to my own devices for days with no means of contact with the outside world. I am wary of the women servants here, who are most ready to steal, lie, drink, or poison their master and mistress, or to join in a plot for murdering us at any moment. Perhaps I am over-imagining, and it seems to be the general impression in England that the Malay nature is treacherous, bloodthirsty, and cruel, prone to running amok at the slightest provocation. But it has been far more peaceful here than in England, no doubt dreary and utterly boring. Life and property are also far more secure in this place than in London, for I know no 'civilised' country where it would be possible to leave my house perfectly open night and day for years as we did, without any serious loss of property.

25 May 2023

The lapse explains it. The lacuna is such and necessary and not obligated to be filled up with news or updates on the writer's life. A bit of mystery goes a long way. Got too busy to even write but I am determined to finish this book. I recently received some good news that a publisher from the Netherlands is interested in this project. And with a grant on the way, this gives me even more impetus to charge ahead and conclude this. I am in Bangkok, as I type this. It is one of my favourite cities and I took a little less than a week off to recharge and be alone and revel in its grit, sleaze, drink, food, bustle, noise and Buddhist respite. The Thais let it be, they are natural fatalists. They famously and historically avoid conflict through guile and smiles and will turn a blind eye as long as they don't disrupt the order of things, but through condition, they are not as depoliticised as us in the island state, and almost like a non sequitur to this sentence: their women too are beautiful.

1:06:05 A brief note. I understand it's a theatrical device, not a filmic one but I wonder what was Yi Sui's intention to suggest a seaview here with the painted backdrop just outside their SIT flat. If a flat is a socialist element of an aspiring working class, then this backdrop is anomalous, place-less and ill-fitting, an incongruent element that makes more sense to a kampung on the beach, or a bourgeois villa or highrise apartment by the waterfront.

1:07:16 Feng Ling feels abandoned by Shao Ming's sudden departure to Indonesia. She wanders off at night to one of my favourite scenes of the whole film, which I call Yi Sui's take of the Rückenfigur,[3] a woman contemplating the pitch dark landscape from a hill. Nothing much is visible, save for city lights and the barren, leafless tree that cuts a central figure complementing the human in the foreground of the composition and the wild *lalang* that grows tall in equal abandon. And just as well, Yi Sui plays romantic classical music in the background to accentuate the melancholy of the scene.

1:08:56 This is definitely Mount Faber, and the car on the hill at night reminds me of the car driving to a morgue in *Sumpitan Rachun*. Cars are the vehicles, actors, icons and media between places. Zhi Xiong and girlfriend are sent to look for his sister at her favourite haunt and find her atop the hill moping under the leafless tree at a godforsaken hour.

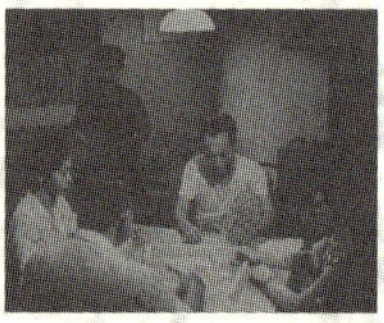

1:12:49 This involves a subplot of the neighbours whose daughter is pregnant by her rich boyfriend. The father is a sarong-clad dude that only knows to gamble and play mahjong and make money illegally. As if intentionally placed in the plot here to espouse the virtues of traditional Chinese values and contrast it to a family with paternal neglect and errant children: the older son is encouraged by the father to capitalise on the rebellion and go into smuggling of goods in ships and the impressionable youngest son asks for money and wields a toy gun. The mother pleads with a matchmaker, who's the father's mahjong *kaki*, to find her daughter a husband, to which the matchmaker retorts that no youngster uses a matchmaker these days.

1:17:13 What ensues later is the punishing spectacle of pain and shame for a 'violent', 'bad', 'morally-laxed', 'money-grubbing' family, when Xiu Lan the daughter is inflicted with unbearable pregnancy pains and had to be taken away by paramedics. Everyone comes out of their flat, as if they never left the *kampung*, to witness the ordeal and find out through hushed tones what had happened. Feng Ling's mother warns the father of consequences when the poor get taken advantage of by the rich and the father claims virtuous Feng Ling is nothing like the wayward Xiu Lan.

26 May 2023

This place is nothing but a mud-swamp. We finally built an attached bathroom, at my husband's behest, and I get to cultivate my garden and flowers in this godforsaken jungle. How do they take this sticky heat, and year-round summer, especially in May. This isolation is sheer imprisonment and loneliness to any Englishwoman, and my fellow Europeans are but a few I would rather not pay constant social visits to, for fear of contempt. When I visit the village town, it is no doubt flattering that I am treated with novelty, by as motley and unpleasant a crowd of animals as the population here, who have never yet seen a white dove with an olive-branch. I would just as soon fly away again hastily!

I am amazed by the sheer proliferation of cannabis bars and dispensaries in the last few years, as if medical pot and weed are as ubiquitous as the bars and bristos in the city. I am very much tempted to enter one out of curiosity, and not need, but the well-warned and well-conditioned citizen in me tells me to take it safe, and I am reminded of the soft oppression upon our bodies.

The plumb weary-eyed waiter from the rooftop bar at the hotel made conversation with me last night. The usual comments about how clean, green and safe my country is and then he ventured that he would like to have worked there if not for the hefty agent fee. I mentioned couldn't he pay the agent through instalments from his salary. That wasn't allowed. I realised then it made sense for fear of defaulting in payment and returning home. I said yes Singapore is good for work and money, and it's very safe. CLUNK CLINK! And there he was this late morning at the cafe, clearing the dishes, as I'm typing this. He apologised, how are you today he asks. I'm good. You are working he says, I smile and I continue writing this.

I told him last night I like Bangkok, I like the rhythm here and people are warm and relaxed, compared to the stressed, workaholic nature of my brethren back home. I like the women too, they're beautiful. No, he says, I like Korean, Japanese and Chinese girls. Ah, so similar to back home I say. Grass will always be greener. Then the conversation went a bit political, I asked him about the Thai monarchy, which is as hushed here in Thailand as it is talking about drugs at home. I spoke a bit about the one-party system rule in Singapore and he seemed indifferent to it. Then he asked me quite a random question like which country will become a developed country the soonest: Thailand, Vietnam or Indonesia. I told him I don't have the knowledge or foresight to predict this. As if waiting for me to reply something short and inconsequential first, he went on to astound me with his parable-like answer, whose wisdom seemed to tether between intelligence and ignorance:

Thailand is last among three. We no like competition, the feeling is same same to my country people—you ask everybody they tell you.

Are you confuse?

Japan is top in all the thing, most modern country in Asia, everything best.

And your country is second place, the best and first in many, I forget.
Why Japan and Singapore have same?

Japan lose war but come back winner in only 70 year, compare to so many superpower last time go down the hill.

And then Singapore throw down the hole by her sister, but still win after 50 year, and all other Southeast Asia country jealous. These two country stories, make people in Thailand think, what if Thailand is rushing to top as most developed nation? But we think, what is happen? How much we pay?

You see Tokyo subway everyone mind own business, no life, so still and quiet, and some in nirvana. Good luck if you settle down as foreigner in Japan.

And your garden city?

Looking beyond tree top and your skyscraper, you see old people push the cardboard, also they do the toilet cleaning, also they collect the dirty plate and cutlery.

I think, if you no job for three months and little saving, how to live in house? How is survive with high cost of living, so fast and furious, like the movie?

I think I can't imagine happen to me if live long time in Singapore.

In Thailand, we the Land of Smiles. My people want to be like this, whatever happen, happen. My people no desire to be the developed nation and suffer.
Thai we smile and *sabai* we famous, the feeling of the world at our feet, where is we have food on the table for our family and we have job that we can pay rent. If lose job, still have fish in the water, rice in the field, no die hungry.

So we be last developed country, it's ok, after Indonesia and Vietnam.

That explains his maturity, the Isan native has probably seen it all. Did he have that revelation when he was tethered to a cruise liner tending a bar that brought him to various parts of the world, or from the marijuana-hazed parties, filled with young European bodies, in Koh Phangan, where he used to work?

1:19:19 I am reading the curious Chinese characters on Feng Ling's straw bag, '西湖', which translates to West Lake, which is a freshwater lake in Hangzhou, East China. I tried to look it up but found nothing on the internet. It could be some cultural branding in that time, considering the place of interest has influenced poets and painters throughout Chinese history for its natural beauty and historic relics, and also inspired Chinese garden design. So it was a bag befitting the most cultured person in the family.

1:23:05 Zhi Xiong is going to the Trade Union, where they are busy with the upcoming elections. Feng Ling is asked by her mother to accompany her sister-in-law to visit her own sick mother in Muar for a few days, and to also get over her grief for Shao Ming. The women: Mother, Feng Ling and Xiao Chen (Zhi Xiong's girlfriend I assume) have perspective here: if Zhi

Xiong stops drinking, changes his lifestyle, and becomes more involved with the Trade Union, he can accomplish more. By this morality, vice is considered ill-equipped for progress.

1:24:09 Yi Sui documents the arduous interstate journey here from Singapore to her laidback cousin, Muar—first across the Causeway to Johor, another scene (the other before being *Che Mamat*) that features the crossover and the observation of the water pipes that feed Singapore from Malaysia. Then they hop on another bus from South Johor and head northwards. Then they take a bumboat to Muar, from then on they take another bus and finally a trishaw to the inner village. Almost like travelling back in time. When they finally arrive at the generously built wooden house, it reminds me of the *kampung* house in the Malaysian film I watched by U-Wei Hj Saari called *Perempuan, Isteri & ....?* Of course, these houses would be ubiquitous in Malaysia then, and possibly now in a modern way.

1:28:59 Back home, Zhi Xiong returns to his flat early from work for dinner, to prepare as driver to pick up an election candidate. Perhaps it was the young charismatic lawyer Lee Kuan Yew. Wouldn't that be a momentous filmic metanarrative? Zhi Hai is also rushing to the harbour for a worker's union meeting. *Merdeka* is in the air. Then the father joins the son to talk about politics. It's a cliché, but only the men talk seriously about politics. 1500 people in the unionists. What does the mother know? Only that her vote is secret, the government tells her, and that she votes for the party not the person. She's listened to the speeches, and she will vote for the party that will serve the people.

I mentioned the key historical event before. The general elections of 30 May 1959, which incidentally will be its 64th anniversary in four days' time. This event marked the landslide victory of the People's Action Party (PAP), in which they won 43 seats out of a possible 51. The party has remained in power ever since the fateful elections.

The Constitution of Singapore was revised in 1958, to grant Singapore self-government and the ability for its own population to fully elect its Legislative Assembly. As an opposition party then, the PAP released their election manifesto entitled *The Tasks Ahead* that lobbied for a series of policies and programmes such as the provision of low-cost housing, the strengthening of education, as well as the development of industries that will improve employment opportunities for the local population. These were in addition to the goal of attaining independence for Singapore through a merger with the Federation of Malaya.

On top of that, campaign issues gathered around the topic of government corruption and independence of Singapore, as well as the communist insurgency led by the Malayan Communist Party (MCP), which had been causing the Malayan Emergency. This desire for independence was reflected in the chant of the Malay term *Merdeka*, which means 'Independence' or 'Free'.

Moreover, a symbiotic relationship between the PAP and the trade unionists formed an umbilical link to the growths of political movements and trade union movements, seen in developing countries with a colonial past. It was certainly easier to organise workers to fight for fairer wage and working conditions than to organise them to fight for the right to vote. Some of these trade unionists are now affiliates of the present NTUC (National Trades Union Congress).

I turned on the tap, even the water from the pipes is heated. I returned to the local skatepark to catch the launch of the new collab line of skateboards with an American skate company, and to catch a glimpse of one of my favourite skaters Corey Diaz, for an autograph, if I buy one of his decks. Turns out, I couldn't find his shape in the size that I wanted and Corey and crew decided to return at 6.30 when it's much cooler. So I didn't buy the deck and I never got to meet Diaz so that's that.

27 May 2023

The Europeans, including my husband and I, were quickly rounded up and thrown into the City Gaol where we were detained until the late afternoon of the 11th. We were then, together with six hostages, transferred to the City Hospital which had been turned into a detention centre. The Hospital and the Police Station formed the centre and pivot of the rebels' defences, according to some of our associates, who spoke Malay and eavesdropped on the rebels' conversations. They were expecting an attack. There had also been talk of executing the hostages.

Jack was well aware that the hostages were poised on a knife's edge, but was sure that assistance from outside would arrive either on the evening of the11th or the morning of the 12th. We considered in a room at the Hospital, which was turned into Cell No. 1, the problem of how best to avoid being shot by would-be rescuers. We were all by ourselves. We decided that help would come either from the Royal Marines or from the Paratroops, so we improvised a ditty from a children's song 'She'll Be Comin' Round the Mountain,' should they come.

We also made one for the Red Berets just in case.

I'm a bit of a flâneur, either through birth, through conditioning or through influence of Baudelaire's modernity and if we go with Nietzsche's concept of the *eternal return*, then two hundred years later, the condition of the flâneur and modernity happens to one of their postcolonial subjects in the present. The whole experience of loneliness, alienation, atomisation, individualist thinking pervades my being as I roam the streets and consort and cavort with strangers.

I had been having dreams that I cannot wake up from. Fictions that realise themselves.

Candy says, "we fall in love so many times but men, they just want to fuck."

She says women's minds and bodies are one whereas men are able to separate their minds from their bodies.

Then her eyes go back to her phone, more interested in ordering her food by the time she gets back.

Her boobs look good but they are utterly fake to the touch.

In the shower, her food arrives through the Grab alert, I peek at her phone and her wallpaper shows falling dollar-bills.

The girl is decked in Prada from head to toe.

She will be back to Korea in a month.

It's a job she says, like mine. In the morning, she gyms, swims. Then she shops, goes to the cafe, and then she waits.

It was at this point I realised knowledge coincides with an exchange for burden or freedom. It is abundant and overwhelming, the *cup runneth over*, the cup that is half empty or half full and one that you can trade in for fictional tokens or emotional truths. Knowledge makes you doubt as you never know enough or, as Socrates says, know that you know nothing. I realised the folly of beauty and desire as a biological need for vitality and reproduction.

Why did I doubt when love came to me? Is it love that I doubt or knowledge that it is not love.

I wake up in my hotel, I am alone. I know it is still early, the light has not yet filtered through the curtains. The room has become the interiority of my head. To nullify existence is to temper the will and alleviate suffering.

I step into the lift. It is clogged with strong perfume that is almost suffocating. In it, a Middle-Eastern couple exchange words, and then exchange gazes with me. In the restaurant, I notice two small mousy men, dark and hirsute, whose physiognomy interests me. They have the scale of two twelve-year-old boys but with small heads, as if they are proportionately correct if you take a picture of them, but appear much smaller in life as if they are of a different species.

The rooftop waiter doesn't seem to take a break. I try to avoid conversation with him at breakfast, by behaving eccentrically. I cough loudly and make weird noises and suddenly start laughing to myself as if in some private joke. At first he seemed amused. Why you laugh he asks. I just ignore him and do a little tapdance to the buffet table. He seems to get the hint and now complies with distant stares from his station from the corner of his eye. I did tell him I was an artist.

1:29:45 At 2.15am, which the fateful clock shows here in cinematic documentation, the PAP had already won 26 seats, as announced on the radio, therefore winning the election. The new regime has taken over. Singapore is finally self-governing.

1:30:01 And almost immediately, the new regime got straight to work in the next scene, cleaning up vice. First up was Lim Cheng Hock's coffee shop that Zhi Xiong frequents. I assume it is for gambling, drinking and prostitution without a license. Police had come to paste the new Government Act notices on the wall, where black Brylcreemed heads gathered to read. Next, they head to the docks.

1:32:04 A very brief restless moment of the night traffic inserted here circa 1959. Brief but pure cinematic bliss here.

1:32:55 We learn from Zhi Xiong's conversations with his buddies at the drinking den that tragedy had befallen the children of his not-so-model neighbours. Da Fei, the son, had been arrested for smuggling contraband at the docks and worse still, Xiu Lan had died from the earlier mishap. Zhi Xiong, flanked by both friends on either side of morality, is told by one of them to focus on his affair with Daisy instead, and by the other, to forget her and stop philandering to find more useful things to do with his time.

1:37:12 This is a wonderful scene that continues Yi Sui's interest in Romanticism, played entirely to the strains of Rachmaninoff's Prelude in C Sharp Minor, on the trope of the fallen woman, or the woman scorned. The Russian composer was only 18 when he composed this piece. The story behind it goes: Rachmaninoff had a dream where he was at a funeral, and in the distance was a coffin. He begins walking towards it, faster and faster, he opens it to find himself inside. I remember this same sequence where the old protagonist in Ingmar Bergman's *Wild Strawberries* also discovers himself in a coffin. This is most peculiar in the Cathay-Keris films I have seen so far, in the use of classical music, which also seems to imply a kind of cultural class and taste on the part of the director.

So Daisy and Zhi Xiong have a private confrontation at a booth in a bar where Daisy flits between flirtation, tenderness, coldness and hysteria while ping-ponging between the seats at the booth—first to sit beside Zhi Xiong to lure him to drink and then opposite him to pry out the truth from him. A truth, that Daisy like Candy, knew all along—that Zhi Xiong just wants to have fun and doesn't really love her. Daisy asks how can a woman who lives in darkness have a bright future.

Yi Sui seems to imply here that Daisy's fate lies in a lifetime of loneliness and certain death. Why is brightness so important when it has been proven that some organisms thrive in darkness?

28 May 2023

At six in the morning, we heard the sound of what sounded like powerful engine boats, like from the Marines. Then we heard shouted commands from the direction of the Police Station. I quickly stood on the bed and saw over the translucent glass, in the pale light of dawn, the silhouette of two cargo boats. Then, a voice speaking in Malay, called on the rebels to surrender. Hurriedly, we put into operation the plan that Jack and I worked out. We scrambled to move our beds to fortify ourselves against any fire, enemy or friendly, which might come through the door, and crawled under them. We had only just reached cover when a machine gun opened fire from the Police Station and was answered immediately from the direction of the river. The window shattered as a fusillade of shots crashed through the glass—from both attacking troops and the rebels. Quite a lot of stuff came through the windows and the windows came with it, most of the stuff that came in was ours. With our mouths dry from the brick and plaster dust which filled the room, Jack and I began to sing:

'They'll be wearing dark green bonnets when they come,
They'll be wearing dark green bonnets when they come,
They'll be wearing dark green bonnets but they won't be singing sonnets,
They'll be wearing dark green bonnets when they come.'

I forgot how Jack, being Welsh, had such a rich baritone, which projected outwards well ahead for the both of us, for I was trembling like a leaf. I was praying maddeningly in between singing.

Nietzsche said that "In music the passions enjoy themselves." I was thinking about this evidentially when I was listening to Led Zeppelin's reggae-infused *D'yer Mak'er,* the song title a play on the words 'Did you make her?' The lyrics go:

Oh oh oh oh oh oh,

You don't have to go, oh oh oh oh oh
You don't have to go, oh oh oh oh oh
You don't have to go
Ay ay ay ay ay ay
All those tears I cry, ay ay ay ay
All those tears I cry, oh oh ah ay
Baby please don't go
When I read the letter you wrote me, it made me mad mad mad
When I read the news that it told me, it made me sad sad sad
But I still love you so
I can't let you go
I love you
Oh, baby I love you
Oh oh oh oh oh oh
Every breath I take, oh oh oh oh
Oh, every move I make
Oh, baby please don't go
Ay ay ay ay ay ay
You hurt me to my soul, oh oh oh oh
You hurt me to my soul oh, oh
Darling please don't go
When I read the letter you sent me, it made me mad mad mad
When I read the news that it brought me, it made me sad sad sad
But I still love you so
And I can't let you go
I love you
Oh, baby I love you, oh
Oh oh oh oh oh oh
You don't have to go, oh oh oh oh
You don't have to go, oh oh oh oh
Oh, baby
Babe, please, please, please, please
Oh oh, oh oh, oh oh, baby
Oh oh, oh I really love you, baby

 Which, effectively, crumbles language to a series of moans

and cries. So much so that the song is essentially the embodiment of sexual desire, loss and pain:

Oh oh oh oh oh oh,
oh oh oh oh oh
oh oh oh oh oh
Ay ay ay ay ay ay
cry, ay ay ay ay
cry, oh oh ah ay
Oh oh oh oh oh oh
oh oh oh oh
Oh
Oh
Ay ay ay ay ay ay
oh oh oh oh
oh, oh
Oh oh oh oh oh oh
go, oh oh oh oh
go, oh oh oh oh
Oh
please, please, please, please
Oh oh, oh oh, oh oh
Oh oh, oh

I am also reminded of the artist Paul Chan's book project *Phaedrus Pron* (2010), which culminates at the limits of intelligibility in the irrational. Chan recasts Plato's text (I'm sure Nietzsche would approve) about the philosopher Socrates and a young man's dialogue on art, erotic love, and madness and turns it into a pornographic prose by typesetting his custom 'Oh Fonts' with the original text to produce an array of erotic idiolects, an example:

SOCRATES: don't be shy *mmm* yes yes faster *mmf ulp* yes yes so big *mmm mmm mmm glupp oooh mmm hhhm ooh mm mmn ulp glupp oh mm mmf oh mm* yes yes *mmn* right there *hm ah* yes yes yes *mmn glupp* right there *hmm* harder harder yes yes so good *glupp* so big so big so…

1:47:25 The bicycles here enact a sense of carefree-ness in the idyllic tropical landscape, just before the encounter of Shao Ming's automobile in Muar. He had driven himself and Zhi Hai all the way from Singapore.

1:48:49 The reunited couple walks through the coconut groves at night, the tropics here, like Shao Ming says, is where "we forget where we are," to indulge in poetry and look at the reflection of the moon in the water. The very purpose of my writing as well, to reflect on some images. The site of the coconut grove, in a memory trigger again, in U-Wei Haji Saari's *Perempuan, Isteri dan Jalang (Woman, Wife and Whore)* however situates the tropics in Malaysia as a site of terror, darkness and the feminine.

The couple, Zhi Hai and family all return in a single car to go back to Singapore, even docking on a cargo boat, during a time when you didn't need a passport to travel from Singapore to Malaysia.

1:53:54 Shao Ming's father makes an appearance again. He does not have a local face, but rather has a face that resembles ones from Korea or Northern China. Perhaps he is a foreign theatre actor. When Shao Ming seeks his parents' approval of marriage to Feng Ling, his father remarks how he too came from a poor family and admires people who work their way up.

1:56:00 Feng Ling's niece sings the National Anthem while doing her homework. I need not say more. The Zhangs, their lot close to done, are counting their kids off to marriage, so that their kids may propagate more useful citizens.

2:00:00 The cars and their roles: Shao Ming and Feng Ling spot another car at their go-to haunt. Little did they know the purity of their love on this symbolic hill will be marred by the thousand lovers' night trysts to come after. I'm kidding, it has always been a place for a lovers' tryst, the automobiles just made it easier.

2:01:46 *Happiness after two hours*

But you know it's taken months and months for me to finish this, so I'm happy. Feng Ling and Shao Ming are happy and are going to get married. They are going to sail the world, as promised by Shao Ming's loaded Dad: crossing the Straits of Malacca, the Indian Ocean and beyond. Hell, they've even renamed Mount Faber the Phoenix Mountains to commemorate lovers and *Flames of the Forest*.

Love colonises.

I was shaking to the core, unable to move. We heard grenades go off and then movements in the hospital buildings. I think someone was coming, but already hoarse from the rubble dust, we still continued to sing. It was then that someone shot right through the sheltered window of the room and it shattered completely. We saw the burly outline of a commando officer. I was close to just giving out, and must have collapsed momentarily after a quick challenge and answer. All I could remember was a husky voice saying, "Out you come, old girl!" And that same voice spoke to Jack, in response to him singing "they won't be singing sonnets" by quipping, "You are wrong, sir" by promptly pulling out a copy of Shakespeare's Sonnets.

We were finally rescued. It was 6.20am when we climbed out of the window. The last eighteen minutes were now part of history, minor history maybe, but terribly important to all those who had played a part in its making. The fire-fight was over, but there was still quite a lot of shooting and the occasional crump of a grenade as the beach-head was extended.

I still have most unhappy reflections when I remember those who were killed in getting us all free again. They, or the ones I saw, were so young, and it is still one of the things I find hardest to forget. Whenever I remembered all that jungle up behind the residency and of what it held and could hold again, I feel convinced I could never go back—and those long stretches of river where we always waved to fellow voyagers—I'm sure I could never travel happily again; where any bend could produce some snipers, hoping to cover themselves in honour and glory for the cause, and for what cause?[4]

29 May 2023

We forget where we are

I was thinking about the coconut grove scene again this morning, and what made this image of the tropics so surreal and compelling was the amount of light needed to shoot the coconut grove at night in darkness, and how light was also reflected off the water, placid as a mirror, forming a shallow *double* image. Back in the day, the lights used must have produced enough heat to augment the already searing humidity that would bake the makeup on the poor actors' faces. This construction in isolation, as artifice, is the thing that punctures the narrative of the film. A falsification of reality contrasted in black and white. Surely, this counts as a most intriguing cinematic study or representation of love and romance in the Malayan tropics.

A postscript

I want to charge this writing against the political backdrop of the time, in retrospect after digging up more information, and also to serve as a prelude to the next chapter for *Korban Fitnah*.

In 1955, 29 Asian and African leaders gathered for a meeting in Bandung, Indonesia on a commonality towards independence. This also marked the birth of the term 'Third World' (now sometimes used derogatorily) that was defined as the "the colonised, neo-colonised or de-colonised nations and 'minorities' of the world whose economic and political structures have been shaped and deformed within the colonial process." Moreover, communist China, represented by Zhou Enlai, signed the *Convention on the Issue of Dual Nationality* at the conference and gave overseas Chinese the ultimatum: choose between taking local nationality or Chinese nationality. Singapore was not part of this conference.

Yi Sui, like many other Chinese-educated people of the time, responded to the climate and lobbied for a 'Malayanised Chinese-language cinema' as well as supported PAP's 'Malayanisation' and multilingual policies, while advocating independence and the merging of Singapore and Malaya. Yi Sui, the idealist and realist, and a mildly-leaning leftist, wanted to map out this cinema in a hybridised melding of the four great traditions of Chinese, Malay, Indian and Western cultures. Its cinema should insist on stories that contain the realities of Malayan people, and also shot by Malayans themselves. However, he also wanted to fuse Mandarin and the other dialects as a broader linguistic language of 'Chinese-language' cinema to unite Chinese audiences residing out of China.

When Yi Sui spent $120,000 of Cathay-Keris' money to make *Lion City*, it took nearly a year to complete and unprecedented promotion at the end of 1960 to tout it as "The first Malayanised Chinese-language film: portrays Singapore as it moves from a colony to self-government." What is more is that the semi-documentary and politically correct film was shot against PAP's Anti-Pornography movement of the time. To add further, before *Lion City*, Cathay Productions had helped the PAP film news documentaries, and employees such as Yi Sui had constantly maintained close contact with government officials.

While Lion City was a success, in contrast, Cathay Productions still made a loss when screened even though it had always made Malay films that cost four times less. Cathay Productions' general manager Tom Hodge supported Yi Sui's film as he believed there was a larger market for Chinese-language films and wanted to diversify film production. The more expensive film however, caused widespread complaints among Malay workers.

Notes

Chapter 5 (cont'd): Lion City (1960)
Rubber rebellion

1. *Elizabeth Choy: More than a war heroine* by Zhou Mei (1995).

2. *Nineteen Eighty-Four* by George Orwell (1949).

3. The Rückenfigur, German for "figure from the back," is a compositional device in painting originally used to convey the sense of longing, emotional isolation, and existential restlessness characteristic of the Romantic movement.

4. The five passages written in 'Englishwoman's Voice' was inspired and adapted both from Emily Innes' *The Golden Chersonese* with the Gilding Off from Eddie Tay's book *Colony, Nation and Globalisation: Not at Home in Singaporean and Malaysian Literature* (2011); and Eileen Chanin's *Limbang Rebellion* (2013).

Chapter 6:

Korban Fitnah (1959)

Angelus Novus in Nusantara

Its fundamental belief must be precisely that society is not allowed to exist for its own sake, but only as a foundation and scaffolding, by means of which a select class of beings may be able to elevate themselves to their higher duties, and in general to a higher existence like those sun-seeking plants in Java—they are called Sipo Matador,—which encircle an oak so long and so often with their arms, until at last, high above it, but supported by it, they can unfold their tops in the open light, and exhibit their happiness.

Friedrich Nietzsche, *Beyond Good and Evil*

In time images of power,
Our emergent selves,
Will be familiar
As, first, the body learns
This other song.

—Edwin Thumboo, last stanzas from *Island*

25 September 2023

Ho Chi Minh City

I've been gelatinous with fatigue. In these latitudes, the light is hard and I wanted to die every day. Everything I did was a struggle. Waiting was endless. I am really walking around like a fool in the scorching heat on an already inhospitable planet. What climate change are they talking about? Only human beings are egotistical enough to think change can be brought upon a whole planet by them, whether for better or for worse. We are already nearing our own extinction. Earth knows this. Perhaps some animals. Except us. And the planet is going to thrive once we are done. We are unable to fathom a beauty that is not ours to behold, and this is my interpretation of the sublime. Because I would be damned.

I am at Factory, a converted workshop on the top floor of an old industrial building, along one of the busier minor roads. A living dusky stairwell uncoils and carries you to an open, large-window-to-attic cafe where locals and expats go to work on their laptops on chic tables and chairs. I am spending a week here, a self-imposed retreat as I could not find the time nor the space to write back home. It gets harder to finish anything. The closer you get to the end of the project with every step you make, two further steps are pulled out before you. I am putting up in the gaudier side of Saigon, along Bui Vien Street, lined with massage parlors, marijuana kiosks, and open-air clubs with dancers on podiums, each blasting their own brand of techno and hip hop across the blue and red light-tinged streets. If I drink enough and maybe have a joint and walk along this street at night, I might just feel like Captain Willard in *Apocalypse Now*, hallucinating through time, 44 years after the film, 49 years after the war, and 34 years after the fall of communism. As a shallow tourist not able to understand its politics yet, I can't find any strand of communism, except for old posters sold in darkened hole-in-the-wall shops. I know it's modeled since the late 80s on a socialist-oriented market economy with free market incentives, but judging from the billionaires and millionaires it's producing, is it not some form of capitalism with private share ownership? Are these, as Godard once said, the children of Marx and Coca Cola? America lost the war but won the market.

As I delve into the final film, my attention steers towards Indonesia and the idea of Nusantara, especially on the shared identity of Malaysia, Indonesia and Singapore. In contention are the links the father of Indonesian cinema, Usmar Ismail had with Singapore through his collaboration with film studios from 1958-1963, which happens to be my period of study and how this period also forms the backdrop of burgeoning nationalism in the three countries. Ismail produced *Hilang Gelap Datang Terang (After Dark Comes Light),* which was shot entirely in Indonesia, and subsequently, the eponymous film, *Korban Fitnah (Victim of Slander)*, under the pseudonym P.L. Kapur with Cathay-Keris in 1959. This was followed by *Bayangan Diwaktu Fajar (Shadows at Dawn)* in 1963, a remake of his first film *Tjitra* (1949). Mohd Erman Maharam, in his thesis on the transnational concept of Nusantara Cinema, writes:

These often-forgotten co-productions seem to suggest that, on the one hand, regional filmmakers like him have always tried to maintain transnational relationships between these national cinemas. These co-productions outline a clear cultural relationship and understanding on certain levels: filmmakers may hope for a larger market based on shared cultural values and codes, envision transnational cooperation between transnational workers and actors, as well as represent two national establishments in one film. On the other hand, co-productions have been side-lined not only by the industry but also by film scholars. These films are more like inappropriate realities which interfere with the right of these national cinemas to define their own cultural identity.[1]

In contention is also the ownership of the classic black and white Malay films made by Cathay-Keris Studio that Singapore has wrested away from Malaysians. Moreover, this has been severely discounted by the different national imaginings and its political foundations fabricated by the political elite. For Singapore, "The strongly top-down approach of the nation-building process is characterised by limited public debate and consensus on national cultural policies and the overlooking of contending national visions."[2]

26 September 2023

<u>Korban Fitnah (1959)</u>

0:00:42 *Hey you, bird in a cage*

To the strains of a repetitive bass line, the film opens overexposed, like *a white, white day* with an elaborately shot scene of two khaki-clad policemen in shorts, escorting a remanded person, in handcuffs, from his cell to the court through several barriers of security. Hock Peng's account details this meticulously as he traced the route they took from what was once Outram prison to the district court in a jeep.

Lahirmu seorang diri
menanggung luka hati tak berhenti
kerana fitnah menimpa diri
Batinmu nangis
hati patah
Riwayat tertulis penuh dengan
titisan air mata

The prisoner wears a pin-striped shirt, as if to mimic prison bars, literally and figuratively. The jeep goes up the long, narrow white-walled road that leads to the civilian world. The scene, now laden with an overcast sky over the greenery, is painted grey. The prisoner looks vacantly at the string of shophouses, as the jeep careens around a bend. The song *Burung Dalam Sangkar (Bird in a Cage)* by Mustafa Osman is not an interlude but a prelude to an end. This works three ways: firstly, it illustrates the emotions that the prisoner is feeling. Secondly, it operates retroactively in that it alludes to a demise of a bygone time and place, effaced by modernisation, by the route from "Pearl's Hill, Keppel Road, the Customs House, Cantonment Road, Fullerton Road, Anderson Bridge, before arriving at the Criminal District and Magistrate Courts at Hong Lim Green along South Bridge Road." This psychogeography dots the political and judicial landscape that informs the film. Lastly, it is analogous to a flashback in which the story is recounted here where the end of the film is actually the beginning of the 'bird in the cage,' embodied here in different ways by the three main characters.

0:04:30 *Criminal District & Magistrates' Courts*

Enters the actor that played the chief editor in *Che Mamat*, Yem Jaafar as the district judge hearing about Case no. 390: *attempting suicide, Hussein Bin Haji Daud*. Hussein, our prisoner, pleads guilty to the charge and does not venture to account for the events that transpired. The courtroom is packed with Hussein's family members and bystanders. Some degree of realism is taken into account by Ismail here in the scene, while some liberty is also taken on his part, for the audience, in portraying this story as a fictional account. Firstly, a portrait of a young Queen Elizabeth hangs above the judge as evidence of a colonial system but the proceedings are conducted in Malay instead. Many of the men don *songkoks* as an emblem and style of Malayhood, which would also be common in Malaysia and Indonesia then. There is no account or medical corroboration that Hussein might indeed be clinically depressed and stigmatised as a criminal by an outdated law. When I first started this project years ago, I had a vested interest in the State's control of what we do with our bodies as a form of biopower.[3] It is as if it is the only 'crime' you can actually get away with, without recourse to justice, if you are successful in committing it, through your death. However, since 2019, suicide was decriminalised in Singapore with the passing of the Criminal Law Reform Bill. This comes after much criticism in the way the country deals with suicide victims and survivors. Lastly, all portrayals here point to the court as a site for melodrama, of which, this film falls under the particular Asian genre.

A pak cik (uncle or older man) pleads with a sullen-cheeked Hussein, amidst tears and visible heartache, to account for his side of the story to the court, which started two years ago, so that we can have a film to watch.

0:09:30 We are transported to what looks like Malaysia, maybe KL and its botanical gardens, I think it's the Pertana Garden because of its proximity to what I assume is the Jamek Mosque as the first landmark to establish this scene.

A mass cycling scene. And this is how I am always led to rabbit holes and taken two steps further towards the imaginary periphery of the film reel. When I first watched it, what struck me in this interlude was the choreographed scene of youths on bicycles singing about *merdeka* and Malaya.

Lalalalala lalalalala lalalalalalala	*Lalalalala lalalalala lalalalalalala*
Bersatu padu kita semua	*Together we are united*
Rakyat Tanah Malaya yang merdeka	*The people of independent Malaya*
Aman Sentosa, rukun dan damai	*Safe and tranquil, harmonious and peaceful*
Kita hidup bersama	*We live together*
Nyanyi bersama sambil menari	*Sing along while dancing*
Ketawa, suka, serta bergembira	*Laughing, being happy, and having fun*
Kita semua warganegara	*We are all citizens*
Hidup bagai saudara	*Living as relations*
Marilah kita membina	*Let us develop*
dan membangun Malaya Merdeka	*and build an Independent Malaya*
Supaya makmur dan jaya	*To prosper and succeed*
Rakyat merasa bahagia	*The people feel happy*
Bersuka-ria atau bekerja	*Having fun or at work*
Mesti dibuat dengan satu hati	*Must be done with a united heart*
Ini semua untuk kepentingan	*All in the interest of*
Malaya tetap merdeka	*Malaya will remain free*
...	...

If that is not reminiscent of communist propaganda imagery, then it must have been borrowed. I must have discussed this with Hock Peng years ago. This scene, perhaps, has the most sentiment of Ismail's nationalistic leanings or at least his political views. And this perhaps is quite close to a *Nusantara* ideology. A quick research online proves otherwise. Ismail had the support of the New Order for his earlier nationalist cinema and was boycotted by the communist party. But the gold pot here is that I discovered another filmmaker, who was almost erased from history by authorities for his 'communist-leaning' films, which tend to portray the working class in their social or historical struggle as opposed to Ismail's Hollywood style that focused on the psychological dimensions of his characters. We all know today the latter form has emerged as a purer, more aesthetic and popular 'cinema', whereas social realist films are relegated to the arthouse and academic crowd, in which it has its own aesthetic form. Both of them couldn't be any more different. Ismail, bourgeois and aristocratic, born into privilege where his father taught Medicine in university, received a Dutch education and later received his B.A. in cinematography form the University of California. Whereas Bachtiar Siagian was a son of a railway worker who grew up in a plantation, and only had primary school education through his benefactor, a Dutch woman, whom he served as a domestic servant. Siagian learnt his craft during the Japanese occupation, watching its war propaganda and also studying Russian cinema, thereby being convinced of cinema's political power.

To return to the scene, this could very well be an ad for Malaya Day. A young multi-racial ensemble singing in harmony with nature, while the wheels of their bicycles are smoothly turning, making loops around the expansive park. Carefree, yet responsible for their futures, the sun smiles upon their tanned cheeks, and Hussein's rich baritone proclaims

Marilah kita membina
dan membangun Malaya Merdeka
Supaya makmur dan jaya
Rakyat merasa bahagia

I compare this route—bright, open, cyclical and merry and social as a stark contrast to the beginning of the film—the dark, dreary, lonely, closed and linear trip in a police jeep.

0:14:45 *Wahab the sleaze bag and impending villain*

As the group park their bikes and rests by the lake, the pak cik from the courtroom is seen with a stalled engine by the

roadside, with the kebaya-clad lass also seen earlier among Hussein's family members. Hussein's weaselly sidekick Wahab steals the opportunity to accost one of the women, played by a stunning Eurasian actress, from the cycling contingent. Pak Cik complains the kids these days don't stop anymore to offer assistance, while Wahab is trying to grope a feel of Julia, the non-actress, in a secluded spot he took her, while a sleazy saxophone plays in the background. *Please let me go* she says twice in English as she tries to prise herself out of his grip. This sexual assault is stopped just in time as Pak Cik steps out to fetch some water nearby. Pak Cik admonishes the lad whom he calls scum and a disrespectful creature and tells him to scram. Pak Cik serves as the proverbial wise man dishing out warnings to damsels like Julia and gullible and honest Hussein, who also gets tricked by his lecherous friend, when he spots yet another prey in the kebaya-clad lady, Rahimah, by the black car. Wahab convinces Hussein she is his lover and pleads with Hussein to tell her to meet him across the park as she is afraid of her uncle. When Hussein approaches her to tell her this, he gets slapped across the face, being mistaken for trying to pick her up.

Like mischievous schoolboys, Hussein gets his revenge by telling Wahab that Rahimah really loves him and asks to meet Wahab at her place at 4pm tomorrow. Feels a bit like a comical plot from the style of the earlier Malay films transposed into this melodrama.

The sun sets an hour earlier here.

Lady...lady...boom boom. A muscular man pulls me aside to let me look at his phone screen of images. I made out a grid of limbs and flesh tones. I demurred politely. I was lost at the junction and I forgot how to cross the road in a sea of scooters and I forgot about the noise and soot of Saigon that I had to wash off from inside my nose the last time I came back. But smell is a visceral memory you can never shake off.

Manila is a smell to me because of a bad experience. I was on a research trip and on a whim to visit Romblon island that produces marble souvenirs (I got one from my domestic helper then). Somehow the resident administrator that booked my flight didn't take into account the layover time for the interconnecting flight. So I missed the connecting flight and had to stay in a cheap airport hotel while I waited for the next available flight, which happened to be in a few days because it is such an obscure island. There was a stench that followed me that I couldn't put my finger on. There was absolutely nothing to do there, a real no man's land, and I was stuck there purely for transit. It felt like purgatory made worse by a smell that the closest I can think of is the smell of petrol and engine oil, and stubbed cigarettes and maybe mixed with a bit of sewerage. The former smells are familiar as I once rented an office space as a studio right above an automobile workshop, and that was horrible too. So I never made it to Romblon as there was a storm and the next flight was canceled too. My week's window was up and I was bound for my return flight. I sought insurance and put this down to a foul experience.

Ho Chi Minh City District 1 is organised like a grid, there is no metro or subway here, and it takes forever to go by car in a traffic jam at peak hour. On scooter, it's much more practical if you are travelling solo but I had forgotten to bring my face mask and I didn't want to seem spoilt or uncool by pulling my T-shirt to my nose. On foot, there are bumps and potholes and broken pavements everywhere which makes for more conscious walking. Those semi-brothels masquerading as barber shops along a street, one woman catches my eye, she's done too much plastic surgery around the lips, such as they balloon like sausages matching her incredible doe eyes and pointy chin, she's singing Karaoke by the shopfront, her pimp beckons me in. They are all singers. I caught one on the second floor on the opposite side of the road drawing the curtains, and though the window was closed, I knew she was singing from the sliver of light that lit her from the street, like a melancholic mime; like from an Edward Hopper scene. Maybe she was waiting for her client to undress (or get dressed) while she looked out the window to practice her singing. I am reminded of the Taiwanese singer that XY told me about, who married an up-and-coming film director, supported and acted in his films, and as they both got busy with their careers, they began neglecting each other. Years had passed, and they ended up in divorce. She found God later, singing for the church, and he went on to become a beloved director. In an interview later on, he would say it was ten long and empty years, a betrayal to her truth when all she remembered was giving her all for him. *It is just a reasonable ending.* A perennial gendered truth.

The whine of mopeds everywhere, it had been pouring like some victory over the sun. And everywhere I dine, there is a leaking roof at some spot I am told not to sit on. This non place. A few years back I visited Ariel here who had followed her newlywed husband to tend to a small business. She had been depressed in Vietnam and wanted badly to come back, suffering from occasional anxiety attacks.

27 September 2023

Overslept. My brain is tired. The sun peeked into the curtain to check what I was doing. It formed a nice reflection on the mirror to inform me it's really a silver object that disappears when you look into it. St. Paul's 'darkly' glasses. It got me to think about subjectivity and objectivity, these lofty academic terms. The mirror's object disappears as you peer into it, but from my angle in bed, my reflection is not there, my subject is missing and the mirror regains its objecthood, so I take a picture of it, as though I am not there. *I am not there.* On my phone, I further manipulate its angles to make it into a perfect rectangle such as if you are a ghost looking straight on at it without your reflection. What technology accords us is novel ways of seeing. There. Now it looks like a perceptual enigma. Maybe I want to be a ghost, and liken the viewer as one if I painted these images. Don't we all desire to be like ghosts in a floating world, in ghost time? But what does painting do other than what the camera does instantly and perfectly. Then the painting is interested in the human—imperfect and durational; contingent and fallible. An image is not captured but painted, built up, constructed, doubted, and looked at intensely over and over again. This agency that one has converts to power in an image. You may choose to also drain its power with restraint, control and form such that it becomes flat and inert, yet open like a valve. I know that I may be painting a dying world or perhaps that I myself fear dying so I consume all these images at once and try to paint them frenetically but it's a physically all-consuming activity. So painting for me is actually a remembering act that involves the whole body, and its subject is that of seeing, of looking into a mirror without a reflection. It's also a vicarious experience that derives its pleasure from the image.

Today I feel like I can chew up reams of paper. Writing is the most intimate form of recording thoughts and feelings. It's truly a medium of human intelligence, a delayed truth in code different from the speech act. It approximates thought but it is not equal to thinking. The speed of thought in my case is extremely fragmented and incoherent. What writing does is that it searches for and organises meaning based on the syntax of the writer, like what I am doing now. It is a technology that organises thought.

The mirror has an accomplice in the bathroom. She tells me the truth today—that I have grown pudgy around the waist handles. They look womanly. I prided myself yesterday on looking young because of my slender build and my cheek pouches. But today I am aging, I look my age no matter how much I try to tuck my tummy in. I can't believe she lied. Just two days ago, she told me I looked like a stud, who had been working out.

0:20:30 Hussein and Wahab live in an idyllic bachelor's house with a painted backdrop of nature by their window. Impressions here tell us that Hussein is a bookworm, focused on studying hard as he is being supported by his brother Hassan, who is withholding marriage so Hussein can complete his studies first. Wahab, on the other hand, is a good-for-nothing entitled fella who wears fancy clothes, who is not interested in working for his money but instead borrows from Hussein so that he can go out on a date with Rahimah.

0:21:57 Wahab trespasses Rahimah's compound and tries to grab and hold her. This second brazen act deserves reprisal but goes unpunished instead. No one thought about making a police report then for his repeat offence. This could reflect the social mores of the time and would not have aged well in today's socially conscious circumstances. Rahimah gets saved again by yet another elderly man in the form of the local Chinese egg-seller played again none other by the inimitable Dollah Sarawak, in a cameo, for yet another portrayal of a Chinese stereotype in the affectations of his spoken Malay. He gives him one *kung fu* chop that throws Wahab to the ground and pummels him with eggs. Wahab swears revenge and flees the scene. Fleeing and taking revenge is something Wahab is tasked to do in this film.

0:26:45 Enters Hassan the big brother as a turn in the film. At once, his presence consumes the screen. Tall and debonair with dark shades, Elvis coif, and a sharp moustache, he cuts the lean silhouette of a movie star walking long strides as he gets down from the bus to visit his sister. Physiognomically, he looks similar to Wahab. Both are tall, lanky and have high cheekbones and a slightly hooked nose. But Hassan's eyes have a doleful quality about them, whereas Wahab with his tight greasy curls and weaselly looks, ends up like a caricature of Hassan. Perhaps these actors are typecast perfectly, one with a worldly air, the other is a petty dandy and a man scorned.

We confirm now Hussein is studying in KL, and his siblings are in Singapore. What accounts for this transnational circumstance? I assume Hussein was sent to Kuala Lumpur to study. Now this makes sense after looking it up. The National University of Singapore was only established in 1980. Its predecessor the University of Singapore was established at the head start of 1962, three years after this film was made, after splitting up with the University of Malaya in Kuala Lumpur, of which Hussein is most probably attending. The University of Malaya, at present, is a public research university and is the oldest and highest-ranking Malaysian institution of higher education.[4]

0:27:58 Hassan spins *the burung dalam sangkar.* I believe this is not a contingent scene by Ismail but carefully inserted as a symbolic point in the film, the cage acting as needle to the spinning wheel. Accompanied by a willowy orchestra, this is the start of turmoil and tragedy, where the real melodrama begins. We learn that Hassan's and Hussein's oldest heavy-breathing sister is sick with a weak heart. Presumably unmarried as she has to mother her two siblings, she maintains the household and has traditional values. She pleads with Hassan to get married as she is seriously ill, and the betrothed family is waiting and sending five letters to her already. Hassan agrees to get married and Big Sister is elated.

A note: Rahimah, Hussein and Hassan are all played by Indonesian or Indonesian-born actors. Big Sister is played by Siput Sarawak, the mother of Singaporean pop singer Anita Sarawak. Maria Medano, once voted the 'Most Beautiful Person in Malaya,' also produced this film in a rare instance by an actress-turned-independent film producer. She was made famous in her portrayal of the Malayan vampire *Pontianak*, Cathay's first Malay film. Hussein and Hassan were played by Sukarno M. Noor and Achmad Nungcik Alcaff respectively, who were already household names in their native country made famous by Usmar Ismail. Bahasa Indonesia has differences in pronunciation and vocabulary from the standard Malay that we know today even though it may be a derivative of the Malay language. They are speaking here in a rather polished way, and because of the silence of the film, I am wondering whether it's similar to earlier Hong Kong cinema where films were typically shot silent first, with dialogue and all other sound dubbed afterwards. This may have been quicker and more cost-efficient than recording live sound, as actors may come from different regions. Dubbing could be a standard way to serve the Malay-speaking market. Their voices may also not have been their own but dubbed by another performer.

0:33:00 After his exams, Hussein returns to Singapore by train to meet his new sister-in-law. We get a glimpse of the now-closed railway station in Tanjong Pagar.

0:33:20 If they are not well-off, then this must be a pretty decent house with two storeys and a compound in which they live. Considering the fact that Hussein could also afford to go to university. Maybe Hassan owns a business which lets him travel a lot. Perhaps they inherited the property from their parents. They have not had to relocate to flats yet and are living in a low-rise estate, not quite a *kampung*. Relocation would be during the major periods of 1960-1965 towards Independence. I notice Siput Sarawak who plays *Kakak* (Big Sister) here is wearing an awful wig and playing someone much older than she is. She has playful and piercing eyes, inherited by her real-life daughter.

0:34:40 Hassan is lying on Rahimah's lap, in full view of her lovely bosom and face. It turns out the kebaya-clad woman is his new wife. A couple in love. I do not think this level of exposure and intimacy will be allowed in today's cinema portraying a Malay couple, following a conservative Islamic resurgence in the 1970s, popularly referred to as the 'dakwah movement.'[5]

0:35:17 *Shock and surprise*

An awkward, dramatic cut of expressions on Rahimah and Hussein's faces when they discover each other's relationship to Hassan. Cinematically, it works, but it's not natural and breaks the flow of the scene and exaggerates the tension between them. They shake each other's hand and pretend to not know each other.[6]

0:36:24 *Kakak* Munah makes them all a meal and I am noticing how really beautiful Rahimah really is as she bends down slightly to reveal a hint of cleavage to put a dish on the table and sit between the two brothers, one dressed in devilish black, the other in plain white. This has some power of position of the woman in the centre here, in a very flattering *kebaya* seated where the head of the household would usually be, from the camera perspective she is a few inches higher than the two brothers. This is deft and masterful by Ismail in setting the tension that is to come. Hussein tells Rahimah that Hassan is a good man and that he is like a father to him and how he is indebted to him. We also find out that Munah got ill after her husband passed away, just as she enters the scene and joins them at the table, her back facing the audience, and lower in position than the rest in camera perspective, denoting her supporting role in the film.

28 September 2023

0:39:30 *Cinema of interruptions*

The first two interruptions come as blissful ones in the form of twin celebrations—Rahimah's pregnancy and the passing of Hussein's exams. They celebrate in a very colonial and modern fashion in a suit-and-tie dinner at the now demolished Wyman's Haven.

Wyman's Haven was a large seafront bungalow where patrons of the restaurant enjoyed a splendid view of the coastline. It was located near the junction of Jalan Haji Salam and the Upper East Coast Road. The restaurant opened in the 1930s and flourished, right after WW2, especially in the late fifties. However, this idyllic lifestyle was interrupted by the government's East Coast Reclamation Scheme, launched in April 1966. The massive land reclamation project, undertaken by the Housing Development Board (HDB), flattened the hills at Siglap and Tampines and excavated 1,525 hectares of land to add a kilometre of coastline to the island. The project would cost $613 million and take 20 years to complete.

Wyman's Haven would have been in the vicinity Temasek Secondary School today.

The next interruptions come in the form of musical interludes, three to be on point, and how this is borrowed as an offshoot of Indian cinema, suspecting that Ismail adopted the Indian pseudonym P.L. Kapur to cater to the distinct style of Malayan filmmaking, away from his nationalistic leanings and Hollywood-influenced style. This transnational influence however might have broken away from the traditional patterns of Malayan Cinema in the colonial implications and labour profiles of Chinese owners, Malay *bangsawan*-based actors, and Indian writer/directors and producers.[7]

Lalitha Gopalan writes that the 'Cinema of Interruptions' is defined by sudden explosions into song-and-dance sequences, half-time intermissions and heavy traces of censorship as devices that assist in the construction of a distinct visual and narrative time-space.[8] I will attempt here to illustrate how Ismail used these devices to his advantage to construct a particular visual and narrative time-space.

0:39:55 First sequence. Spatial.

This is the establishment shot where the singer is a vehicle that introduces the viewer to the interior space, the patrons and the social setting. She is singing a form of *dendang* or love song borrowed from the style sung by Portuguese sailors in Malacca. She wears a shiny reflective dress and goes from table to table, serenading her multi-racial, formally-dressed audience. One guest, an Elvis lookalike, checks her out intensely as if enthralled by both her figure and her voice. The camera work and edits are done seamlessly, then the camera cuts to Rahimah and the brothers' table, another one of a Chinese group and then the singer returns to her band of boys dressed in batik shirts.

0:43:03 Second sequence. Poetic.

Instantly recognisable as the classic song *Bengawan Solo*, the next singer is a cherubic young lady dressed in a traditional *kebaya*, with the house band. She stays put, and so does the camera, except dollying slowly to a close-up on the singer and Rahimah's table, with Hussein chain-smoking all the way, and the Chinese table.

The Indonesian song written by Gesang Martohartono in 1940, is a description of the longest river in Java, Solo River. The song became popular in Indonesia during the WW2 and was heavily promoted in the newly-independent country after the war. It gained widespread popularity in Japan and other Far East and Southeast Asian countries, existing in many versions of the song. One would remember Rebecca Pan's version used in the soundtrack of Wong Kar-wai's film *In the Mood for Love*.

The song is a poetic description of the river which flows through the central and eastern part of the island:

Bengawan Solo
Riwayatmu ini
Sedari dulu bikin
Perhatian insani

Musim kemarau
Tak berapa airmu
Dimusim hujan air
Meluap sampai jauh

Mata airmu dari Solo
Terkurung di gunung seribu
Air mengalir sampai jauh
Akhirnya ke laut

Itu perahu
Riwayatnya dulu
Kaum nelayan selalu
Menyimpan riwayatmu

Mata airmu dari Solo
Terkurung di gunung seribu
Air mengalir sampai jauh
Akhirnya ke laut

Itu perahu
Riwayatnya dulu
Kaum nelayan selalu
Menyimpan riwayatmu

Bengawan Solo
This is your story
You have, since the beginning
Attracted people's attention

In the dry season
Your water is not as much
In the rainy season
It overflows far and away

Your source comes from Solo
Confined in a thousand mountains
Water overflowing far and wide
Finally, reaching the sea

The boat
Its history
Fishermen were always
Saving your history

Your source comes from Solo
Confined in a thousand mountains
Water overflowing far and wide
Finally, reaching the sea

The boat
Its history
Fishermen were always
Saving your history

This song could be read as a love song about independence as much as it's a poetic symbol of national independence.

0:46:30 Third sequence. Infectious and intimate.

Joy and celebration is in the air. Everyone is all teeth and smiles. Hassan gets up to ask Rahimah to dance, but she's too shy. Whether he is aware of this or not, in the din, Hussein impishly pulls Rahimah out to dance and she obliges. We have to understand here that these are the moments that feed on Hassan's blind jealousy later. Earlier on he catches the two in an intimate moment where she is adjusting Hussein's tie.

On the dance floor, there must be like seven or eight couples doing the *joget*. The camera is stationary, establishing the mood and atmosphere.

0:47:00 An enthralling track shot of a Caucasian woman's nimble bare feet as she teaches her partner how to do the Irish stepdance to the music.

We become included as part of the patrons watching three full-length performances.

0:47:57 Three consecutive events spark the revenge that is to ensue and sow the seeds of tragedy, as Wahab the louse steps back into the picture.

Wahab arrives at the family gate looking for Hussein but is surprised to see that Rahimah lives there too. He has the nerve to still accost her and asks her to invite her in. She gives him another slap and Munah hears the din, oblivious to what has happened and invites the devil into her home instead, thinking he is just Hussein's harmless friend. I still do not understand the etiquette here, first of Wahab arriving unannounced, maybe it's because there were no handphones then and that's what people do in the community. Second, Rahimah restraining her disgust and displeasure of having this man in her home, where she's even made to serve drinks. Wahab meets Hassan who also has just returned home, who tells him he just got married to Rahimah. Hassan already senses something amiss when Rahimah feigns a headache and refuses to speak with Wahab.

0:51:50 Next, Hussein receives his first paycheck and is excited to give his brother and sister-in-law a treat. He asks Rahimah to accompany him shopping without Hassan, as he will be back late. They shop at the old CK Tangs and along Orchard Road before arriving at a plant nursery in Bedok I presume from both the location and the events that are to follow. It seems like this is the old Bedok nursery that is still around. I may be wrong. By pure chance, Wahab spots the two and follows Rahimah to the nursery, and proclaims yet again how much he loves her. This harassment does not abate and he grabs her again and she slaps him yet again and screams. Hussein arrives in time and wallops him in the bushes after Wahab disses Rahimah for being 'just another girl'.

0:55:12 By coincidence too, Hassan happens to be outside the nursery just as he catches Rahimah and Hussein hailing a taxi back. I speculate here he might be having money problems, that's why he is always moping and walking around and arrives home at erratic times. When he sees a bruised Wahab coming out, he coaxes him into telling him what had happened.

At the Bedok Restaurant over drinks and a cigarette (this now establishes Bedok and the East Coast as a predominant location site), Wahab tells a livid Hassan that Hussein and Rahimah had been having an illicit affair since their school days, having stolen Rahimah from Wahab. Wahab painted a picture where he stopped them from eloping because he knew Rahimah was marrying Hassan. And just about a while ago at the nursery, he got punched by Hussein for trying to stop them from carrying the affair. And so Hassan drank the poison from the devil's drink without even questioning it. He believed the story. If this is not a display of two petty chauvinistic men letting their emotions get the better of them, then I don't know what is.

Doesn't the plot remind you of the Shakespearean story of Iago and Othello, replaced by Wahab and Hassan?

It just dawned upon me that *Slander!* has taken on a new meaning in that I'm akin to a storyteller here, of the oral tradition, of telling you the reader some gossip either about myself or what had happened in the film so you don't have to watch it. I am envisioning a cheap pulp fiction kind of book now. Hmmm.

A whisky bar on the floor below the cafe! Smells of cigars, darkly masculine finish, black leather seats, kids in black. I had an old-fashioned by the window, staring down at the afternoon scene like the sun himself. A pretty girl in a tight white *ao dai* with a pamphlet, is outside what seems like a fishing resort tourist shop. I take a scooter back to the hotel and contemplate what to do next.

Two hours later, Ni, who hails from the Mekong, looks at my painted nails while giving my hands a rubdown. She asks what's this or rather she meant *what's this for* and I said, *beauty*. She giggles and kisses me on the nipple, tells me to get dressed and escorts me out affectionately on my arm, tall on her platforms. I don't know whether to feel like I'm her puppy, her uncle or her boyfriend. Before dinner I stop at the makeshift kiosk to check out the cigarettes.

During dinner, I serendipitously take refuge just before another torrential downpour and return to the hotel just as the rain subsides.

On a hallucinogenic infused night, my rational brain tries to fight it at first, still trying to compartmentalise thoughts into neat little boxes. Then it starts to whirl and I don't know if things are real or am I imagining things. My thoughts are scrambled and lost and come back again. I tell myself to stub the little brown cylinder, and then I watch it again, so it doesn't catch fire. Then I turn it to the other side of the ashtray so I remember I did it so it's real. Then I feel like I'm floating and flying. My rational brain comes back to tell me to close the windows in case I fall off. Or am I imagining it? They are still open. Lose Your Smile by the Beachhouse is playing and it's sublime, I want to use the song title for my next painting show. Then I start to take pictures with my handphone, thinking they will make good pictures to look at when I am sober. Then I am reading the lyrics on my phone and making notes for some of my paintings. Then I am looking at my camera roll memories. I save one of Jean, Jagger and myself together in some shot of his kindergarten. He looks so happy. Jean messaged me a few days ago to tell me she cannot handle him anymore. I want to show him this. I crop a picture of Jaxxon on his birthday so that it's just his smile filling the image against the candle flame. I drift out of consciousness. Then my attention shifts to the door. What if I don't wake up, and they are unable to get in. Shall I unlock and unlatch the door. And I am thinking dying feels like absolutely letting go and I am still afraid of what is going to happen. I still want to write this and paint. But I am feeling such ecstasy. Then I find myself in a crucifix position on my bed. I am a martyr. How I have suffered. My body is telling me something in this symbolic position. I feel such bliss. I know my fate now, I know what I want, I know what I feel. I got to keep moving. Repeating some actions. Drink water. Yes, I will drink water. What if they find me in bed and my last camera roll are strange images—some whisky bottles on a rack, two close-up images of three Persian horses on a cigar ashtray; seven images of really blurred-out ceilings and walls of a hotel room; a couple with child of five or six; a tightly cropped picture of a face with a flame in front of it.

But these images, "they're not mine, they simply exist..."[9] An hour later, I am chomping away on BBQ pork ribs and drinking mixed fruit juice on the street. I take a walk again along Bui Vien Street, with an open packet of potato chips bought from 7-Eleven. This is where it begins: the birth of the 21st century nightmare. It is not about Vietnam, but the world on this street. The digital and virtual world are manifested in this world of hyper-stimulations. Every colour of light, every pixel, and soundwave flood the cacophony of bodies—podium dancers, bouncers, Western tourists, peddlers, fire-breathers, pimps, ladyboys, shoe-shiners, streetwalkers in a backdrop of LED sign boards and huge screens of soccer and tennis telematches—sports, recreation, hedonism all exist at once in this LED river. I am thinking of *Blade Runner's* (1982) intro scene or *Enter the Void* (2009). At least four times, I am pulled by the arm to take up a massage or a streetwalker. A young Australian backpacker with his T-shirt flipped behind his shoulders says to a skinny Vietnamese man crouching down to wash his shoes, *but I don't have change mate!* But the man continues washing them anyway. Outside one of the boutique hotels, a bald American man has also removed his top in protest, taking up space everywhere, kicking his luggage, shouting *well I'm not leaving no matter what you tell me to do!* Happy hour seems to be from 5pm to 3am in the bars outside since they are still making announcements. At my hotel, two pudgy and scantily-clad Russian women in their late thirties, with thick make-up are trying to book a room but their credit cards don't work. I overhear the manager taking a call, and one of them saying *don't worry my friend has guarantee he will give you number.*

There are only two kinds of people left in the world—buyers and sellers—a world full of buyers owned by sellers. A businessman can ultimately be a buyer, while a philosopher can be the seller. My favourite quote by Nietzsche comes to mind:

> I know my fate. One day there will be associated with my name the recollection of something frightful—of a crisis like no other before on earth, of the profoundest collision of conscience, of a decision evoked against everything that until then had been believed in, demanded, sanctified.[10]

What does it mean to live like a 21st century man now? *The horror, the horror* as I chomp on my wagyu-beef flavoured spicy chips.

A record of male loneliness and desire might be cliché, unfashionable and decried today, but Herzog once spoke about "adequate images."[11] I understand this by authentic representations not heard, read, and seen before—what, who and why they represent in representations of the world that are a resistance against the patterns and currencies of images. And that to me, makes it a *novel*.

As I was spacing out on the sofa, X messages me out of the blue from Instagram about his new work in a shopfront in Bangkok for Pride Month. I see exquisite shapes and drapes made from monk robes. I am both happy he is finally showing and that I have some social contact from home.

0:57:48 A monumental shot of a moody brooding Hassan by himself, going down a staircase that leads to the coastline. Five films ago, it was a brooding Mamat contemplating his plight around the area. We too are mourning with him for this whole stretch of coast that has been reclaimed. Hock Peng describes this passage aptly:

> After hearing of Wahab's slanderous revelation of his brother and his wife's affair, Hassan leaves the Bedok Restaurant and walks towards the promenade by the sea. Here, the shot lingers on as Hassan walks down the staircase in despair and strolls towards the bench in the distance as 'tragic' music plays in the background. The camera then pans from a mid-shot of a contemplative Hassan on the bench, over the empty East Coast promenade, and on to the expanse of the sea…

Achmad Nungcik Alcaff plays Hassan brilliantly as his countenance gives way, as he walks and walks till the evening, to one that is filled with rage and jealousy, changing his devilish good looks to one of menacing evil.

1:00:57 Hassan enters his home to find Rahimah and Hussein in jovial banter. He ignores and chides Rahimah, retires immediately to change into his striped pajamas and proceeds to chain smoke. He even pushes her aside and refuses dinner when she enters the room to find out what's going on and asks her to go away. This hostility and *merajuk* extends to Hussein when he attempts to bring dinner to him, flinging the tray of food violently to the floor. *Girls would not know man's problem,* Rahimah chides Hussein back upon his return after he having earlier mansplained how women do not understand men.

Later in the night, Hassan completely flips, the true deed of slander is fulfilled, when he accuses Rahimah openly in front of Hussein of having an affair with him, having 'caught' them in the room when she was just merely asking him to stop playing the saxophone (a rendition of *Bengawan Solo*) so as not to wake Hassan. This event triggers three different emotions in the protagonists:

1:05:58 An image. This is the exact point of slander! Rahimah is hysterical with pain after being awfully and falsely accused of adultery with her husband's brother. She laments to *Tuhan* (God) why this has befallen her. The figure of the chaste and good woman being wrongfully accused of illicit behaviour.

Hussein is sullen and hurt with tacit grief for something his brother is capable of accusing him of. He is like the perpetual sulking martyr of the film. The misunderstood, honest, good but simple-hearted man.

Hassan is literally possessed by jealous relentless rage and cruelty, and he is unstoppable. He drives both Hussein and a full-term pregnant wife—literally throwing her to the porch to fend for herself—out of his home. He is a temporary villain and accomplice to Wahab's character of the antagonist. Munah is unable to stop one brother from driving them out, and the other from leaving. Sweeping strings accompany the drama and tears, grab your tissues.

This is the exact point of slander! Rahimah is hysterical with pain after being awfully and falsely accused of adultery with her husband's brother

I wish to take a break here to borrow from Malay epistemology, two forms of masculinity, namely *rajuk* and *amok* and their connection to male loneliness and why men brood.

Rajuk is a form of sulking that can be seen as a melodramatic emotional expression seen in many old Malay melodramatic films. *Rajuk* is usually foregrounded in depictions of 'the fictitious adventures of human relationships' in films that reflect culturally familiar forms of behaviour and also to generate drama in these Malay films. Traditionally, there is a male protagonist as a suffering 'victim-hero' frustrated by a class-impeded romance, opposition from a feudal-conscious family to an unsanctioned match, the self-sacrifice of women, and some weakness of the men. So this culture-bound disposition of *rajuk* is due to social marginalisation and vilification. *Rajuk* can be suffered by both men and women.[12]

Then there is *amok* (derived from the Malay meng-âmuk from which the British borrowed for terms like to 'run amok'), which became a colonial construction through the likes of someone like Frank Swettenham.[13] In his writings, *amok* was depicted, via colonial rationality, as an action of an individual who, suddenly and without apparent cause, seizes a weapon and strikes out blindly, killing and wounding all who come in his way, regardless of age or sex, whether they be friends, strangers, or his own nearest relatives.

According to Swettenham the cause of *amok* lies in the psychology of the Malays, that consists in a proneness to chronic disease of feeling, resulting from a want of moral elasticity, which leaves the mind a prey to the pain of grief, until it is filled with a malignant gloom and despair, and the whole horizon of existence is overcast with blackness. *Amok* has a very masculine physicality to it but is a colonialist stereotype and essentialist category created out of the disavowed and suppressed elements of the European self.

So neither *rajuk* nor *amok* is racially specific.

In Usman Ismail's *After The Curfew*, a woman called Laila, who also works as a prostitute, cuts pictures of Hollywood films stars and longs to be loved by a man, Iskandar, whose former ideals as a soldier are unable to match up with a newly independent nation that wants to put the former war behind it. Iskandar, in turn, is unable to love his fiancé, Norma, who pines and waits for him. Norma herself and her brother seem to be stuck in a perennial bourgeois fantasy of song-and-dance parties, while Iskandar and Laila, both socially marginalised and vilified by war and patriarchal economy respectively, sulk constantly at their realities. Both have dreams that are broken or unfulfilled—one is consumed by memories and the other is buried in images; Laila has no one to give her love to and Iskandar is unable to love.

The former soldier, haunted by the war, is unable to forget the past and is eventually defeated by it. He had become a victim of his country's independence, which he fought for, and the new nation has moved on without him. Even though the two women are sympathetic to Iskandar, all three want different things and are unable to have a relationship in the present. Throughout the film, Iskandar suffers from bouts of *rajuk* that finally ends in a bout of *amok* when he kills his former comrade. What he needed in this instance was a good therapist to help him out of his depression.

Incidentally, the actor that played Iskandar is also the same actor that plays Hassan in *Korban Fitnah*, A. N. Alcaff. Hassan had just lashed out in a fit of *amok* at Hussein and Rahimah, having been slighted earlier. Hassan also moped, sulked and brooded over long stretches of beach, and this is not strange to the history of *rajuk* men. There have been thousands of such portrayals in film and painting. My two favourite seems to be the painting *Melancholy* by the Norwegian painter Edvard Munch, the father of expressionist painting, that features a man with his face on his palm, brooding by the shoreline.

He painted a few variations of this theme, but I like the 1893 version the best. It is reportedly inspired by his friend's failed affair but I am pretty sure it was his.

Then there's the most beautiful depiction of male loneliness and sexuality ever captured on 16mm film and it's no other than Vincent Gallo's minimalist *The Brown Bunny* (2003). The film features a bike racer who travels cross country to participate in a race, while dealing with the ghost of an unresolved relationship. There is a scene where his lone bike pierces through the Salt Flats of the desert in deep brooding sensuality. Bud the biker, has all the trappings of masculinity, but suffers in silence. He also encapsulates the broken promise of another masculine mode of being, the *merantau* or 'the wandering.' Because only men are known to wander in search of knowledge and adventure, but in the demise of patriarchy, we only wallow and sulk in broken promises.

A common attribute of melodrama is that it is usually dominated by an active female character that represents the questions, problems, anxieties and difficulties of women living in a male-dominated and patriarchal society, so much so that it's usually defined as a woman's genre. I speculate that the genre also critiques unstable forms of masculinity that project anxieties about modernity onto female characters. In the 1990s, the slew of Malay films coming out of Malaysia especially, focused on female protagonists that were modern and independent, in pursuit of vocational, romantic and sexual emancipation, while negotiating patriarchal rules. Cinema combined both Western and Asian concepts of melodrama to portray the complexity of female protagonists and signify their new roles and social dimensions in the market economy. I don't need to go further than to highlight U-Wei Hj Saari's seminal 1993 film *Perempuan, Isteri Dan Jalang (Woman, Wife and Whore)*, of which the female protagonist, the former *kampung* girl Leha, exploits her newly empowered sexuality to the fullest and subverts and upsets the whole patriarchal system that she is subjected to. There is no self-victimhood or pious morality here like Rahimah but for Leha to embrace her inner slut for survival. Incidentally, her husband kills her finally in yet another fit of *amok*. I go further to South Korea to briefly mention controversial director Hong Sang-Soo's truly modern depiction in *On the Beach at Night Alone* (2017), of a washed-up actress, Young-hee, who retreats to and ponders at a beach, her affair with a married man, also a film director. The scenes include a mysterious man who kidnaps her and cleans her window (I suspect is a figment of her shadow self or subconscious imagination), and one where she drunkenly berates her friends with the truth during a dinner. In what becomes a case of art imitating life, Sang Soo had a much-publicised affair with the actress, Kim Min-hee, that played Young-hee.

Lahirmu seorang diri
menanggung luka hati tak berhenti
kerana fitnah menimpa diri
Batinmu nangis
hati patah
Riwayat tertulis penuh dengan
titisan air mata

Wahai, kau burung dalam sangkar
Hatimu sakit jiwa kesan
Tak seorang pun turut rasakan
Asap yang kau deritakan

It's unthinkable for a person
to bear such grief without end
because of slander
You're crying within and
your heart is broken
Your past was filled
with tears

Hey you, bird in a cage
Your heart in pain and your soul in grief
no one can empathise
What you have been suffering

1:08:46 A cage with two parakeets spins by itself. Might be the devil of slander doing it, as the tale continues.

Both of them take separate lonely routes in the dark night but still end up at the same place. The fate lines that meet. They still manage a duet to *Burung Dalam Sangkar* to accentuate their psychological state to the audience in another interlude. The beautiful woman of Malaya has to endure walking alone in the night, being wrongfully accused, and being accosted yet again in this film, while pregnant here, by a drunken driver, who looks like a businessman of Chinese ethnicity, who has spotted her and pulled over at the secluded track of the beach. Hussein hears the damsel's distressed screams again at the foot of the road by the beach and goes to her rescue. He pummels the driver and gets him to scram. I don't know if this scene is trying to tell us something metaphorically. Rahimah succumbs to labour and is attended to by a fisherman by the beach who comes to their aid and brings them to his *kampung* shed, whose wife also happens to be a midwife. *Hassan, Hassan,* Rahimah cries.

1:16:04 Somewhere in 1959 in *Kampung Loyang* in the East Coast, the sun rises, and a newborn's cries are heard coming from the midwife's shack by the sea. Rahimah gives birth to a healthy baby boy, a new hope, in a place still untainted by modernity. Hussein goes to relay the good news to the fisherman who is returning from sea. Kind of messianic as I read this line again.

Meanwhile Munah's heart isn't able to handle the recent spate of events and takes ill, and is attended to by the doctor. She pleads with the doctor to post a letter to Rahimah's Pak Cik in KL to help resolve the matter of slander that Rahimah and Hussein had been accused of.

Back in KL, Pak Cik, who seems like he is either a land owner or a lawyer handling land deeds for vegetable farmers, chances upon Munah's letter on his table while speaking with a farmer, and proceeds to open it. Reading that Munah is in dire family trouble, he makes plans at once to go to Singapore.

In the lift to the club, I am surrounded by men. A multi-racial group of three late 40-somethings on my left and a white dude in his 20s and his Vietnamese friend. White dude presses a button, but the lift doesn't close so I try again and it does.

The White dude goes, *Thanks bro I never know sometimes which button is 'door close' or 'door open.'*

I smile and say, *No worries.*

Quite a way up, waiting.

White dude quips again to one of them in the group on the left, *Oh is that a G-Shock bro?*

No one replies.

He goes again, a little louder, *Must be a rare piece, a transparent G-Shock!*

The trim man on the left, who looks Filipino, realises he's being addressed. *Oh this? Yeah man. I have had it since 1997.*

His buddies snigger loudly. One of them goes, *It's as old as he is.*
White dude and his partner laugh.

Another of them adds, *Yeah, he's 26.*

Now everyone laughs. I feel loosened up.

At the Hideout, dancing and mingling bodies thicken like cell walls to downtempo music and drinks. I order a whisky sour, but the bartender stares blankly at me at my lack of club etiquette. *No cocktails at this hour!* He offers me a whisky coke instead. I take up the offer and hang around the bar with my glass in hand. I survey the circular-like space with a view of the skyline. It looks like an expat joint. What is so underground about it? Where is my techno? I am about to leave when I see a bunch of bodies going through a curtained opening that leads to what looks like another room. I head in and find a much darker and enclosed space, and people are raving, I see a pair in drag and top hat, and balloons. Deep house is on. After a few minutes, my eyes transfix upon a Latino woman's bare back as she's gyrating. I am mesmerised by where the definitions of the lower trap muscles of her back are and how they move as she dances.

The last text I read for the night from the thin paperback I brought along with me: *The loneliness is deeper than usual today. I'm developing a dialogical rapport with myself. Rain can leave a person blind.*[14]

In bed, in my daze, thoughts fill my head: It is when you are prepared, then you can die; it is when you are responsible, then you are free.

30 September 2023

What is that pungent leaf that epitomises Saigon? The internet says it's the Vietnamese fish scale herb or *rau giấp cá/ dấp cá* and describes it as a polarising herb. Those who love it and those who hate it. It gets its name from how the leaves look and also how it tastes and smells like fish.

XY made me aware of my narcissistic tendencies even as I indulge in these qualities to feed my art. Can they ever be separated?

I arrive early at the airport. A petite and well-dressed Vietnamese woman, with a Louis Vuitton luggage, at the line asks me if I am taking the 3pm or 5pm flight. *5pm* I say. Am I in priority she asks. *No I'm not*, I respond and she directs me to the next line, beside an older German couple. *They are not flexible*, she says, *the gate only opens at 2.20pm*. She volunteers to explain that she arrived early with her mother on separate flights to escape the long immigration queues so that her mother could have a smooth departure to Taipei en route to Texas. *Nine million people living here*, she says, *the airport needs to be at least double the size*. What is her mum doing there, the couple asks. *Oh, she was a Vietnamese refugee, now she's American*. And herself? She's Vietnamese, she says. The old German couple, strangely enough, are en route to Adelaide, where they live. The Vietnamese lady goes on to explain how it is always a little confusing when she travels with her mother, and they always think Vietnamese women are prostitutes going to America to work even though they resemble each other. When she was in school, they used to tell her America is the enemy, and she used to think, is her mother the enemy? She has decided to remain Vietnamese as she does not identify with American values even though her mother loves Michael Jackson very much. She works in Singapore instead where she has a very stable, high-paying job. *Texas is incredibly racist* she says. At Customs, she always gets into fights with the officers who condescend and look down on this tiny woman. She says unless she marries Mike Tyson, and learns to dodge and fight, she's never going to America. *And Vietnamese*, she whispers, *are hypocrites. They teach one thing, but they do another. The rich send their kids to America and launder their money there but say other things about them. When the kids come back, they are so spoilt thinking they can get a job with the parents and that they always think they are right.* When her mother became American, she had to swear allegiance and bear arms to defend her new country. She laughed when she asked her mum, *so then are you going to shoot your own daughter the enemy*. And her mum says, *why choose me? There are over 300 million Americans to do that. It's not my problem.* The Vietnamese lady just as quickly disappeared the minute the priority counter was open, as she swiftly ordered the staff around to check in her branded goods in double-quick time.

1 October 2023

1:19:41 *The Truth*

It is always, always hard to hear and one has to suffer the truth of one's abuse of power. One has to live in regret for the things one has said to others, when you banish the other from their own home.

In Singapore, Pak Cik finally reveals to a remorseful Hassan that he had been manipulated and deceived by Wahab, and had made a terrible mistake to accuse his brother and wife of having an illicit affair and throwing them out of his house.

There are three acts here:

In search of lost time

1:21:48 For a few minutes this scene involves a literal search for Rahimah and Hussein around the newly developed Opera Estate with Pak Cik and Hassan, without any wireless communication back in the day. In his blog, Hock Peng would describe this as 'Potential Destinations for the Banished' in the form of 'Private Houses, Hotels, Motels and Police Stations.' I see it, over 60 years later, as a performed operatic walk of reminiscence and loss, recorded on film. Popular landmarks and houses mark Fidelio Street, Frankel Estate and Siglap Road, all of which may still exist or not today.

The roots of Opera Estate, whose streets are named after both European operas and *bangsawan* (traditional Malay opera), lie 135 years ago when a poor Lithuanian man developed 500 acres of land on the east coast into coconut and rubber plantations. He became a prominent and wealthy merchant eventually and his sprawling landholdings in Siglap included a family home by the sea right until WWII. In 1947, Crédit Foncier d'Extrême-Orient, a pioneer Franco-Belgian land developer in the Far East and Singapore acquired the land for about $1.1 million. The developer proceeded then to cut up the land and sell plots to other developers, that included Crédit Foncier itself, the Singapore Trading Company and Nassim & Co, to construct housing projects on the estate. Back then, a one-storey terrace house would sell for just under $10,000. Opera Estate was not targeted at the wealthy but the working-class and professionals (this could perhaps explain the siblings' house). These were the kind of houses they could afford to buy—off the beaten track, where no buses would go and where it constantly flooded. Those were the days when you could see cows grazing on a grassy field, where one could collect the cow dung to be used as fertilisers for one's plants. There was even a small, rocky hill on Aida Street with goats on it and an Indian goat milk peddler selling his products on bicycle. Other houses would probably cost one over $100,000 in the other parts of Singapore.

One famous resident was Singapore's first president Yusof Ishak, who lived along Aida Street. He and his wife were fondly remembered for gestures like giving an orchid from their garden to a neighbour, or delivering *kueh* during Hari Raya.

My own history embeds with the estate via my first family home in the Jalan Remis area. My earliest conscious memory as a child was in the house. I vaguely even remember being in a pram (though this could be in another place). I was impressed upon by the undulating hills of Opera Estate, unaware then that it was unaffected by the great flattening of Bedok. I think at some point, and this memory needs some corroboration from a family member, my father moved us to a flat in Bedok, and my father's brother and family continued to stay in the house. I remember visits to Jalan Remis and the estate shops before the bends. I remember the accidents my cousins had, one of them badly burnt behind the knee by the exhaust pipe of a passing motorcycle while she was trying to cross the road. Both my father and uncle worked for an oil company then, and I think we lived decently for some time. When I was married, I used to drive to Tosca Terrace in the area to visit my sister-in-law, and it must be at least over a million dollars to own a landed property like that these days.

Over a two-day search they pass by Hong Chew Hotel (once the site of illegal activities and prostitution) in Telok Kurau and Singapore Hotel in Geylang, which was burnt to the ground in 1971. They are also seen emerging from Joo Chiat Police Station, headquarters of the eastern division of the Singapore police force then.

This scene is poignant as Ismail combines both strands of operas in the soundtrack accompanying Pak Cik and Hassan's search of lost time, and persons.

1:25:28 Later in the family home to rest and take respite from the futility of their endeavour, Pak Cik consoles a distraught Munah, who unwittingly makes Hassan suffer the full weight of remorse and bitter regret—for being cruel to his wife; not bothering to listen to her explanation; and for allowing her to roam the streets alone in full-term pregnancy.

1:26:39 *Snapshot*

Day 3 of the search at the beach along Nicoll Drive, Hassan and Pak Cik take a rest on a bench by the water. The viewer also spots Wahab with a bevy of girls on a picnic mat on the other side, his saxophone-playing friend serenades the picture with a jazzy version of *Bengawan Solo* (is Hussein the secret soundtrack musician here?). One of them takes a picture of Wahab and a woman friend on her rolleiflex. It is such a striking scene of a woman in a 1950s bathing suit and cat-eye shades almost pointing to the audience to take a picture, that we partake in being caught in that moment of time in the past, and forget about Wahab, who interrupts the scene again by trying to get cozy with his woman friend. She playfully rejects his advances, and he begins to chase her around trees and along the beach; they end up where Hassan and Pak Cik are and the soundtrack then turns to a suspenseful warrior drum beat.

1:27:52 Hassan confronts Wahab about his slanderous lies and pounds him and thrashes him into the water. Wahab, weak and depleted, can only struggle in the water. When I slow down this scene forwards and backwards, it does seem like an epic fight in the water, and a contrast of black and white, good and evil. Hassan fights his demon even though the demon here is portrayed as cowardly and weak. And this demon ultimately has to seek forgiveness from God, as Pak Cik says, being so damned and beyond human forgiveness.

Hit and blind

1:29:47 But in the end Hassan pays the real price of the tragedy here when he goes blind after being hit by an automobile around the bend in the estate while trying to chase after someone who resembles Rahimah from behind. Academic Timothy Barnard identifies this as a trope in Malay films that conveys the onslaught of modernity and the inability to envisage the ugliness within developing societal mores.[15]

2nd October 2023

Never underestimate walking. Not Hassan's, not Herzog's, nor mine. It's the great companion to solitude. In Rajasthan, in the desert, I was surrounded by death. Animal carcasses lying every 100 metres was something I was not used to. I am not used to being reminded of the life-cycle of death in my everyday life. I would panic if I got lost, more still if I had no water with me. So I ventured not to go too far away from my station alone. It means I do not want to venture too much into the unknown or to a death. But I have always, always enjoyed long walks on my own. One thinks and walks. One walks and thinks. Hassan, Hussein and Rahimah all did their fair share of walking and thinking. Who remembers Truffaut's self-inspired protagonist in *The 400 Blows* whose long walk at the end breaks into a runaway to the sea, or Tsai Ming-liang's female character, Lin, and her closing walk where she finally releases a flood of emotions, in a park created after the eviction of longtime squatters and the demolition of illegal buildings on municipal land, or the breathtaking walk of a pair of men in the wind in Béla Tarr's seven-hour masterpiece *Sátántangó*. But Herzog takes the cake for walking as an ecstasy of endurance, as an act of faith, to save his mentor Lotte Eisner from dying. His religious but arduous journey from Munich to Paris that spanned 776km and 21 days, took the burden and pain for Eisner's sake, and demonstrated his will and sacrifice for her to live. It didn't make rational sense but it affected me deeply, that maybe faith exists as an act, not a belief system. As I read and walked further with him, I delayed my reading and didn't want him to finish his walk just yet. Was I being selfish to the memory of Lotte Eisner? Eight years later she pleaded in sickness with Herzog, *I am saturated with life. There is still this spell upon me that I must not die—can you lift it?* He did, and eight days later, she died.

Sometimes, you don't have the time to walk. Who remembers Ahmadpour starting to run to Poshteh from Koker, just to pass a notebook back to his schoolmate so that he will not be punished by the teacher, and reach back home before dinner in time so that he will not be punished by his mother? [16]

I received the paper bag from a tall Pan-Asian kid who wears a basketball jersey. I said, *ok I'm gonna pay you now*, and whipped out my phone. Then I remembered. *Oh, can I check out the T-shirt first?* I pulled the article out and first noted the extremely faded graphics. That I can live with as its character. Then I discovered yellow stains around the hem and especially around the armpits. *But there're stains all around*, I said. *I don't know*, he says sheepishly. *It was lying in my cupboard all this while, I only wore it once, but it was too small for me.* On his account, it had claimed "thrifted in the US, no holes no stains." Was he trying to pull a fast one on me to make a quick buck? *Ok best price*, I asked? Yes, 50. I don't know how to haggle and don't know how to confront, and I dislike being petty, especially with a kid. So I transacted. *Thank you, sir,* he said and I felt my age again. And slowly I made my way home to the other side of the island.

4 October 2023

> *After the war, it was only through a baptism of war and suffering that I regained my soul and returned to the East. I recovered my sight. I can see now that my country is Malaya, though my blood is Chinese and my education English. And that I have an active part to play, however small, in the rebuilding of a new and better Malaya for my children's children.*[17]

The prelude of this book and its title alluded to how certain imaginations, in our rapid modernisation and decolonisation, in parallel with the decline of cinema, had been silenced to make way for other forms of imaginings. You remember the idealistic university students cycling in the first quarter of the film, those cycling in the spirit of *Merdeka*. I thought of the *Fajar* generation. *Fajar* means the 'dawn' in Arabic and also refers to the first of the five Muslim prayers of the day.

Fajar was the organ of the University Socialist Club, a left-wing student group made up of English-educated intellectuals that played an important role in the politics of colonial Malaya and post-colonial Malaysia and Singapore. The club began its life with medical students of the University of Malaya, which later expanded to include students from the arts and science faculty at the Bukit Timah campus. The organ, which mainly circulated magazine issues within the campus, was active from

1953 to 1971. In May 1954, the members of the Fajar editorial board were arrested for sedition, in reference to publishing an article titled "Aggression in Asia."[18] They were subsequently released after just three days of the trial, defended by D.N. Pritt, the lead counsel in the case, assisted by two junior counsels, Tann Wee Tiong and a young lawyer called Lee Kuan Yew. Around that time, Chinese Middle School students were being prosecuted for their demonstration and opposition against national conscription. These two events that formed the basis of the widespread agitation against British rule also laid the basis for the formation of the People's Action Party (PAP) in 1954. It was even claimed that the student leaders of the club were founding members of the PAP. Some of the leading members that were detained in the mass arrests in 1956 were subsequently released following the PAP victory in the 1959 elections. However, these members were sidelined by the party leadership after these elections.[19]

The club's fate suffered under Operation Cold Store in 1963, when Fajar was banned. In its ten years of operation, its rise and fall marked the political tempo for openness and repression in the country. Its demise was to leave a lacuna in the political discourse that would not be filled again, at least not in the same way. But think about this. The club existed in the same period as the Golden Era of Singapore Cinema. And these were tumultuous times for an island at the cusp of seeking its nationhood. Both public political discourse and cinematic imagination were closed for the making of only one through path that we know now. "It marked a closing of the mind from which a new opening must surely come at some future time."[20]

Poh Soo Kai, one of the founding members of the University Socialist Club, also one of the members stated earlier arrested for sedition, was detained without trial by the International Security Act under Operation Cold Store.[21] Soo Kai asserts that Lee Kuan Yew wanted to oust his left-wing opponents and use the 1963 Merger with Malaysia, in conjunction with independence, as leverage.[22] Dr. Poh, who trained as a medical doctor, in an interview with Kirsten Han, recounted his 17 years in detention as a political prisoner, and the general climate of fear that Singapore, like the rest of Southeast Asia might fall into Communism:

> But they said we were against merger, and therefore we had to recant that our stand was wrong. And we had to say that… condemn the Communist Party. We had to condemn the Communist Party, the Communist Party was wrong, and then we had to go on TV to say these things, and on the private side, you had to talk about your friends. You know?
> They were not interested in facts. They knew a lot, but they wanted you to say something which was not factual.
> For instance, they would say, "Do you know this person, your friend, is he a Communist?"
> I said, "I do not know! How do I know if he's a Communist?" Nobody ever told you he was a Communist, nobody ever told you that. Nobody ever told you, "I'm a Communist." They didn't say it, they couldn't. So I said, "Nobody ever tells me this."

They would say, "But what do you think? Is it possible?"

> I mean, you wanted to go out, right? You wanted to go out. So you thought, it's possible, it's not possible, right? So if you said, "It is possible. It is, I do not know, but it is possible." Then that was good enough for them. They'd write it down, then the record would say that I said he was possibly a Communist. And that was good enough. And then when you went out, they played one against the other. Then your friendship was gone and you didn't feel nice about it.

Indefinite detention without trial is probably the ultimate form of control and the scariest political tool ever, that could be used by the state against individuals. National security, a legitimate aim, may contravene human rights in an action where justice may not be proportionate to law.

A few weeks ago, I got lost on a bus and ended up at a familiar place I had seen online in pictures. On the overhead bridge, I caught a glimpse of what seemed like the former Whitney Detention Centre, now an eerie plot of land with deserted buildings undergoing construction at a busy and indifferent intersection of an expressway. It's urban legend that this center was the site to infamous stories of detainees being tortured and the highly publicised escape of Mas Selamat Kastari, the notorious fugitive who was arrested in Indonesia for terror-related activities.

2 November 2023

What sin we've done that all these happened to us?

1:30:38 Rahimah gets wind of news from the fisherman and the newspaper, that her husband was looking for Hussein and her but has gotten into an accident and lost his eyesight. Rahimah immediately sets out for the hospital.

Back in the siblings' home, an illness-ridden Munah laments about the tragedy into which the family had fallen.

Typing this away really sleepily in a deserted Indian-Muslim joint by the beach. I got stuck paying with my card for a good ten minutes. Finally, someone in the establishment realised I could pay through a QR code.

As I am typing. My mind is so tired it is confusing the words 'sleepily' with 'simply'. I tell myself not to finish the *teh halia* I ordered lest I cannot sleep. Ten minutes later I finished it anyway to stay awake.

Throughout the six days that I stayed with him, Pok Su never once turned on the radio. He would, instead, sit in the living room, smoking and staring at his two empty cages. His head was itself a cage, in the cage was a jungle, and in the jungle was music, both private, and faraway.[23]

23 November 2023

I arrived in Jakarta like a newborn baby on his first week—vulnerable, weak and jaundiced, needing lots of sustenance. On the plane I thought I had left the last symptoms of Covid, having contracted it a second time round. But I was plagued by bouts of diarrhea and fatigue after I landed, coupled with the stress of travelling and maybe the exuberant street food. But my body was having none of it, and would plead to sleep every hour in the hotel room. I amused myself looking at the buildings through a gauzy veiled curtain on the 22nd floor, and lulled by the five prayer calls, of this ridiculous representative of a cheap hotel chain—they checked me twice into a twin-bed room instead of a double-bed room, and proceeded to provide a solution by joining the beds together. Their recycling policy proved dismal as I struggled to fill my bottles with much needed hydration at the dispenser outside, they wouldn't fit between the tap and the tray. I easily ran out of toilet paper and the shower head is screwed, stuck in position and I have to stoop respectfully whenever I attempt to wash my hair.

I had been paying a lot of attention to the Israel-Hamas conflict and was morally affected by the quandary: how do we weigh the senseless slaughter of innocent Jews on October 7th with the daily oppression and suffering of Palestinians made even more disastrous by Israel's subsequent retaliation and relentless bombardment of Gaza? I paid a lot of attention listening to commentators, philosophers and politicians on both sides of the debate and their antinomies, its *differend*,[24] no side can be taken without diminishing the other, besides taking in known facts and events of which you may also fall to disinformation, of a reality or affinity that is not familiar to you.

With some time to spare. I opened the files to watch the film that the curator kindly sent me on WeTransfer. On my VLC player, *Violetta* (1964) by Bachtiar Siagian had the kind of glow that Murat Nemet-Nejat spoke of in 19th century photographs, which had to do with a nascent and flawed technology of the paper and chemical process of the time.[25] In this case, this artefact had a painterly yellow glow of forgotten celluloid. The reels themselves were discovered in celluloid storage facilities, located precisely on the river's edge and were subjected to frequent flooding. This *bengawan* light made out of both water and photons and caressed and marinaded these reels gently with time. This is a peculiar case though. It most definitely would have been a black and white film, three years older than *Korban Fitnah*, so where did the yellow tint come from? Did someone try to colourise this in the 90s again and then it fell into obscurity or did it get its aura from the veneration of time and 60 years of neglect? I couldn't help being mesmerised by this effect. And its montage cross-fades and superimpositions, inspired by Russian filmmaking, were so dreamlike.

Here was a man who fell victim to the anti-communist purge and was imprisoned without trial for 12 years, despite claims that his films did not contain communist propaganda. Violetta spoke of a tragic love story about a paternal-starved girl with a much older soldier and her domineering, overly protective mother. Even though he made other films, the 1962 feature is the only surviving film of his. I felt privy to a precious, forgotten cinema from Indonesia that made its halo even more luminous.

I think about the new flat digital light of our present networked images. With the loss of aura comes the loss of punctum.[26] This new light has another destination. It has to reach as many souls as possible and hence does not travel in the straight pinprick line because we have built complex networks of infrastructures. For the first time it travels in a circuitous manner, a labyrinth of light to all your mobile devices. But light is ever faster than what the human eye can ever register so it always looks the same in representation. Yet today, it's become completely permeable as if to forgo material and media altogether, deceptively different in form, media is light itself that doesn't need the natural sun. It's weightless, semi-erotic.

Coming back to Siagian and Ismail. I think about who gets to be remembered and embedded in a national identity and culture. This can relate to any nation as well. Who gets to assert prominence of national interests and agenda within the film industry and political sphere. Who gets to construct what will form the basic features of a common cinematic culture, or not. Who gets to produce new understandings and perceptions that concerns the geopolitical environment of their time, where a newly independent nation was located. One cannot also deny the soft power of the 'Hollywood' influence in providing the technical and business model for film industries in the region as opposed to local cultural values that would shape the identity of a more vernacular cinema.

And like a riff off Benedict Anderson's notion of imagined communities, de Leon Espena's paper on *Cinema and politics* talks about a transnational Southeast Asia where local filmmakers and producers formed an informal network of technology, people and ideas that invigorated the maturation of national cinemas.[27] Also transnational collaborations would have been made easy with the region's collective historical, social and cultural attributes.

24 November 2023

Like all pilgrimages in a baptism of rain and mud, the visit to Joyland, the Mecca of music goodness is a must, its pronounced slogan in uppercase letters, worthy of any Jenny Holzer artwork or religious institution:

UNFOLD THE MAGIC
AND SEEK NEW ADVENTURES
IN OUR LAND OF JOY

In the cab before, I already felt like puking from virus-related car sickness. Everywhere is three times further in reality here, than what was on Google maps. Because of the huge delay brought by the traffic jam exacerbated by the heavy torrential downpour, the driver got impatient and dropped me at the wrong stadium. So there I was walking and finding my way in the rain, sick to my stomach, till a kind and entrepreneurial rider sold me a poncho from his scooter. That wasn't the end of it. At the gate after queuing and being body-checked, I was told to return to the booth as my ticket was 'early bird' and I was a late worm. I couldn't qualify to come in. But I was sick, I protested. It's policy rules, she said. I smiled sardonically. My smile stretched from policy-driven Singapore island to the ticket touts hanging out just a hundred metres away from me. So I paid a late-charge fee and entered the mud-soaked arena. You got to be joking to hold a middle-aged man hostage in a stadium of music and activities for nine hours without re-entering.

Perhaps my pampered Singaporean mind cannot take it, this is Southeast Asia, after all, chaos rules, and you go with the flow and make your own time. I don't know if the virus had taken its toll on me and made me leave the festival an unbeliever. At the burger stand, I made my order with the 'R' initial, thinking it was easier for the staff to remember or pronounce. When I received my burger and fries, the server uncannily called me 'Remy', and I was jolted from my anonymity. I was ready to head back after checking out the scene, when I was beckoned from the main stage by a gorgeous and shy siren on her guitar. What sounded like grunge meets shoegaze was headlined by the text 'FAZER DAZE'. And for the next 45 minutes I was enthralled by this lanky and mixed-race chanteuse, and her whole band, even though rock solid, seemed negligible.

When I finally made my way outside, there was a chorus of Grab and Gojek riders approaching me, *Pak, nak pergi mana, pak?*

I picked the one that resembled an Indonesian John Candy. I bargained his price by one-third, which he suggested! He took up more than half his space on the scooter and scraped another motorcycle on our trip back—besides a few exchanged sentences of (no apology)—*what were you thinking*, or, *you were too close to me*—there was none of the dagger stares and taking down of particulars and claiming of insurance, that Singaporean motorists are so used to. I looked at his side mirrors. The one on the left was just an empty holder and didn't even have a mirror and the one on the right was bent out of sight.

In bed, I thought of the most peculiar and fascinating observation that happened to me watching the films of Usman Ismail and Bachtiar Siagian, in relation to Indonesian film history through the figure of the soldier played by Indonesian actor Bambang Hermanto in a form of a meta-narrative. You see, he was cast as a disgruntled vigilante soldier from the Indonesian Armed Forces in the late forties that fought for independence against the Dutch, who turned to petty crime as he resumed civilian life in Ismail's seminal *After The Curfew* (1954); and he returned, possibly, as a benevolent communist soldier in Siagian's *Violetta* (1962), just before the purge of 1965 in the coup d'état, under the *Lekra* programme called TURBA, assisting farmers and urbanised leftists to village life.[28]

25 November 2023

1:34:04 As Rahimah walks along the corridor of Alexandra Hospital, I am reminded of my father's short stay at the same hospital, possibly for a fall, and I remembered the sun hitting upon the butter yellow-painted walls of their halls and corridors. I remembered the distinct colonial architecture of the hospital and found out it was the site of a massacre when the Japanese occupied Singapore in 1942, then known as the British Military Hospital. In 1998, the National Heritage Board marked it as a historical site.

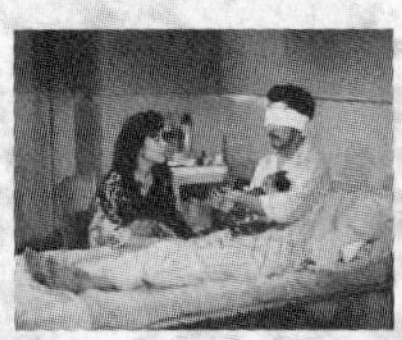

1:36:09 Rahimah walks into Hassan's ward and hands over her newborn to an attending nurse. Hassan, reunited with Rahimah, pleads for his wife's forgiveness and attests to Wahab's wrongdoing. He hears a baby's cries, to which Rahimah places their son in his arms. He is content to hold him, as his eyes, he says, only see wrongdoing. Pak Cik walks into the picture and introduces the Caucasian eye specialist Dr. Wyman to Rahimah. Is he the owner of Wyman's haven too? He looks like one of those present-day bespoke barbers with the trimmed full beard, horn-rimmed glasses and fade haircut.

1:37:13 Dr. Wyman explains that in order for Hassan to see again, he needs an eye donor. Rahimah foolishly offers hers but the doctor says, for good reason, it has to be from a dead person.

1:37:30 The camera pans and dollies to reveal Hussein eavesdropping behind the window blinds.

26 November 2023

There is no language that shapes any world or civilisation. There never has been. All is left is the brutality of illusions. The metaphor, starved of magic, is now reduced to sideshow whorism. Sentences are now the cunning conceited castraters of your once-holy silences.[2]

Weakened, I feel the virus gnawing in my gut, as resilient as I am to it. It's an internal war of survival, and one cannot recover without the complete annihilation of the other.

I started out more innocent, gullible and ignorant than what I am now and this book would have changed considerably if I started out at this point in time. I started out insecure. In my proposal, I also made a lot of presumptions that I wouldn't make now. But we don't live our lives by 'what-ifs' and what better way than to explore the contingent nature of thinking and writing; a journey of thought, through writing. A record of consciousness perhaps. I am also using footnotes more considerably than before, not just as acknowledgments of references and cross references, but also to locate knowledge outside the self, as supplementary information and readings that function as *para*-sites.

1:37:59

So I come to this particular scene in Korban Fitnah *when Hussein (Sukarno M. Noor's character) who plays an Orpheus-like archetype, backs against a blank wall and faces the prospect of confrontation or suicide. It is precisely at this point of entry into consciousness, I argue, where the transitional, suspended status of being in time produces a dynamic of prospective transformation. Like Paul Klee's* Angela Novus, *or the Angel of History staring back into the past, unable to stop the irrevocable change of progress.*

Hussein comes up against a brick wall, literally, but it's the most abstract scene in the film. Framed against the white background, Hussein stands out into the foreground. This is brought out expertly and psychologically by Ismail. As the camera zooms in for dramatic effect, with music (dramatic as it's the first time it's being used here), to a quarter-body shot, the 'closest' to a filmed object, it flattens depth to an imaginary point. Note, the camera zooms in and not tracks or dollies; there are differences here in technique, not being pedantic or geeky here. The camera draws him in quickly by its lens, and not the other way round where the subject draws the physical camera slowly as it tracks or follows the subject. There is an aspect of 'realism' but intrusion in a forward tracking shot (dolly), Godard was famously opposed to this, *tracking shots are a question of morality* he said. To break this down, Godard wants to put the viewer in an ethical and critical position of judging instead, where his technique does 'justice' to the scene. This creates a construct in which the viewer stands outside the image and must examine it critically, to accept or reject. I don't know if a zoom lens violates this even more as it closes in from a distance quickly, discreetly though without 'asking', objectifying its subject. I see a paradox though: a zoom-in technique, though abrupt and less physical, provides and accords the subject an instantaneity through its own unconscious as an abstract image of thought,[30] as opposed to an intrusive camera physically following the subject and therefore making him conscious of being in a film. To be fair, Ismail wanted to make an emotional and psychological point, and whichever way, would be uncritical in Godard's opinion as the viewer is drawn into the image and has to make choices within the image, such as sympathising with the character. The closest analogy here, of my fascination, would be provided through the complex affect of Deleuze's time image. Here, Hussein functions as my double, my memories become his in a crystal that produces a time-image. The psychological dimension of Hussein's character affects me. It is an image that helps me recognise, recollect and dream, hallucinate. The same way I kept revisiting that *Orang Minyak* image. The time-image ruptures the present, the narrative, with a difference of significance.[31] It's the only scene where his subjectivity becomes pronounced, at the exclusion of others, and my identification intensifies. For the impasse is mine, and does not belong to the character of Hussein here. The 'I' here becomes most evident, the figure as 'I' as self is the point of identification. I am the locus of determination and history, and in this sense, time, and Hussein is my vehicle and my eyes. I have been unable to look forward, running up against a wall, so I can only turn back. How a person as mute as me has managed to write a book like this. But…

Words elude me
Language is a trick
Burroughs says

But I get stuck on a word with emotion
So I comfort lack of word with more words
Perhaps then, difference between speaking and writing
Derrida says
One comforts but one speaks

As Hussein contemplates, I had been waiting for him, and for this scene. I had also been waiting to receive the words so that they speak through this page and not of me. Hussein becomes Remy and I become words. These words will eventually be outside my death, after the end of my time, Remy's, Hussein's, Sukarno's. This scene only takes up half a minute but 720 frames of the cinematographic self can be suspended within an image and text to produce a being in time.

> A Klee painting named Angelus Novus shows an angel looking as though he is about to move away from something he is fixedly contemplating. His eyes are staring, his mouth is open, his wings are spread. This is how one pictures the angel of history. His face is turned toward the past. Where we perceive a chain of events, he sees one single catastrophe which keeps piling wreckage and hurls it in front of his feet. The angel would like to stay, awaken the dead, and make whole what has been smashed. But a storm is blowing in from Paradise; it has got caught in his wings with such a violence that the angel can no longer close them. The storm irresistibly propels him into the future to which his back is turned, while the pile of debris before him grows skyward. This storm is what we call progress.[32]

Here, 'history' is self-directed where the self is the only constant, a self that contains time: a duration that never passes, and at this instance, in its infinite sadness, is aware of its authentic being. This is the redeeming moment of his vision, in the 'look of resolute disclosedness,' he takes action for this life, by choosing a self-determined death, to end time. However, this action is sheer folly, an exaggerated subjectivity that is to be short-lived, without foresight, for it cannot encapsulate that which lasts—the fragrant length of time, and being.[33]

1:38:58 Hussein writes a simple note to Dr. Wyman: "Dr. Wyman, I wish to donate my eyes to my brother, Hassan. Hussein." He passes it to a nurse and makes his way down the same dark corridor that Rahimah just walked previously in the other direction. Pak Cik and Dr. Wyman receive the note and hurry to find Hussein, who is walking along the compounds, making for the top of the tower block. The camera emphasises that the building is eleven floors high. Hussein proceeds to climb up the stairs. Pak Cik and Dr. Wyman spots him in his ascent. The older man pleads for him to come down.

Hussein's action, brash it might be, is decisive. Suicide, more often than not, in the cultural sense, except in instances of radical religious and nationalist fervour that go by other names of 'martyrdom' and 'patriotism', is frowned upon as a negative and morbid action. I think it has to do with the violent collapse of life onto the horizon of death, which goes against beliefs of humanity: god, law, fate etc, through a sheer act of will and self-determination. It is one of the only times that we would value hesitation and lingering. However, Hussein believed that his death would make Hassan 'see' again, and would bring him a new vision. Again, in this case, however preposterous it may be, of *rajuk* gone extremely bad, in favour of self-imposed fratricide, suicide succumbs to an act of piety, love and sacrifice.[34]

Suicide then, is justified, by the person committing it, by meaning that death would bring something back in return. Applying a Heideggerian perspective, suicide is not the affirmative 'being-towards-death' because it does not mobilise mortality as a condition for free action in the world, but rather negates it. It violates at least two of the formal criteria set by the philosopher for the very conception of 'being-towards-death.'[35]

27 November 2023

1:41:26 As Dr. Wyman looks on, Pak Cik pleads with two patrolling policemen in the scene to go up and 'arrest' Hussein at once. It's strange in the sense that in the moment of impending death Pak Cik resorts to the enforcement of the law to intervene. In the English subtitles, it says 'arrest', though there are nuances and differences between Malay and English and their translations. In spoken Malay, Pak Cik told the officers: "Tolong, tangkap dia." 'Tangkap' could mean either to 'catch' or to 'arrest' him. Why wouldn't he use 'stop' instead, as you would have asked any abled person to do it. Perhaps that would be too formal when translated in Malay to say 'hentikan'. As if to say, by this scene here, that either there must be some authority to intervene, or it is to provide the narrative connection to why he was arrested at the beginning of his story. The State takes over the subject.

A crowd of bystanders gather on the field with the doctor and the old gentleman. Hussein sees this and continues anyway. He struggles with one of the policemen, breaks free and continues back up his ascent. Surely to die now would only be a spectacle. On the tenth floor, he is finally restrained by the policemen and brought back down the building.

Earlier the situation with my digestive system had taken a beating for the worst, and I was in and out of the toilet before the situation became quite untenable. I needed medical attention immediately, or at least some antibiotics. One can never prepare for a situation like this, especially when traveling. The medical clinic I had googled to be half a kilometre away was shuttered down for good, replete with graffiti, when I arrived urgently by taxi. Through the kindness of some locals, I was whisked away on a scooter to the nearest small clinic. On the bike, I remember always enjoying my ride in every ghetto, alley, street corner, dirt path, main road and thoroughfare of Southeast Asia, sans Singapore. Over at the clinic, they spoke no English and I had to use my

So I come to this particular scene in Korban Fitnah when Hussein who plays an Orpheus-like archetype, backs against a blank wall and faces the prospect of confrontation or suicide

halting Bahasa at best to talk about my condition, and Google Translate if needed be. *Sakit*, I said, *sakit perut* (stomachache). Thank God words like 'diarrhea' and 'antibiotics' are universal, and I was given a cocktail of different capsules by the good doctor and made my way back to the hotel. A few hours later at my keyboard, I am wondering if I should admit myself to the nearest hospital. The pain, weakness and bowel movement do not seem to be going away. I am flying back home tomorrow, and the medley of *maghrib* prayer calls sound even more distantly foreign. The typing is actually effectively distracting me from the reality of my condition.

1:43:01 We are transported back to the film's present, and the courtroom as Hussein recounts his story solemnly. He is that same person with the stony glare of 1:37:59, the *Angela Novus*, the *last man*, a time machine of past, present and future.[36] He is me, my *ecstasies*, also recounting *my* story in these pages.[37] Art is always beside itself. Hussein exchanges a glance with Rahimah from the stand. The judge is wiping away his sweat or tears; he acknowledges the tragedy of Hussein's story but he must "abide by the law and order," in spite of both Hassan and Wahab's calls for their respective culpability. However, he shows mercy and puts him under observation for a year instead of imprisonment. This is forthright. And we should all hope as citizens under any democracy to be granted justice, tempered with mercy, in systems that uphold the written law.

I had been thinking alot about this actually. Justice and mercy are values and qualities that are derived from even higher values of courage and compassion respectively and exist outside the letter of the law. In a way, I propose here that courage and compassion are ecstasies in their own right, one bearing consciousness for the other. It might be my attempt to reconcile any moral conflict, and in a deeper sense, to also reconcile a double, perhaps triple consciousness.

Here, Hussein functions as my double, my memories become his in a crystal that produces a time-image

Initially meant as a footnote, the following grew way too chunky to talk about it there as I thought about it here. What is this 'double consciousness'? I borrow this term from W. E. B. Du Bois' autoethnographic work, *The Souls of Black Folk* (1903), in which double consciousness is expressed as the dual self-perception by subordinated or colonised groups. I refer to this as a peculiar sensation as a conflict of identity—of always looking at one's self through the eyes of others, including one's own. This split in consciousness or in one's sense of self contributes to how we behave differently in different situations, 'performing' an identity for others, and how this might be affected by power. Additionally, I bring out Eddie Tay's *Colony, Nation and Globalisation* (2011), which in the first chapter he suggests that "the work of history, in particular Southeast Asian history, has to be dissociated from colonialist historiography, as the latter conflates modernity with colonialism." And further: "This suppression of pre-colonial history creates the fallacious notion that the price of modernity in Singapore and Malaysia was colonial rule…Through this process, indigenous subjectivity was construed as inferior to that of Europeans. This is the core of colonialist ideology, for a home without its own history, and which is portrayed without the benefit of its inhabitant's collective memories, is a home that can be easily appropriated by others."[38]

Jean-Pierre Bekolo, the Cameroon film director, wrote about how this can exist in literature—the literature of the colonising culture distorts experiences and realities and inscribes inferiority on the colonised people, or, the literature of colonising countries appropriates the language, images, scenes, traditions of the colonised countries. His project then is about how literature or film from the colonised can articulate their identity and "re-appropriate their past in the face of the inevitable otherness of that past."[39]

Double-consciousness could also be, take for example, the story of a young Black man whistling Vivaldi in a White neighbourhood, to assure the folks he is non-threatening.

I am the locus of determination and history, and in this sense, time, and Hussein is my vehicle and my eyes

Or Asian-American women scoring more on Math test papers when they identified as Asian-American and less when they identified as women.[40] But this double consciousness could also mean my non-identity, my null identity, my bi-triple-racialness of which I have no roots to the Father race and no recollection (a lack) of the Mother race, with or without colonialism. Where do I start as one and finish as the other? Identities produce conflict when they do not adhere to any one system or tradition, or stability. It produces a moral conflict. Perhaps that was the original ideal of the State, to neutralise and modernise these tensions. What of appropriation? I appropriate everything, being nothing. I am the modern subject par excellence. I pass for all things Southeast Asian in Asia, and Asian in non-Asian places. We are the oppressed, but we are also the future because miscegenation is inevitable as we always desire and subsume the other.

This in-betweenness in what could potentially mean for our cinema's history is elucidated again by Mohd Erman Maharam's paper, which proffers a 'Sinema Nusantara' an alternative regional outlook based on Singapore, Malaysia and Indonesia's cultural likeness and historicity. The proposed label looks to cultural spaces around the Southeast Asian archipelago which exists beyond political boundaries, well before independence was granted to the three countries. This is useful in studying the complex relationships between cinematic productions and film representations by regional filmmakers who share comparable cultural values as well as similar struggles over social and cultural identities.

He quotes both Paul Basu and Homi Bhabha in defining this 'in-betweenness' as a way to escape the "methodological essentialism that continues to dominate Western logic; the relentless search for the singular and true nature of things; the desire to certainty, for dividing the world into this or that (one 'fixed' essence separated from another)." Basu attributes a double-consciousness born from "histories of borrowing, displacement, transformation, and continual reinscription."

This double-consciousness, defined by an 'essential connectedness', is not characterised by symmetry, however, but by 'syncretic complexity'.

Bhabha, Erman notes, highlights 'in-betweenness' as the metonymic presence that lies in articulating those social divisions and unequal developments that disturb the self-recognition of the national culture, and its anointed horizons of territory and tradition. Bhabha's concept privileges a kind of superior cultural intelligence owing to the advantage of this in-betweenness, which is the straddling of two cultures and the consequent ability to negotiate the difference.

1:44:50

My advice to all, let this be an example to us
and try to avoid being succumbed to slander and wild accusations.

The needless morality at the end, however, by the judge, the authority, always inserted at the start or end of many of these Malay films, begs another philosophical question:

But is it still *slander* if you avoid succumbing to it? Are they only words then? Wittgenstein says that words have no meaning other than their 'applications'. We may have recourse to the law to prove slander but we are also quite familiar here, with how slander has become an apparatus of the state to sue and quell political opponents.

28 November 2023

All relationships in this world begin with an encounter.[41]

In the dream a faceless woman leads me up the roof of an old walk-up apartment. What are we doing there? We are kleptomaniacs. Is it XY? I'm not sure. But we are…breaking into the next apartment through a window. First, the woman goes in, then me. I think she has a bob, I think we are a couple. Ok no, we are just housebreakers…burglars? Apparently, we just break in, to have a look around the apartment and so the woman can feed the cat that she saw from the window. This feels like what XY would do. I'm anxious as fuck. When we leave, I follow behind her, back through the window. When it's my turn, I hear the door to the apartment unlock. *Shit.* I panic and I fall three storeys down.

Boom.

Like Saigon, the sun sets and rises an hour earlier in Northwest Java. But it took me two days to realise this. At first I thought there was something wrong with my iPhone clock (though this was also highly impossible if it is based on real-time data). I thought I had overslept, since it was so bright as the sun peeked harshly from the curtain, but it was still six in the morning, according to the screen. My alarm had not sounded yet. At eight, I went outside to one of the room service staff. *Sekarang jam berapa?* I asked and she corroborated the information on my mobile phone.

At the contemporary museum, in spite of my gastrointestinal woes, three works in the current exhibition catch my eye and made my short gamble before the airport worthwhile. In one of the galleries, Amin Taasha, a young Afghan artist who makes works well beyond his years has a beautiful series of ten miniature paintings in gouache, silver and gold. A simple but intricate recurring motif of a horse in various positions of repose and activity and a string of marigolds—together with other motifs of cacti, and poppy plants—run through ten stations of an epic poem that capture the trials and tribulations of a thirsting soul. I swear Abbas Kiarostami produces the same equivalent in his films. Upon closer reading, I find out they are inspired by the Persian poet Hafez and his book of poems called *The Divan of Hafez.*

Next, Balinese artist Wayan Jana reproduces the mythology of the Mahabharata in a wood carving: a sage-like warrior lies on a bed of arrows that pierce his wooden flesh as his body floats meditatively above the platform. The Mahabharata tells of the love encounter between Prabu Santanu of Hastinapura and Dewi Satyawati, and of Santanu's only son from his previous union with the river goddess. Dewabrata, the son and heir-apparent, renounces his birthright and takes a vow of lifelong celibacy so that his father can be happy and his other descendants with Satyawati can claim the throne. Because of this selfless act, the gods honour him with the ability to decide the time of his own death. This ability to know one's fate and grasp immortality, through some form of ascetic renouncement of the self, surely, has occupied human thought forever, across cultures, and generated conceptions of being. I am curious too, and intrigued by stories of both filial piety and patricide in mythologies across cultures that perhaps serve as loose metaphors for the upholding of tradition, or a violent overturning for change or revolution.

You remember again how Hussein told Rahimah that Hassan was a good man who was like a father to him and to whom he is indebted, to the extent he was willing to donate his eyeballs to his older brother. Anyway, back to the Sanskrit lore, one day Dewabrata, who is renamed Bisma by the gods, accidentally kills Dewi Amba, a princess, who gets reincarnated decades later as a war commander to have her revenge. Bisma, fighting on behalf of opposing forces, recognises the reincarnation and lowers his weapon, and is subsequently hit by a barrage of arrows that pierce through his body. As he lies speared and propped up by the arrows majestically above ground, he succumbs to his destiny eight days later.

Lastly, in another instance of filial piety, I am struck by S. Sudjojono's painting *Selamat Jalan Pak (Goodbye Father*, 1971) on how it reminds me of both Goya's *The Third of May 1808* and his late work (the Black Paintings). In deft yet haphazard strokes of paint in primaries and darks, with barely two discernible figures on a field by a dirt track, Sudjojono, the father of Indonesian modern art, recounts the story, an ecstasy in itself outside of his own body and time, to visit the moment he kissed his slain father's forehead as the revolutionary lay dead by the bushes in a ravine, after having being shot in the stomach by Dutch soldiers. The almost abstract and atmospheric painting shares a historical background—The Second Military Aggression of 1948 in Yogyakarta—with Usman Ismail's *The Long March (Darah dan Doa*, 1950), merging the painter's humanity in the former, and the flawed resistance hero's humanity in the latter, with the fight for independence.[42]

In the taxi to the airport, because of the horrendous traffic jam (and one can never underestimate the traffic in Jakarta), I try to make small talk with the driver in Bahasa Indonesia. I ask him how long before getting ourselves out of this jam. He shows me a long stretch of red in the route on his GPS before a smooth blue line traverses all the way to the air terminal. He asks me where I am from. He asks if I am Indonesian or if I am Malay. I said I am a mix of *Orang India* and *Cina*, and he gets slightly amused. He buys two raw clusters of soybeans in a junction from a street peddler, and offers me some. I politely decline. *Sakit perut* I say. He is amused. I ask him yet again how long more he thinks this jam will last. He asks me what time my flight is. *Bisaaa* he says confidently after I reply. He slips the beans off the brown shell contently, with his tongue and teeth, and discards the empty pods on the front passenger seat. I don't understand how this traffic works in this overpopulated city—you have formal road tolls where you pay with a card at the junction of a major road or expressway and you have informal road tolls at a little crowded intersection where it's just a dude, like any peddler or beggar, standing in the middle collecting cash from you.

Do viruses have a consciousness? Is memory a human faculty? Vampire bats are known to remember who have fed them in the past and would return the favour to those in need of blood. This behaviour promotes long term social cohesion and memory. Of course, we never talk about humans this way. We are never taught to think of memory as biological and evolutionary and social, because it's always been a case of individual transcendence for us. Perhaps memory has become selfish for us. Or memory could be repressed for other causes. What if we are meant, and condemned, to perpetually colonise, consume and infect worlds we visit, the way genes and memes and viruses do their thing, to bring some sort of balance to the universe?

On the plane, 10,000 metres above Java island, I revisit two images from my iPhone I had received earlier. Three nights ago, my godmother had gifted me something long lost and precious. *At last Aunty B found some photos* the WhatsApp message said. It was my biological mother. I had been asking my father, my stepmum, and relatives, probably for years. The first image is a picture of a tall, slim and light-skinned woman in a lace-sleeved bridal gown, standing beside a dark skinned, curly haired man, in a light grey suit, with large tinted glasses, her arm wrapped across his, holding a bouquet of roses. Flanked to the bride's right was Aunty B, 40 years younger and on the groom's left was another dark-skinned curly haired, bespectacled man that resembled the groom. I remembered this scene a long time ago in a photograph which I lost, but here again…the bride is beautiful, I say with pride and a slight surprise, but I stumble upon that look of apprehension on her face. *Yup…she a fairy princess* my godmother says. She would take her life four years later, two days before her husband's birthday. I think there was a long, eternal silence in the family after that.

The second image featured a host of relatives crowding around two mothers and their newborns in the centre. My young godmother was there, and a motley of cousins, uncles and aunts that I recognise, some of them have passed and some of them are still around; I assume the kids who I am not in touch with are around somewhere. Aunt B was there again too on the left, she had a baby in her arms. And again, seated right in the middle, is the fair-skinned woman in a light sleeveless dress, carrying a baby as well, a shade darker than she is. They have named him after P. Ramlee, or rather the nickname the Malay movie star goes by, Remy. This time she is smiling at me. That cheek and jawline is mine. The smile is one of pride, but her gaze is distant, or aloof. I zoom in on the baby. He looks like Jaxxon the first time I saw him.

8 December 2023

And life goes on

Kuala Lumpur.

In the Grab taxi, I meet a lovely driver by the name of Fadly. Initially, I meant to talk about this book at a pre-launch at the book fair but I was unable to make it. I decided to help out my publisher anyway, and to also find out how book fairs work with independent publishing. Because the shipment was delayed, we were unable to get the books delivered in time for the fair, and so I offered to pick them up from the airport cargo complex myself. What was meant to be quite a straightforward task in theory and instruction, proved to be harrowing for me in dealing with the Malaysian customs. Yesterday we managed to claim two boxes but one box was still stuck in custom limbo. Today I am here alone to make the trip to pick up the last box, so we can at least make the stock for the second day of the fair. Fadly had been kind, but sharp, to offer to drive me to and fro, with waiting time, as long as I pay him in cash. Luck and stupidity would have it, that I have forgotten to bring my passport in exchange for an entry pass, and security was having none of what I offered them in its stead: my credit cards, my mobile phone and digital I/C (which is useless out of Singapore), my possessions, everything, except my life. I have to go back and retrieve my passport and half the day is gone already. So this will be four cross-country trips of 50 km of road, the length of Singapore, each time, in a situation created by many unforeseen factors.

In the vehicle, we speak about many things. I am surprised I could hold a conversation in my halting Malay, but I realise one thing—that my thoughts are peppered with Chinese words when I struggle to find the Malay words. This is so strange as I do not think in Chinese, but I figure that it has to do with the brain switching code to another language, as Chinese and Malay are 'other' languages that I speak.

Fadly is from Johor but he works in KL. Sometimes on the weekend, like tonight, he will drive back to Johor to catch up with an event. He tells me he used to work in Singapore. But ever since Covid when he had to return back, he hasn't been able to find employment in the island city. *Singapore ada duit* he says and before it used to be so much more mobile. He is very young but he speaks of the fluidity and movement of people and goods from Johor before Singapore was separated from Malaysia in 1965. After that, his family members and friends had to relocate. Now it has become especially hard for foreigners. I stare out the window, on the trade highway, endless tarmac, industrial stretches of building, on my left a barrier separates me from another endless stretch of palm trees and peatland.

At the customs just before closing, I'm in total disarray when they tell me I cannot check out the box I just collected as it has to be detained by the KDN. What the hell is the KDN? This wasn't the case yesterday. Why are they stopping me now? *Kementerian Dalam Negeri Malaysia*, a Chinese man in bermudas, holding on to a package, tells me. *Usually it's for contraband* he says, *yours is books how come ar?* He scratches his head. Was it something I said? I was told to cut open the box and declare the items and I said they were books from Berlin, meant for a fair and showed them my lanyard. *No! Sorry it cannot leave today, come back tomorrow*, a haughty customs officer in a tudung tells me off. How come? It's not 5.30 yet I say. *KDN sudah tutup. Besok balik lagi.* And she walks away.

Dejected and empty-handed, I return to my taxi. Are you ok, my driver asked? I said *this is life* in English, how do you say that in Malay? *Inilah kehidupan* he says after thinking for a bit. I smile but it doesn't sound quite right.

We pass by large tracts of land, and he shows me where they have special roads that are built and closed for Formula 1 races. In Singapore he hears that there is somewhere near the marina where they close the roads just for such races. Yes, I said it's true. *Singapore takde tanah. Tapi Singapore ada duit.* He reiterates again. His brother who also works as a driver in KL sends his kid for Chinese language classes, because he thinks China is coming up and wants to give his son an edge and head start in life. We pass by another stretch of land where there is a drift race going on.

We get stuck on the Jalan Istana highway because there is going to be a big football match. Johor is playing Terengganu. The conversation then crosses over to football and he mentions Hasnim Haron, a Singaporean that played for the JDTs. So in my limited football knowledge, I mention Fandi Ahmad, our most well-known player ever. I felt a little foolish after mentioning how he married a South African Model, and how both his sons are tall and big and now playing for foreign leagues. But I recover and remember the tremendous roar of Singapore football in the 90s, even for a plebian like me. I was at the match in '94 when Singapore and Fandi beat Kedah at the National Stadium. The same superstar team with Malek Awab and Abbas Saad would go on to take the double later that year with the Malaysia Cup in KL, ousting Pahang. The conversation moves on to the Crown Prince of Johor and how benevolent he is to his people. What is that? I point to a phenomenally tall skyscraper, with a futuristic geometry reminiscent of lattice and *songket* design, that soars majestically towards the evening sky. *Itu Menara Warisan Merdeka* he says. He gives me a bit of political history and their iconic symbolism, bordering on the phallic, in how the former tallest buildings in KL, the Petronas Twin Towers, was a project of Mahathir. Not to be outdone two prime ministers later, Najib built the Merdeka 118. Nearing the end of the journey I hear him talking softly on the phone if he could borrow a 100 ringgit.

I reach the fair, now thronged with visitors, to shrug off my account to Diana, our bright and able intern. There's a term in Malay, she says, that means when something is not meant to be yours, and it's said like this:

tak ada rezeki

Rezeki, the notion of one's lot in life as being based on God's providence.

That's what I meant when I asked the driver just now, and not the literal translation of *This is life*. In the giddy buzz of the fair, someone grabs my attention and it's Wee Beng, a Malaysian writer, critic and artistic director I haven't seen in ages. *What do you mean?! Haven't seen me around?* He says incredulously. *I was thrown out of Singapore. I cannot enter or work there anymore. That's what it means.*

I feel foolish the second time. Or was it the whole day I felt that way?

Back in the hotel, I am totally spent.

I think about the events that transpired just now. It feels like part of a Kiarostami film. It was Bernard Stiegler who proposed "life is always *already* cinema."[43] The philosopher Jean-Luc Nancy wrote a beautiful treatise on Kiarostami's film *And Life Goes On* (1992). In the film, a filmmaker father and his son travel in a car in the aftermath of an earthquake in Iran, to find the boys who were in a previous film of the filmmaker. The filmmaker himself is played by an actor. The blurring of life and art and the use of metanarratives produce a new kind of image which is not a copy but a continuation of life. Sight here does not 'capture' the subject but rather throws itself out there to search and deliver the subject. This is where philosophy takes place: sight, or, the gaze, is compared to Being as something that goes on, that is stranger to, but continues nevertheless, in the discontinuity of moments, events, singularities and individuals. Cinema too, is inscribed in the exterior outward gaze, both as subject and object, of life. I mention this too because of my affinity for this text, for Kiarostami, and my own relationship, in this late stage of writing, to the proximity between writing and cinema. Similarly, writing is *already* inscribed in the author. Without writing, my subjectivity will not exist. In this sense, writing operates on two registers:

Firstly, it is a register of the movement of life: movement and rest, speed and slowness; continuation and interruption, the way life is.[44] The other register is that of the "passage through the image," of cinema and other images, or the gaze that moves and throws itself out there to search, question, re-visit and deliver the subject. Perhaps this whole document is "the continuous and intertwined movement of these two registers that overlap at the same time." There is life, and nothing but life, that continues and discontinues continuously, as evidence, in this document. But one remembers Benjamin as well: consciousness of history occurs when there is a juxtaposition of two discontinuous events, one in the present moment, the other of a past, that give each other meaning in its newfound semblance. Like my pivotal scene of Hussein confronting suicide. The past event remains incomplete without the present moment of juxtaposition. In this case it is my intentionality that creates this new image. What I want to say is this: meaning is chancy, as is meaning in history, be it from film or anywhere else. In the beginning I said emotion can be a powerful thing against facts. They are real things;

they can go around and meander in a book. Then you can sense how emotions move compared to written law. As artists we invent, manipulate and appropriate and we work with chance and the arbitrary. 'Arbitrary' involves a discretionary judgment, not one fixed by law. The 'powerful thing', though opposed to facts, is distilled from them to create this book made up of documents, which in turn are made up of an array of sequences, elements, discontinuities and reactions. Content that may be arbitrary but also critical.

How do you explain *rezeki* to a Western audience? How do you explain *rezeki* to events happening 8000km away from us; how do you explain *rezeki* to the Israeli victims of the October massacre; how do you explain *rezeki* to the longstanding suffering and carnage upon the Palestinian people? I realise each of my near-interstate trips just now was even longer than the whole length of Gaza. Nancy only attempts to broach the conundrum of catastrophe and tragedy through an anecdote in the film:

> The child says to a woman whose daughter died: "God does not like to kill his children." The woman: "So, who does?" The child: "It is the earthquake." And the child goes on to tell the story of Abraham and Issac, which is, in every tradition of the Book, the emblematic story for justice that springs forth and decides in the midst of injustice.

Images of life, as evidence, puts the imaginary at a distance, to speak on the level of the immediate real, to speak at the right distance, as just or a form of justice.

Can images ever, *ever*, do justice to life and its vagaries and to its great tragedies? I think this was what Godard, or Kiarostami, and Nancy, and Benjamin, strove and fought for.

Life would still have to continue and go on.

I run a bath and lie in it for a long time. My hotel has seen better days and it's in a slightly shabby state. I find strands of long hair, not mine, on the edge of the tub and lay my iPhone there. In the bath I think of tigers, yellow and black but crossing the narrow Straits of Johor to come into Singapore. These tigers I only read about. Driven out of forest boundaries, by colonialism and agricultural expansion, into plantations. Where they used to roam freely, they became a menace when they started attacking plantation workers. Then they were hunted down, sometimes for their hides, and then hunted recreationally, and then held in captivity for entertainment. My mind drifts with every *splish-splosh* my hands make with the water. I think about the woman in those two magenta-tinged images that have lost their cyan halos. And all the zinged memorial photons, delayed but never untimely nor knotty, that once crossed and met, caressed, hid in and bounced off her face, 47 years of light though only stored recently, discrete and surrogate in data, have finally reached me, and pricked me nevertheless with a gentle truth. I took as long to understand what Barthes meant in *Camera Lucida*. This *noeme*, my lack. This techne of image. My ghost. It punctures, freezes, captures me. My hallucination, short of the unbearable, that produces a catatonic state in Rohiah, staring at the *Orange Minyak*, himself a Medusa turning her to stone. But there is no horror here. Yet 'she' returns to haunt me, for the longest time shunted me, my repressed. The mental image is the return of the image object. Yet I'm forever on the outside as a spectator; I can never become her, yet I can become Hussein at the point of entry into consciousness, where I speculate my own death.

> *The present gives to the past a form it otherwise lacks. Yet the present requires some fragment of the past to provide its own direction.*[45]

Her parents were from Johor. I think I understood the apprehension. She was not a fairy princess. The bride was a deer caught in the headlights. I could never forget nor could

I remember. Meaning and curse are inscribed in the same coin of memory. That's why I'm so hung up on objects and things lasting. I had given up on the closest humans to me. The slander of memory.

Yellow and black are the colours of imagination. Magenta is the colour of memory. And art is an outlet toward regions which are not ruled by time and space.[46]

Notes

Chapter 6: Korban Fitnah (1959)
Angelus Novus in Nusantara

1. Mohd Erman Maharam, *Between National Cinemas: Reframing Films from Malaysia, Indonesia, and Singapore*, Faculty of Arts and Social Sciences, The University of Nottingham, 2020.

2. Ibid.

3. Michel Foucault's concept of biopower describes the administration and regulation of human life at the level of the population and the individual body—it is a form of power that targets the population.

4. I gathered this source from Wikipedia: The University of Malaya was the only university in newly independent Malaya. The university has graduated five prime ministers of Malaysia, and other political, business, and cultural figures of national prominence.

   The predecessor of the University, King Edward VII College of Medicine, was established on 28 September 1905 in Singapore, then a territory of the British Empire. In October 1949, the merger of the King Edward VII College of Medicine and Raffles College created the University. Rapid growth during its first decade caused the University to organise as two autonomous divisions on 15 January 1959, one located in Singapore and the other in Kuala Lumpur. In 1960, the government of Malaysia indicated that these two divisions should become autonomous and separate national universities. One branch was located in Singapore, later becoming the University of Singapore (renamed to the National University of Singapore) after the independence of Singapore from Malaysia, and the other branch was located in Kuala Lumpur, retaining the name University of Malaya.

5. Southeast Asia has witnessed the emergence of religious resurgence amongst the Malays, popularly referred to as the 'dakwah movement' since the 1970s. Essentially an urban phenomenon, it is marked by an assertion of Islam in the public sphere that differs radically from how religion has been understood and experienced in the past. Characterised by a defensive, authoritarian and puritanical understanding of Islam in response to the problems of change and modernity, it is strongly manifested in the domain of Muslim law known as 'syariah'. While there has been considerable research on syariah revivalism in neighbouring countries, the same cannot be said for Singapore where the Muslims are subjected to the same laws as non-Muslims in all areas except in matters pertaining to the domains of marriage and inheritance. Source: Noor Aisha Abdul Rahman, "Religious Resurgence amongst the Malays and Its Impact: The Case of Singapore", *Alternative Voices in Muslim Southeast Asia*, ISEAS Publishing, 2019.

6. Again, this will not be possible for a man to shake a conservative Muslim woman's hand today, and etiquette will demand that this embarrassing *faux pas* is not committed.

7. Darlene Machell de Leon Espena, *Cinema and politics: the creation of postcolonial self/other and the shaping of strategic cultures in Southeast Asia, 1945-1967*, School of Humanities and Social Sciences, Nanyang Technological University, 2017.

8. Lalitha Gopalan, *Cinema of Interruptions: Action Genres in Contemporary Indian Cinema*, British Film Institute, 2002.

9. Paul Virilio, on Alduos Huxley's "The Art of Seeing," in *The Aesthetics of Disappearance*, p. 52. Semiotext(e) 1991.

10. Friedrich Nietzsche, *Ecce Homo*, 1908

11. Werner Herzog: “Give us adequate images. We lack adequate images, our civilisation doesn't have adequate images. And I think our civilisation is doomed, is gonna die out like dinosaurs if it does not develop an adequate language or adequate images.” From *Werner Herzog Eats His Shoe*, a short documentary in which directors Werner Herzog and Errol Morris make a bet which results in Herzog being forced to eat his own shoe. The bet was not Herzog's attempt of a jab against Morris, but rather to support a struggling but gifted Morris in his quest to do whatever was required to finance a movie project. In the process of eating the shoe, Herzog wants to encourage other aspiring filmmakers, and to set an agenda of increasing what he calls adequate images as a true reflection of the world.

12. Norman Yusoff, *Contemporary Malaysian Cinema: Genre, Gender and Temporality*, 2013.

13. Sir Frank Athelstane Swettenham (28 March 1850–11 June 1946) was a British colonial administrator who became the first Resident general of the Federated Malay States, which brought the Malay states of Selangor, Perak, Negeri Sembilan and Pahang together under the administration of a Resident-General based in Kuala Lumpur. His book *Malay Sketches* was a vivid account of Malay scenery and Malay character drawn from his experiences spending the best part of his life in the scenes and among the people described.

14. Werner Herzog, *Of Walking in Ice*, 1978.

15. Timothy Barnard, “Decolonization and the Nation in Malay films, 1955-1965,” *South East Asia Research*, Vol. 17 No. 1 (2009) p. 65-86.

16. *Where Is the Friend's House?* (1987), directed by Abbas Kiarostami.

17. A quote from the Raffles College student Lim Ewe Hock, extracted from *The Fajar Generation, The University Socialist Club and The Politics of Postwar Malaya and Singapore*, SIRD (2010), edited by Poh Soo Kai, Tan Jing Quee & Koh Kay Yew.

18. Ibid.

19. Ibid.

20. Ibid.

21. Operation Coldstore was the code name for a covert anti-communist security operation that took place in Singapore on 2 February 1963.

22. Kirsten Han, *An Interview with Dr. Poh Soo Kai*, medium.com, 2016.

23. Alfian Sa’at, “Village Radio,” *Malay Sketches, Ethos Books, 2012.*

24. Lyotard's notion of the *differend* can be analysed as a philosophical theory of radical disputes, that is, disputes with no possible resolution other than the silencing of one of the parties.

25. Murat Nemet-Nejat, *Peripheral Space of Photography*, Green Integer, 2000.

26. What was unique to the photograph, according to Roland Barthes, was its punctum, which he defined as the sensory, intensely subjective effect of a photograph on the viewer: “The punctum of a photograph is that accident which pricks me (but also bruises me, is poignant to me).”

27. Darlene Machell de Leon Espena, .op.cit 7

28. Large-scale killings and civil unrest primarily targeting members of the Communist Party (PKI) were carried out in Indonesia from 1965 to 1966, as an anti-communist purge following a controversial attempted coup d'état by the 30 September Movement. Lekra or The Lembaga Kebudajaan Rakjat (Institute for the People's

Culture) was a prolific cultural and social movement associated with the Indonesian Communist Party. TURBA is an acronym for 'turun ke bawah', which translates as 'descend from above.' Part of the goals of the program was to transform urbanised leftists by introducing them to the physical deprivations and psychological hardships of village life.

29. Kelvin Tan, *the Nether(r);* R, Aporia Society (2001).

30. Gilles Deleuze, *Cinema 2: The Time-Image* (1985). Translated by Tomlinson and Galeta, 1989.

31. Ibid.

32. Walter Benjamin, *Theses on The Philosophy of History, IX* (1940).

33. I get my inspiration for this paragraph from Byung-Chul Han in *The Scent of Time* (2009), who in turn was influenced by the thought of Martin Heidegger in *Being and Time* (1927). I expand this a little on the next page.

34. In the Shiite tradition of Islam, Muhammad the Prophet made Ali the first Imam to succeed him, and Hassan and Hussein were said to be his descendants.

35. The four formal criteria in Heidegger's conception of 'being-towards-death' is: it is non-relational, certain, indefinite, and not to be outstripped.

    Death is non-relational in the sense that before one's death, one has cut off all relations to others. Death cannot be experienced through the deaths of others, but only through one's relation to one's death. Secondly, one can run away from the facticity of death, but one cannot doubt that life comes to an end in death. Thirdly, death is indefinite for no one knows when it is going to happen. Fourthly, death is not to be outstripped as it is the limit against one's 'potentiality-for-being' to be measured, as in it outstrips all possibilities that one's power of free projection possesses.

36. The last man, as defined by Nietzsche, is tired of life, risk-averse, and seeks only comfort and security. Therefore, 'the last man' is the archetypal passive nihilist, unable to build and act upon a self-actualised ethos. He is also a start and end point of humanity's socio-political development, according to Francis Fukuyama, in which there is no viable and ideological alternative to liberal democracy and free-market capitalism. See *The End of History and The Last Man*.

37. Ecstasy means 'outside-itself' in existential philosophy. Consciousness is considered to be 'outside itself', as its object of thought and perception is not the object itself. This enables one to be 'outside of oneself' with time. Heidegger uses this as a way of temporalising a unity where the three dimensions of time: past, present and future are grasped in and out of themselves as 'ecstasies'.

38. Eddie Tay, *Colony, Nation and Globalisation: Not at Home in Singaporean and Malaysian Literature*, NUS Press and Hong Kong University Press, 2011.

39. Jean-Pierre Bekolo, *Cinema as a Transformative Tool for the Therapeutic Intellectual: Putting Postcolonial Theories in Motion*, Miss Read, 2023.

40. I take these two examples from Brian Lowery's online article for *Big Think* (28 March 2023) entitled "'The self' doesn't exist. Instead, you constantly shape multiple selves," in which he relates 'self' to examples and tests conducted by psychologists.

41. An introductory quote by I Wayan Jana, describing his wood-carving work *Bisma* (2023).

42. Cited as the first Indonesian film, *The Long March* is a 1950 Indonesian war film produced and directed by Usmar Ismail. It tells the story of the Siliwangi Division and its leader Captain Sudarto on a march to West Java after being attacked by the Dutch.

43. Jacques Derrida and Bernard Stiegler, *Echographies of Television: Filmed Interviews*, Polity, 2002.

44. I get this idea from Gilles Deleuze and Felix Guatarri's book, *A Thousand Plateaus: Capitalism and Schizophrenia,* 1980.

45. This quote is lifted from a piece of writing for Art Forum from art historian Richard Shiff called *Critical Reflections* (October 1995). He was inspired by Walter Benjamin's concept of history.

46. I attribute this line to Marcel Duchamp.

Set Margins #25

Slander!
an autotheory of six malayan films
by Remy Shah

ISBN
978-90-834041-3-4

Editor
Susie Wong

Designer
Billie Sng

Translations & Transcriptions
Sarah Noorhimli
Zuraidah Ehsan

Illustrations
Billie Sng
Sarah Noorhimli
Jeremy Sharma

Publisher
Set Margins' publications

Project Management
Sarah Noorhimli

Editorial and Design Advice
Freek Lomme

Printer
Petro ofsetas

Fonts
Arial
BiauKaiHK
Delvon
Minion Pro
Rakesly

Made possible thanks to the generous support of the Research Committee LASALLE College of the Arts, University of the Arts Singapore.

First edition, 2024

Set Margins'
www.setmargins.press

Acknowledgements

I would like to thank Sarah Noorhimli, Billie Sng and Susie Wong, whose care and commitment to this book made it all the more special than it is. I am grateful to Toh Hun Ping, whose immense research on Singaporean film history and locations was the initial spark that triggered all three iterations of *Slander!*. I am also thankful for the support of time and funds from the LASALLE College of The Arts research committee, and the Asian Film Archive for the perusal of their material.

I also wish to thank Louis Ho for kickstarting the first iteration, A White, White Day, with an invitation for an exhibition on film; Kenneth Tay, my curator for the second iteration for SAM Mini Mobile Museum, for the opportunity and excuse to embark on the writing; and most importantly, to Freek Lomme, for taking a chance on this publication.

Joanne Lim, thank you for interning for the second iteration, your tireless research and the title font! And not forgetting Shibani Gaikwad, who rendered those formidable exhibition structures at the libraries. A shoutout to Hendra Hermawan as well, for his silkscreen expertise, Bunga Siagian for her research and precious film artefact, Januar Rianto of Further Reading for publishing an excerpt in their fourth volume, and Faridah Ahmad for checking through the translations and transcriptions with Sarah.

Lastly, I extend my gratitude to whoever has supported my practice, and all family, friends and loved ones who had to put up with me, so I can go on this strange journey that has occupied me for a few years.

Notes